EARTH BIBLE COMMENTARY

Series Editor
Norman C. Habel

PSALMS BOOK 2:
AN EARTH BIBLE COMMENTARY

"As a Doe Groans"

Arthur Walker-Jones

LONDON • NEW YORK • OXFORD • NEW DELHI • SYDNEY

T&T CLARK
Bloomsbury Publishing Plc
50 Bedford Square, London, WC1B 3DP, UK
1385 Broadway, New York, NY 10018, USA

BLOOMSBURY, T&T CLARK and the T&T Clark logo
are trademarks of Bloomsbury Publishing Plc

First published in Great Britain 2020
Paperback edition first published 2021

Copyright © Arthur Walker-Jones, 2020

Arthur Walker-Jones has asserted his right under the Copyright,
Designs and Patents Act, 1988, to be identified as Author of this work.

For legal purposes the Acknowledgements on p. vii constitute
an extension of this copyright page.

Cover design by Irene Martinez Costa
Cover image © Borut Trdina/istock

All rights reserved. No part of this publication may be reproduced or
transmitted in any form or by any means, electronic or mechanical,
including photocopying, recording, or any information storage or retrieval
system, without prior permission in writing from the publishers.

Bloomsbury Publishing Plc does not have any control over, or responsibility for,
any third-party websites referred to or in this book. All internet addresses given
in this book were correct at the time of going to press. The author and publisher
regret any inconvenience caused if addresses have changed or sites have
ceased to exist, but can accept no responsibility for any such changes.

A catalogue record for this book is available from the British Library.

Library of Congress Cataloging-in-Publication Data
Names: Walker-Jones, Arthur, author.
Title: Psalms book two: an earth bible commentary / Arthur Walker-Jones.
Description: New York: T&T Clark, 2019. | Series: Earth Bible commentary |
Includes bibliographical references and index.
Identifiers: LCCN 2019016124 (print) | LCCN 2019017011 (ebook) |
ISBN 9780567689429 (ePUB) | ISBN 9780567676290 (ePDF) |
ISBN 9780567676283 (hardback: alk.paper)
Subjects: LCSH: Animals in the Bible. | Bible. Psalms, XLII–LXXII–Criticism,
interpretation, etc.
Classification: LCC BS663 (ebook) | LCC BS663.W35 2019 (print) |
DDC 223/.20859–dc23
LC record available at https://lccn.loc.gov/2019016124

ISBN: HB: 978-0-5676-7628-3
PB: 978-0-5677-0069-8
ePDF: 978-0-5676-7629-0
eBook: 978-0-5676-8942-9

Series: Earth Bible Commentary

Typeset by Newgen KnowledgeWorks Pvt. Ltd., Chennai, India

To find out more about our authors and books visit
www.bloomsbury.com and sign up for our newsletters.

CONTENTS

Acknowledgments	vii
List of Abbreviations	viii

Chapter 1
INTRODUCTION ... 1
    Reading like a Mountain ... 2
    Turtle Island ... 4
    Animal Studies ... 8
    Anthropocentrism and Binaries ... 12
    Lost in Translation ... 14
    Identification ... 15
    A Reader's Concerns ... 16
    Coevolution and Niche Construction ... 18
    Canon and Genre ... 21

Chapter 2
"AS A DOE GROANS" (Pss. 42–44) ... 25
    Deer ... 26
    Spiritual/Material Binary ... 31
    Water ... 32
    God, My Rock ... 35
    Sheep and Goats ... 38

Chapter 3
URBAN EMPIRE (Pss. 45–49) ... 51
    Perfume and Ivory (Ps. 45) ... 51
    Urban, Imperial Ideology (Pss. 46–48) ... 54
    Embodiment (Ps. 49) ... 58

Chapter 4
SKIES PROCLAIM (Ps. 50) ... 61
    Asaph ... 61
    Sun, Earth, and Skies ... 63
    Sacrifice ... 65
    Bulls and Goats ... 69
    Right Relations ... 73

Chapter 5
EARTH AS REFUGE (Pss. 51–55) — 77
   Za'atar — 78
   A Green Olive Tree — 79
   The Wings of a Dove — 82

Chapter 6
EARTH AS ENEMY (Pss. 56–60) — 89
   Wings — 89
   Lions — 91
   Dogs — 96
   Of Wild Dogs and Mad Humans — 105
   Scientific, Religious, and Economic Reasons — 110
   The Dog as Liminal Figure — 111
   Summit Socioecology — 113
   Earth Creatures and Earth — 116

Chapter 7
GOD AS ROCK AND EARTH'S JOY (Pss. 61–64 AND 65–68) — 119
   Rock — 119
   Wing — 121
   Jackals — 125
   Thanksgiving and Earth's Joy — 126

Chapter 8
EMPIRE'S GREENWASH (Pss. 69–72) — 133
   Psalm 69 — 133
   Psalm 71 — 135
   Psalm 72 — 136
   Empire — 140
   Conclusion — 147

Bibliography — 151
Author Index — 159
Biblical Index — 162
Subject Index — 166

ACKNOWLEDGMENTS

I am grateful to the University of Winnipeg for granting me a research leave that was crucial to the research and writing of this commentary. The research, which was originally proposed to finish writing the commentary, gave me time to take a detour into animal studies when I decided I had to know more about the animals mentioned in the Psalter. I have found it fascinating and productive and hope the reader will think so too.

It was through the detour into animal studies that I began reading about coevolution. I am grateful to the Templeton Foundation for funding that allowed me to study evolutionary anthropology as part of the Human Distinctiveness Project led by Agustin Fuentes (Anthropology) and Celia Deanne-Drummond (Theology) of the University of Notre Dame.

Several parts of this book were initially presented as papers at the Society of Biblical Literature Annual Meetings. Parts of Chapters 2 and 4 were read to the Book of Psalms section. Part of Chapter 8 was read to the Ecological Hermeneutics section. Parts of Chapters 1 and 8 were read to the Islands, Islanders, and Scriptures section. I am grateful to the participants in these sections for their constructive feedback. I would particularly like to thank Jione Havea of the Islands, Islanders, and Scriptures section of the Society of Biblical Literature for asking me to present a paper on Turtle Island that helped me to begin to think through the intersections of my own social and ecological context with animals, race, colonialism, and the reading of the Psalms.

I would also like to thank Carriera Lamoureux, Ellen Henry, and Carrie Walker-Jones for proofreading and commenting on earlier versions of the manuscript. They saved me from many errors, and those that remain are solely my responsibility.

ABBREVIATIONS

AB	Anchor Bible
ABL	Robert Francis Harper, *Assyrian and Babylonian Letters* (1900)
ANET³	*Ancient Near Eastern Texts Relating to the Old Testament*, 3rd ed.
BA	*Biblical Archaeologist*
BAR	*Biblical Archaeology Review*
BBR	*Bulletin for Biblical Research*
BCE	Before the Common Era
BDB	Brown, Driver, and Briggs, *Hebrew and English Lexicon of the Old Testament*
BHS	*Biblia Hebraica Stuttgartensia*
CBQ	*Catholic Biblical Quarterly*
cs	common singular
EA	Bezold and Budge, *Tel-El-Amarna Tablets in the British Museum* (1892)
HALOT	*Hebrew and Aramaic Lexicon of the Old Testament*
HSM	*Harvard Semitic Monographs*
HTR	*Harvard Theological Review*
ICC	*International Critical Commentary*
Int	*Interpretation*
JBL	*Journal of Biblical Literature*
JNES	*Journal of Near Eastern Studies*
JR	*Journal of Religion*
JSOT	*Journal for the Study of the Old Testament*
JSOTSup	*Journal for the Study of the Old Testament Supplementary Series*
KAI	*Kanaanäischen und aramäischen Inschriften*
MT	Masoretic Text
NICOT	*The New International Commentary on the Old Testament*
NIB	*The New Interpreter's Bible*
NIV	New International Version
NRSV	New Revised Standard Version
Ps.	Psalm
Pss.	Psalms
SJOT	*Scottish Journal of Theology*
TDOT	*Theological Dictionary of the Old Testament*
TNIV	Today's New International Version
TNK	New Jewish Publication Society TaNaKh
UF	*Ugarit-Forschungen*
VT	*Vetus Testamentum*
ZAW	*Zeitschrift Für Die Alttestamentliche Wissenschaft*

Chapter 1

INTRODUCTION

Of the writing of commentaries there is no end, but this is a very different type of commentary. Different not only because it is an Earth Bible Commentary but also because it integrates the interdisciplinary and intersectional perspectives of animal studies with ecological biblical interpretation. Unlike traditional commentaries, this one will not comment on every aspect of research on each psalm. The commentary will focus on aspects relevant to animals and ecology. Even in this regard there is so much evidence from biology, zooarchaeology, anthropology, and cultural studies relevant to the many species mentioned in Psalms, and so little of it is known in and integrated in Psalms studies that this commentary will have to be content with a few exploratory probes designed to show the extent and promise of the work that could be done integrating nonhuman animals and ecology into biblical interpretation. My hope is that readers will come away with a greater appreciation for the importance of Earth and Earth creatures for biblical interpretation in an age of species extinctions and catastrophic climate change.

When I began writing this commentary, our family dog Jojo was nearing the end of his life. We got Jojo from the Humane Society shortly after we returned to Canada from living in Fiji. We were struggling to reintegrate into Canadian society, and our son David was having a particularly difficult time because he had spent most of his first six years in the South Pacific. He had a dog named Jojo in Fiji and we thought getting a new dog might help him with the adjustment to Canadian society. David named the new puppy we got at the Humane Society after his dog in Fiji. David says that Jojo was an important friend for him during this time. This is all to say that Jojo had become an important member of our family. But for several years he had had arthritis and was obviously in pain. He became so crippled that I had to carry him outside so that he could relieve himself, sometimes in the middle of the night. Still, there were accidents and a growing number of stains on our floors and carpets.

People had been telling us for several months that it might be time to "put him down," and I had been struggling with how to make this decision for a sentient being and member of our family. At the same time, there was a national debate going on in Canada about medical assistance in death that helped raise in my mind the ethics of medically assisted death of a nonhuman animal such as Jojo. When I was going to be away for a number of weeks, he was too heavy for my partner to carry outside, and we decided to put him down. We took him to our veterinarian and he administered an injection. When the drugs started to take effect, Jojo struggled to get up. The veterinarian had to administer another shot to get him to "go to sleep." Even then Jojo continued to struggle for some time. I did not feel Jojo had decided he was suffering and it was time for him to go. Instead I felt I had decided to kill him because he had become inconvenient to look after.

As a result of this experience, I realized that my previous work in ecological hermeneutics focused more on environmental issues than on animals and the ethics of human relations with other species. In the introduction to the Earth Bible Commentary, Norman Habel says that "the most obvious dimension" of identifying with Earth "is to identify with non-human figures in the narrative, empathising with their roles, character and treatment, and discerning their voices."[1] Commentaries on Psalms make few comments on the many animals mentioned in the text, and, when they do, these comments tend to assume the nonhuman animals are objects of the human story, background to the human story, or mere metaphors for humans. While I have occasionally discussed other animals in my work,[2] I have not given sustained and systematic attention to nonhuman animals and the ethical issues raised by current relations between humans and nonhuman animals. While I sought to move beyond anthropocentrism, I tended to apply this to the environment. While I sought to blur the binaries that legitimate oppression, I gave little thought to the human/animal binary. While I sought to avoid treating Earth as an object and background to the human story, I may have assumed nonhuman animals were background and objects to the human story. I will suggest below that according to modern evolutionary biology and anthropology, other animals are integral to the human story and the ancient writers of the Psalms may have had more of an awareness of interdependence than many modern, urban humans suspect.

Reading like a Mountain

The pioneering environmentalist and nature writer Aldo Leopold wrote in *A Sand County Almanac* about learning to "think like a mountain." Leopold recalls shooting a wolf at a time when people assumed that fewer wolves would mean more deer and better hunting. He began to have doubts about this thinking as he watched the "fierce green fire" die in the wolf's eyes. He says,

> Since then I have lived to see state after state extirpate its wolves. I have watched the face of many a newly wolfless mountain, and seen the south-facing slopes

---

1. Norman C. Habel, *The Birth, the Curse and the Greening of Earth* (Earth Bible Commentary Series 1; Sheffield: Sheffield Phoenix Press, 2011), 11.
2. "The So-Called Ostrich in the God Speeches of the Book of Job (Job 39,13–18)," *Biblica* 86 (2005): 494–510.

wrinkle with a maze of new deer trails. I have seen every edible bush and seedling browsed, first to anaemic desuetude, and then to death. I have seen every edible tree defoliated to the height of a saddle horn ... In the end the starved bones of the hoped-for deer herd, dead of its own too-much, bleach with the bones of the dead sage, or molder under the high-lined junipers ...

I now suspect that just as a deer herd lives in mortal fear of its wolves, so does a mountain live in mortal fear of its deer ...

... The cowman who cleans his range of wolves does not realize that he is taking over the wolf's job of trimming the herd to fit the range. He has not learned to think like a mountain. Hence we have dustbowls, and rivers washing the future into the sea.[3]

Learning to "think like a mountain" thus means understanding the interconnections of species in an ecosystem and the long-term consequences of actions. Learning to think like a mountain is similar to the work a commentator needs to do to write an Earth Bible Commentary that identifies with Earth and Earth community.

But how does a human reader identify with Earth and Earth community and speak for them? On the one hand, this is essential to an ecological hermeneutic because a failure to listen to and identify with Earth community has contributed to climate change and the environmental crisis. On the other hand, this may be fraught with dangers. Feminists have recognized that when white feminists thought they were speaking for all women, they were often excluding women of color. Similarly, when a white male thinks he is speaking for Earth community, he may be excluding some members of Earth community or other members of the human community.

As an example of the hermeneutical difficulties in thinking like a mountain, consider the quote from Leopold. When I read Leopold's passage about thinking like a mountain, I can identify with the absent environmentalist who, like Leopold, understands ecology better than the "cowman." Like many urban environmentalists, I might think the solution to an eroded mountain would be to remove the cowman, create a park, and restore the wolves. This has often been the solution advocated by urban environmentalists. But where are Indigenous peoples in this quote, or in the *Sand County Almanac* for that matter? The quote could function to legitimate the removal of Indigenous peoples from the land in order to create parks on the mistaken assumption that humanity and nature are separate and that preserving nature means removing humans, even the humans who have been there for millennia. If humans are, and always have been, part of the ecosystem, then ethical decision-making becomes more complex and ambiguous.

What about the cowman? Do ranchers not understand that a herd needs to be trimmed to fit the range? Or is it just that they have added cattle to the deer on

---

3. Aldo Leopold, *Sand County Almanac with Essays on Conservation from Round River* (*Sand County Almanac* [Oxford: Oxford University Press, 1949]; *Round River* [Oxford: Oxford University Press, 1953]; New York: Ballantine Books, 1970), 138–40.

that range? Leopold's passage that advocates for a more ecological way of thinking could function to support a particular group of humans, urban environmentalists, over and against Indigenous people and ranchers. A green passage that should move beyond anthropocentrism ends up functioning in a new, narrowly anthropocentric way. That this quote from a famous conservationist and nature writer could function to favor one human group is a warning that an ecological hermeneutic needs to be suspicious of the socioecological locations of readers.

Turtle Island

The suspicion that my own reading might be anthropocentric requires a critical analysis of my own socioecological location, as I have already begun to indicate by identifying as an urban environmentalist. The Sierra Madre Mountains of Leopold's quotes are much different than the lands east of the Mediterranean of the book of Psalms, and much different than the ecosystems that I inhabit. I live in the city of Winnipeg in the Canadian province of Manitoba, which sits on the junction of the Red and Assiniboine Rivers, the meeting place of Anishinaabe, Cree, Oji-Cree, and Dakota Peoples for centuries and the homeland of the Métis Nation. While climate change and pollution are worldwide phenomena, they affect different ecosystems in different ways. The Assiniboine River runs 1,070 kilometers (665 miles) through the rich agricultural land of the Prairies until it joins the Red River. The Red River runs north for 885 kilometers (530 miles) along the border between Minnesota and North Dakota and through Manitoba into Lake Winnipeg. Settlers in the 1800s made massive changes to the ecology. They killed the once massive bison herds, sometimes just for sport, plowed up the indigenous tall grasses of the prairies, drained marshes, and replaced the bison and tall grass prairie with domestic plants and animals. Today, the runoff of fertilizers from agricultural lands along these two rivers causes massive, toxic, algae blooms in Lake Winnipeg during warm summers. Netley Marsh, on the delta of the Red River as it enters Lake Winnipeg, might have filtered water running into the lake, but most of the marsh flora has died off, probably partly due to the way water levels are maintained to produce hydroelectric power. The many aquatic birds that used to congregate in Netley Marsh, when Leopold visited in 1941,[4] are now largely absent. To the east and north of Lake Winnipeg is the Precambrian Shield with its many rocky lakes and rivers and boreal forest. As I write this, over a thousand people have been airlifted from Little Grand Rapids and Pauingassi First Nations because forest fires threaten their communities. Forest fires are normal in the boreal forest, but the more severe droughts predicted by climate change models will increase their severity. The Prairies to the south and west of Winnipeg are prone to both drought and flooding.

---

4. Leopold, *Sand County Almanac*, 168–73.

Winnipeg lies on Treaty One territory, the traditional lands of the Anishinaabe, Cree, Oji-Cree, Dakota Peoples, and the homeland of the Métis Nation. As a service hub for many remote Northern communities of Anishinaabe, Oji-Cree, Cree, Dene, and Inuit Peoples, it has the largest per capita Indigenous population in Canada. I am among the settler peoples who colonized and continue to benefit from the colonization of Indigenous peoples and lands. The local news frequently features examples of racism and colonialism and the interrelationship of those issues with environmental issues. For instance, my drinking water comes from Shoal Lake 40 First Nation. In 1915, the city of Winnipeg annexed 33,000 acres of Shoal Lake 40 First Nation in order to provide drinking water for the growing city. Indigenous burial grounds were excavated as part of the project. In 1980, the city of Winnipeg opposed a plan by Shoal Lake 40 First Nation to sell vacation properties in case they polluted Winnipeg's water supply. Since 2011, when Shoal Lake 40's water treatment plant broke down and the federal government refused to pay for its repair, the community has been relying on bottled water. In a compromise, the provincial and federal governments recently agreed to begin construction of a road to Shoal Lake 40 First Nation so that a new water treatment plant could be built.

Another example that has been in the news is the Idle No More movement. In 2012 three Indigenous women and one non-Indigenous woman, Sylvia McAdams, Nina Wilson, Jessica Gordon, and Sheelah McLean, respectively, created the Idle No More Facebook page and held an Idle No More conference to oppose the federal government's omnibus budget bill that eroded Indigenous land rights and reduced environmental protections. This movement that started in Saskatoon rapidly became one of the largest Indigenous movements in Canada with teach-ins and protests across the country. At the University of Winnipeg where I teach, two Indigenous students, Sadie-Phoenix Lavoie and Kevin Settee, were leaders in the campaign to ask the university to divest from fossil fuels, because fossil fuel companies often ignore Indigenous rights and pollute Indigenous land and water. These are just a few of the many examples of the local intersections between Indigenous rights and environmental issues that have propelled Indigenous activists to become leaders in protecting the environment in Canada.

Because of this particular ecological context, the hermeneutic that I use in this commentary is interested in the intersections between colonialism and environmental issues. The Bible has been used to colonize Indigenous peoples and the environment. Settlers like myself have simultaneously used the Bible to denigrate Indigenous culture while appropriating parts of Indigenous cultures that suited our interests. This commentary, therefore, seeks to attend to the ancient and contemporary intersections between colonialism and the environment.

One of the Indigenous peoples of the area where I live, the Anishinaabe, also known as Ojibway or Saulteaux, is among several Indigenous peoples who refer to the continent as "Turtle Island." Or, at least, that is the translation into English and other settler languages of Anishinaabe words and myths. References to Turtle Island are all around me in Winnipeg. There is a Turtle Island Community Centre and a *This is Turtle Island TV* show on the Aboriginal Peoples Television Network.

About a hundred miles from Winnipeg, there are large, exposed, flat rocks in the boreal forest with petroforms that were made by Indigenous peoples up to two thousand years ago. Petroforms are figures and shapes created by the placing of rocks. Some of the most iconic are in the shape of turtles. The local Anishinaabe consider them physical reminders of teachings given by the Creator. Local elders of the Midewewin, or Great Medicine Society, regularly lead vision quests and other ceremonies at the site and tell stories of profound spiritual experiences.[5] Colorful prayer sashes left by worshippers hang from surrounding trees. The large, flat rock on which the petroforms sit is part of the Precamabrian Shield, which is made of 3.96 billion-year-old rock that was the base of an ancient mountain range that has been worn down by the glaciers of successive ice ages, and covers an area of over 3 million square miles, or 8 million square kilometers, of North America and Greenland. I have visited some of these, and as I meditated on the petroforms on this ancient rock of the Precambrian Shield, it was easy to feel I was sitting on the back of Turtle Island.

For Dan Snyder, the white author of the Pulitzer Prize–winning book of poetry, *Turtle Island*, referring to North America as Turtle Island seems to represent a way of imagining and working for a future beyond colonialism and ecological exploitation. A note on the back of Snyder's book says, "The poems in the book share a common vision: a rediscovery of this land and the ways by which we might become natives of the place, ceasing to think and act (after all these centuries) as newcomers and invaders." There are few explicit references to Turtle Island in the book, and I have found no extended discussion in Snyder's poetry and essays of what he means by Turtle Island, but the preface to the book gives a few hints. Snyder says the "'U.S.A.' and its states and counties are arbitrary and inaccurate impositions on what is really here," and the name Turtle Island may help us "see ourselves more accurately on this continent of watersheds and life-communities." He goes on to say, "The land, the planet itself, is also a living being—at another pace. Anglos, Black people, Chicanos, and others beached up on these shores all share such views at the deepest levels of their old cultural traditions—African, Asian, or European."[6] In an essay towards the end of *Turtle Island*, Snyder says: "The return to marginal farmland on the part of longhairs is not some nostalgic replay of the nineteenth century. Here is a generation of white people finally ready to learn from the Elders. How to live on the continent as though our children, and on down, for many years, will still be here (not on the moon). Loving and protecting this soil, these trees, these wolves. Natives of Turtle Island."[7] Snyder seems to be suggesting that the name indicates a return to right relations with Indigenous peoples and Turtle Island.

---

5. http://www.winnipegfreepress.com/opinion/fyi/whiteshells-sacred-stones-126445578.html (accessed November 8, 2013).

6. "Introductory Note," n.p. in Gary Snyder, *Turtle Island with "Four Changes"* (New York: New Directions, 1974). *Turtle Island* was originally published in 1969.

7. Snyder, *Turtle Island*, 105.

There are different versions of the Turtle Island myth among different peoples and geographical areas. The story I am familiar with is from Basil Johnston, an Anishinaabe elder. The story is that the water creatures—loon, beaver, fisher, muskrat—took pity on sky-woman and asked a large turtle to come to the surface so that sky-woman could come down and rest. Sky-woman asked the water creatures to dive down and get mud from the bottom. Each in turn failed. When muskrat volunteered, they laughed at the idea that the small and weak muskrat might succeed where they, the strong, had failed. Muskrat was gone for a long time but, just when all hope seemed lost, floated to the surface almost dead, with mud clutched in her hand. As the animals revived muskrat, sky-woman spread the mud around the edge of the shell and breathed the breath of life into the mud so that soil grew and covered the back of the turtle.[8] The water animals brought plants to sky-woman who breathed life into them and they grew and covered Turtle Island. When the time was right, sky-woman gave birth to twins, one male and one female, the first humans. That winter, quoting Basil Johnston, "the spirit woman and her children depended upon the care and good will of the animals. The bears, wolves, foxes, deer, and beaver brought food and drink; the squirrels, weasels, raccoons, and cats offered toys and games; the robins, sparrows, chickadees, and loons sang and danced in the air; the butterflies, bees, and dragonflies made the children smile."[9] At this point in Basil Johnston's story, Kitchi Manitou has already created the manitous that are in all things. "God" or "spirit" is an inadequate translation of "Manitou" but gives a sense of the presence of the divine in all things. Unlike European culture, where animals are valued only for their use for humans, and spirit is separate from matter, Turtle Island and its creatures have intrinsic value and nobility apart from their value for human beings and spirit is in all things—all life is sacred.

Those who are familiar with the Earth Bible series and other volumes of the Earth Bible Commentary will recognize that contributors speak of "Earth" rather than "the earth" to treat Earth as a subject and that, similarly, the Turtle Island myth treats Earth as a subject. This commentary will note where psalms do not use an article with Earth and speak of Earth as a subject or other parts of Earth community as agents. The Turtle Island story expresses a number of Earth Bible principles that will be used in this commentary. Earth and Earth's creatures have intrinsic worth because they all have spirit in them (the principle of intrinsic worth). The animals are dependent on each other and work together (the principle of interconnectedness). Turtle Island and the animals are subjects capable of speaking (the principle of voice). The animals cooperate in providing rest for sky-woman and caring for humans (the principle of purpose). The animals cooperate in creating the land and its plants (the principle of mutual custodianship). While the story does not express the Earth Bible's principle of resistance, the agency of other animals and human dependence on them certainly indicates the basis for the

---

8. Basil Johnston, *Ojibway Heritage* (Toronto: McClelland & Stewart, 1976), 14.
9. Ibid., 15–16.

idea expressed in other Indigenous traditions that Earth and Earth creatures have agency and can resist human injustices. This reading of Psalms from a particular ecological context on Turtle Island thus pays attention to evidence of Earth as a subject, human dependence on other animals, and the interrelationship of ecological issues with colonialism and empire.

Animal Studies

A reader comes to the Psalms not only with culturally informed assumptions about the relationship of humans with other animals, but also culturally informed perspectives on particular members of Earth community. For instance, a reader comes to Leopold's quote with a long history of cultural associations with the words "mountain," "deer," and "wolf." Western culture has a long history of treating the wolf as an enemy, but Leopold points out that this leads to a misunderstanding of the role of wolves in a mountain ecology. An ecological reading is suspicious that these cultural readings are ideological distortions that may result in readings that favor particular members of Earth community or the human community. It is, therefore, important for an ecological hermeneutic to identify cultural assumptions about "wolves" and "deer." A critical awareness of contemporary cultural narratives through which we read the text is important, in order to avoid projecting human interests while identifying with the nonhuman figures in the Psalms.

In addition, it is important to learn as much as possible about the species mentioned and their interrelationship with other species and the environment in order to avoid human cultural distortions and hear the stories of the other animals. In order to tell the story of a mountain, it is necessary to try to understand the stories of wolves, deer, sage, juniper ... and the way they interact on the ecological niche of a mountain. Or, in the case of telling the story of Earth community in the book of Psalms, it is necessary to tell the stories of the many members of Earth community mentioned in the Psalms and their interrelationship in the ecological niche of Ancient Israel.

There are numerous references to animals in Book Two of the Psalms. In what follows, I will use the verse numbers of the Hebrew Bible. Many English translations have different verse numbers, because they do not include the superscriptions[10] in the verse numbering. I put the verse numbers of these English versions in square brackets. The many references to other animals in the Psalms include multiple references to animals living in close relationship with humans, including a mixed "flock," *tso'n*, of sheep and goats (Pss. 44:12, 23[11, 22]; 49:15[14]; 65:14), "goats," *'atudim* (Pss. 50:9, 13; 66:15), "rams" *'elim* (Ps. 66:15), a "young bull," *par* (Ps. 50:9; 69:32[31]), "young bulls," *parim* (Ps. 51:21[19]), "mighty bulls," *'abirim* (Pss. 50:13;

---

10. Superscriptions are the information like "of David" that precedes psalms. Most scholars think they were added long after the writing of the psalms either during or after their collection in the Psalter.

68:31[30]), an "ox," *baqar* (Ps. 66:15), another word translated as "ox," *shor* (Ps. 69:32[31]), and a "dog," *kelev* (Ps. 59:7, 14[6, 13]) or "dogs," *kelavim* (Ps. 68:24[23]). There are references to animals humans might encounter less often such as a "deer," *'ayyal* (Ps. 42:2[1]), "jackals/foxes,"[11] *shu'alim*, and a "snail," *shablul* (Ps. 58:9[8]); hope to encounter less often like "lions," *leva'im* (Ps. 57:5[4]), "young lions," *kephirim* (Ps. 58:7[6]); as well as references to a snake, variously translated "adder," "viper," or "cobra," *peten* (Ps. 58:5[4]), and perhaps "jackals" or "sea monsters," *tannim* (Ps. 44:20[19]). There are also more general references to "every living being of the forest," *kol chayeto ya'ar* (Ps. 50:10), "every living being of the reeds" (Ps. 68:31[30]), and even more generally "birds," *'oph* (Ps. 50:11), and "animals," *behemot* (Ps. 49:13, 21[12, 20]). There are even references to parts of animals such as "ivory," *shen* (Ps. 45:9[8]), "wings," *kenaphayim* (Pss. 57:2[1]; 61:5[4]; 63:8[7]) and "wing feathers like a dove," *'eber kayonah* (Ps. 55:7[6]) and "wings of a dove," *kanphe yonah* (Ps. 68:14[13]). The alert reader may have noted that I have tried to avoid imposing a domestic/wild binary on these animals by speaking of the frequency of encounter in order to begin to indicate relations with humans that are part of a particular ecological niche, though this remains anthropocentric. This commentary will have occasion to say more about this socioecology in the context of each reference.

There are only a few works on the natural history of biblical animals, and the information in these is seldom if ever integrated into commentaries. There are works on the animals of the Bible like those of F. S. Bodenheimer[12] and George Cansdale[13] that include important biological information, though that information is sometimes outdated. Edward Hope's book for translators is more recent.[14] The works of Oded Borowski[15] and Aharon Sasson[16] are particularly important for this commentary because they present zooarchaeological information on human relations with other animals in the Levant. Yet these books have relatively brief treatments of each species. Brent Strawn's book on lions[17] is an example of the

---

11. This word in Hebrew covers three species of fox and jackals, which look like large foxes.

12. F. S. Bodenheimer, *Animal Life in Palestine: An Introduction to the Problems of Animal Ecology and Zoogeography* (Jerusalem: Mayer, 1935); *Animals and Man in Bible Lands* (Leiden: Brill, 1960).

13. G. S. Cansdale, *All the Animals of the Bible Lands* (Grand Rapids, MI: Zondervan, 1970).

14. Edward R. Hope, *All Creatures Great and Small: Living Things in the Bible* (Helps for Translators; New York: United Bible Societies, 2005).

15. Oded Borowski, *Every Living Thing: Daily Use of Animals in Ancient Israel* (Walnut Creek, CA: Altamira, 1998).

16. Aharon Sasson, *Animal Husbandry in Ancient Israel: A Zooarchaeological Perspective on Livestock Exploitation, Herd Management and Economic Strategies* (Approaches to Anthropological Archaeology; London: Equinox, 2010).

17. Brent A. Strawn, *What Is Stronger Than a Lion? Leonine Image and Metaphor in the Hebrew Bible and the Ancient Near East* (Orbis Biblicus et Orientalis 212; Fribourg: Academic Press, 2005).

depth and extent of research that could be done on many other species mentioned in the Psalms, though he is the exception that proves the rule, because work in biology and zooarchaeology is not widely read or integrated in biblical studies. Brent Strawn briefly mentions that lions are extinct, threatened or endangered in many areas of their former range, but generally these works do not raise the question of the ethics of human-animal relations and what guidance the Bible might have for faith communities that understand themselves to be formed by these texts. Commentaries seldom make use of even these limited, mediated resources much less the extensive resources of natural history, zooarchaeology, biology, and cultural studies to understand the interdependence of humans with other animals and query the ethics of those relations.

References to animals are not mere metaphors. Even when they are used in similes and metaphors, they have power for the author and readers because of lived relationships with those particular animals. As Claus Westermann says, "In animal similes/metaphors it is a question of *real* animals; otherwise the comparison would lose its point."[18] There are many metaphorical uses of sheep in the Hebrew Bible because sheep were so important in the socioecology of ancient Israel. Moreover, experiences of real sheep tend to be filtered through cultural understandings. For example, the ancient and widespread idea that sheep are dumb or passive may serve to justify human use of them.[19] Even shepherds with extensive lived experience may find reasons to think sheep are stupid.[20] It makes little difference whether the references to sheep being dumb are literal or metaphorical in this context. The two interact as the metaphorical uses are part of the cultural assumptions through which people experience literal sheep. Recent research, however, indicates that, in areas suited to their kind, sheep have greater intelligence than dogs and are on par with some primates.[21] Given the history of exploitation, an ecological hermeneutic is suspicious that the references distort the relationship. Allusions to sheep as stupid or passive may justify mistreating and killing them. This underscores again the need for an ecological hermeneutic to be informed both by scientific studies and cultural studies in order to understand what biblical references tell us about the relationships of humans with sheep, their ecological niche, and the sheep's story.

There is a growing body of interdisciplinary research and writing relevant to understanding the relationship of humans to other animals in the Psalms. Since Darwin, the lines that were drawn between humans and animals have become less distinct. This blurring of the lines has accelerated recently with a growing body of scientific and popular literature examining intelligence, language, morality,

---

18. Claus Westermann, *Genesis 37–50: A Commentary* (Minneapolis: Augsburg, 1986). 228, cited in Strawn, *What Is Stronger than a Lion?*, 27.
19. Philip Armstrong, *Sheep* (Animal Series; London: Reaktion, 2016), 10–13.
20. Ibid., 45–6.
21. Ibid., 49–50.

and religion[22] in animals—those areas that were traditionally cited as unique to humans. This raises questions about what it means to be "human" and the ethics of human relationships with other animals. Major contemporary philosophers like Peter Singer, Jacques Derrida, J. M. Coetzee, and Giorgio Agamben have written books about animals.[23] Leading cultural critics like Donna Haraway have focused on animals.[24] A number of schools like NYU and Michigan State have developed institutes, minors, majors and graduate programs in animal studies, human-animal studies, and critical animal studies. These programs are interdisciplinary, with contributions from various disciplines in the social sciences (sociology, anthropology, archaeology, psychology, and political science), the humanities (history, literary criticism, philosophy, and geography), and the natural sciences (ethology, veterinary medicine, animal welfare science, and comparative psychology). As a result, some are now speaking of an emerging field of animal studies—the interdisciplinary and intersectional inquiry that examines the relationship of humans with other animals, and the story of animals themselves. Volumes in Reaktion Books Animal Series were particularly useful to this work, as they provide summaries of interdisciplinary animal studies research on individual species relevant to this commentary.[25]

A few biblical scholars have now begun to engage animal studies. Stephen Moore used animal studies in a chapter in *Mark as Story*[26] and he edited a volume that included papers by biblical scholars entitled *Divinanimality: Animal Theory, Creaturely Theology* that examines the boundaries between divinity, humanity, and animality.[27] The Reading, Theory and the Bible Section of the Society of Biblical Literature had a panel on animals a few years ago that resulted in *The*

---

22. For the research on religion among other species, see Ken Stone, *Reading the Hebrew Bible with Animal Studies* (Stanford: Stanford University Press, 2018), 148–54.

23. Peter Singer, *Animal Liberation: The Definitive Classic of the Animal Movement* (Revised ed.; New York: HarperCollins, 2009); Jacques Derrida, *The Animal That Therefore I Am*, ed. Marie-Louise Mallet (Perspectives in Continental Philosophy Series; New York: Fordham University Press, 2009); J. M. Coetzee, *The Lives of Animals*, ed. Amy Guzman (The University Centre for Human Values Series; Princeton: Princeton University, 1999); Giorgio Agamben, *The Open: Man and Animal*, trans. Kevin Attell (Meridian, Crossing Aesthetics; Stanford, CA: Stanford University Press, 2003).

24. Donna Haraway, *When Species Meet* (Posthumanities, 3; Minneapolis: University of Minnesota Press, 2008).

25. See, for instance, Erica Fudge, *Animal* (Focus on Contemporary Issues; London: Reaktion, 2002); John Fletcher, *Deer* (London: Reaktion, 2013); and others in the footnotes and bibliography.

26. Stephen D. Moore, "Why There Are No Humans or Animals in the Gospel of Mark," in *Mark as Story: Retrospect and Prospect*, ed. Kelly R. Iverson, and Christopher Skinner (Atlanta: Society of Biblical Literature, 2011), 71–93.

27. Stephen D. Moore, *Divinanimality: Animal Theory, Creaturely Theology* (Transdisciplinary Theological Colloquia; New York: Fordham University Press, 2014).

Bible and Posthumanism, edited by Jennifer Koosed,[28] that explored the ethics of the human use of animals and illustrates the potential of animal studies for biblical scholarship. The New Testament scholar Michael Gilmour wrote *Eden's Other Residents* exploring the biblical resources for a Christian animal ethics.[29] Ken Stone's book *Reading the Hebrew Bible with Animal Studies* explores the ways engagement with animal studies could help rethink the discourses of gender and ethics, the interpretation of particular texts, the Bible's material and social history, as well as the history of Israel.[30] A tremendous amount of work will be necessary before this information is synthesized and integrated into biblical studies and will require many people with specialization in various areas of the sciences, social sciences, and humanities. Until then, I will not be able to synthesize and integrate all the information from the sciences, social sciences, and humanities that might be relevant to understanding each of the animals mentioned in the Psalms, but I try in this commentary to give a sense of the richness and potential of animal studies for biblical interpretation.

Anthropocentrism and Binaries

Animal studies shares many similarities with ecocriticism and some ecocritics are beginning to include animal studies in their theory and practice.[31] Animal activists and environmentalists have sometimes been at odds. For instance, environmentalists may advocate for the culling or removal of invasive species to protect an ecosystem or the removal of diseased individuals to preserve a population. Ethical decision-making becomes more complex and ambiguous. Nevertheless, there is much overlap in theory and practice between animal studies and ecocriticism. Both animal studies critics and ecocritics identify anthropocentrism as a problem. They cite Lynn White Jr.'s seminal argument that Western Christianity's anthropocentrism and treatment of humans as separate from and superior to Creation has legitimated the exploitation of Earth and other animals.[32] This commentary attempts to provide less anthropocentric readings of the Psalms by showing the interrelationship and interdependence of humans and other animals. It admittedly remains anthropocentric to the extent that it does not

---

28. Jennifer L. Koosed, ed. *The Bible and Posthumanism* (Atlanta: Society of Biblical Literature, 2014).

29. Michael J. Gilmour, *Eden's Other Residents: The Bible and Animals* (Eugene, OR: Cascade, 2014).

30. Ken Stone, *Reading the Hebrew Bible with Animal Studies* (Stanford: Stanford University Press, 2018).

31. Greg Garrard, *Ecocriticism* (The New Critical Idiom Series. 2nd ed.; London: Routledge, 2012), 146–80.

32. Lynn White, Jr., "The Historical Roots of Our Ecologic Crisis. *Science* 155, no. 3767 (1967): 1203–7; Fudge, *Animal*, 14–15.

attempt to read from the perspective of other species, because I do not yet know them well enough to do that.

Both ecocritics and animals studies scholars understand several interrelated binaries in Western language and culture (human/nature, male/female, spirit/matter, etc.) as functioning to legitimate exploitation and, therefore, seek to blur those binaries. Though ecocritics may neglect the human/animal binary, and animal studies critics often add a concern for the ethics of human animal relations, such as the suffering of animals in factory farms and scientific experiments. I have been influenced by Donna Haraway, who works with the intersections of feminism, environmental issues, and animal studies. In her classic article "A Manifesto for Cyborgs," Haraway argued for developing an "ironic political myth faithful to feminism" that could be used "for *pleasure* in the confusion of boundaries and for *responsibility* in their construction."[33] Thus I have an interest in stories and interpretations of stories that blur the boundaries between binaries and construct them in ways that might lead to a better future. Haraway coins the term "naturecultures"[34] to indicate the way nature and culture are interrelated. This will be a recurring concern of this commentary. I sometimes also use the word "sociecology" to indicate the interrelationship of society and ecology. This commentary, therefore, adds attention to the human/animal and nature/culture binaries and the ethics of human relationships with other animals to the ecocritical analysis of binaries that oppress.

In his book *The Spell of the Sensuous*, David Abram suggests that anthropologists have read the Western dualism between spirit and matter into animist religions. He realized this in the process of doing a doctorate on the psychology of perception and field work with the traditional shamans of Indonesia.[35] He argues that many Indigenous peoples understood themselves in relationship and constant conversation with all parts of Creation and the modern West has narrowed our horizon to relationships with other humans or, in other words, has become increasingly anthropocentric. "The medicine person's primary allegiance," he says, "is not to the human community, but to the earthly web of relations in which that community is embedded—it is from this that his or her power to alleviate human illness derives—and this sets the local magician apart from other persons."[36] Traditional shamans understood themselves as doing ceremonies not just to heal individual humans, or even the human community, but as maintaining right relations between the human community and Earth community.

---

33. Donna Haraway, "A Manifesto for Cyborgs: Science, Technology, and Socialist Feminism in the 1980s," *Socialist Review* 80 (1985): 65, 66.

34. Donna Haraway, *The Companion Species Manifesto; Dogs, People, and Significant Otherness* (Chicago: Prickly Paradigm, 2003).

35. David Abram, *The Spell of the Sensuous: Perception and Language in a More-Than-Human World* (New York: Random House, 1996), 12–16.

36. Ibid., 8.

This commentary will explore the possibility that the same may be true of the priestly writers of the Psalms who officiated at ceremonies in the temple. A commentary is not the place to make an exhaustive argument for this, but it will point to evidence the writers and collectors of the Psalms understood themselves to be maintaining right relations between humans and the rest of Earth community. That this is the case may have been lost in translation, disregarded as remnants of an older religion assumed to be inferior, or treated as mere metaphor. Yet Creation language is frequent in the Psalms and the temple was understood as a microcosm of the cosmos.[37] If the temple was understood as the microcosm of the cosmos, then the priests may have understood the singing of these Psalms and performance of rituals as maintaining relations not just between humans and God but also between God and Earth community. This commentary points to evidence that the writers of the Psalms may have assumed humans were in relationship with all Creation, did not have as strong a binary between spiritual and material as modern translators and commentators, and, as leaders of temple worship, had a special role to play in maintaining right relations among all parts of Creation.

Lost in Translation

Both animal studies and ecocriticism are concerned with language and how it functions to construct reality and inform ethics. As mentioned earlier, the Earth Bible Commentary refers to Earth, rather than the earth, in order to treat Earth as a subject rather than an object, because the assumption that "the earth" is an object has facilitated exploitation. In the first volume of the Earth Bible series, Edgar Conrad argued that "rendering the Hebrew word *mal'akh* as 'angel' introduces a dualism characteristic of the Western perception of reality, which makes a sharp demarcation between heaven and earth."[38] In *Exploring Ecological Hermeneutics*, Theodore Hiebert argued that translators had imposed a Western dualism by translating one Hebrew word in different places as "wind," "breath" or "spirit." He argued that "within the biblical conception of *rwch*, the air of atmosphere and the air that we breathe are at the same time united, sacralized, and granted ultimate significance."[39] Thus, this commentary is attentive to the naming of Earth and points to Hebrew words that blur the boundaries between Western binaries.

Similarly, animal studies scholars use a variety of expressions to attempt to get around the human/animal binary. Jacques Derrida has pointed out that the use of one word, "animal," to designate the incredible diversity of species that are not human is absurd and coins the word *animot* to replace animal.[40] By using this

---

37. Jon D. Levenson, "The Temple and the World," *JR* 64 (1984): 275–98.
38. Edgar W. Conrad, "Messengers in the Sky," in *Readings from the Perspective of Earth*, vol. 1, ed. Norman C. Habel, Earth Bible (Sheffield: Sheffield Academic Press, 2000), 95.
39. Theodore Hiebert, "Air, the First Sacred Thing," in *Exploring Ecological Hermeneutics*, ed. Norman C. Habel and Peter Trudinger (Atlanta: Society of Biblical Literature, 2008), 19.
40. Derrida, *The Animal That Therefore I Am*, x, 34, 47–51.

word that sounds like a plural in French he hopes to alert readers to the diversity of species it represents and call into question the human/animal binary and the violence it does. Derrida wrote originally in French, but the issue is largely the same in the English language. The human/animal binary in the English language functions to legitimate exploitation by bolstering the cultural assumption that humans are separate from, and superior to, other animals. While it is not the only or perfect solution, this chapter has been using "other animals" and will sometimes use "nonhuman animals" to blur the human/animal binary and indicate that humans are also animals. The Earth Bible often speaks of Earth community and Earth kin. This commentary sometimes also uses the more biblical language of "creatures" to indicate that humans and other animals are all created beings in the Bible.

Sometimes cultural assumptions about Earth creep into translation. For instance, translators often add a definite article to Earth even when there is no definite article in the Hebrew.[41] By contrast, other volumes of the Earth Bible Commentary consistently use "Earth" without an article to promote an understanding of Earth as a subject. This commentary adopts a slightly different approach in order to explore why the Hebrew Bible uses, or does not use, a definite article with Earth in each passage. The commentary, therefore, translates "the Earth" when the Hebrew has a definite article and "Earth" when the Hebrew does not have an article. The presence or absence of an article on Earth seems open to a number of explanations on a variety of levels and further study is needed. I want to suggest, however, that the absence of an article on Earth combined with evidence that Earth speaks or acts may be evidence of an understanding of Earth as a living subject.

The translations from Hebrew into English are mine unless otherwise noted, and, because the oppression of Earth and women are interrelated, I often choose inclusive language to translate the Hebrew, though the translations are fairly literal so sometimes I use gendered pronouns for accuracy. In these and other ways, the commentary discusses translation choices relative to Earth and Earth community and sometimes proposes alternatives.

Identification

Both ecocriticism and animal studies are concerned with various forms of identification with Earth and other animals. Habel's introduction to the Earth Bible Commentary speaks of the "task of empathy or identification."[42] Animal studies has given considerable critical attention to the way humans are identified with animals in literature and science that may be relevant to thinking about identification with

---

41. Examples of places in Book Two where the Hebrew has no definite article on Earth but English translations add them are the following: Pss. 46:7[6], 11[10]; 50:1; 65:6[5]; 67:7[6], 8[7]; 68:9[8]; 69:35[34]; 72:6, 8.

42. Habel, *The Birth*, 10.

Earth generally. Some forms of identifying other animals with humans may not lead to better lived relations. The Pilgrimage Window (ca. 1300) at York Minster has a bottom border with a fox preaching to a cock, monkeys carrying a coffin, a monkey doctor examining a urine flask, and another monkey doctor examining a sick monkey. This might seem like an identification of animals with humans that blurs the boundaries between humans and other animals. Paul Hardwick argues, however, that in its historical context the monkeys were understood as aspiring to human behavior, in the same way humans aspire to divine behavior so that the monkeys were being used to talk about humans, not monkeys themselves, and maintain a hierarchy between humans and other animals.[43] By contrast, William Hogarth's four prints *The Four Stages of Cruelty* (1751) that depict shocking cruelty to animals (including humans) in the streets of London are an example of the visual representations that help people identify with the suffering of other animals and played a key role in improving animal welfare.[44] Hogarth's prints are about animals themselves rather than just about humans. A number of artists have explored having other animals create art so that the animals become subjects rather than objects in the making of art.[45] Greg Garrard proposes a typology for the different ways humans represent other animals in literature and culture. Broadly, other animals can be portrayed as either like or unlike humans. If they are portrayed as unlike humans, then they may be portrayed in ways that suggest inferiority, as in Cartesian objectification of animals as machines. Or rarely, other animals may be portrayed as numinous, superior others. If they are represented as like humans, other "animals may be understood in human terms (anthropomorphism) or humans in animal terms (zoomorphism)."[46] There are both critical and uncritical forms of anthropomorphism and zoomorphism. Ecocriticism would do well to develop a similar critical analysis of different types of human identification with Earth and whether the identification is anthropocentric or biocentric.

A Reader's Concerns

Both ecocriticism and animal studies bring contemporary information and concerns to the reading of texts. For ecocriticism, this includes scientific information about ecology and a concern to address contemporary environmental issues. For animal studies, this includes biological information about species, cultural criticism, and a concern to address the suffering of other animals. These contemporary concerns

---

43. Paul Hardwick, "The Monkey's Funeral in the Pilgrimage Window, York Minster," *Art History* 23 (2000): 297, cited in Fudge, *Animal*, 151–2.

44. Fudge, *Animal*, 152–3, citing Diana Donald, "'Beastly Sights': The Treatment of Animals as a Moral Theme in Representations of London, c. 1820–1850," *Art History* 22 (1999): 523–5.

45. Fudge, *Animal*, 156–8.

46. Garrard, *Ecocriticism*, 154.

with environmental issues and animal ethics are a particularly acute issue for an ecological hermeneutics of the Bible, because many faith communities consider the Bible foundational for theology and ethics. Biblical scholars, however, often express the idea that such contemporary information and concerns should be set aside when reading the biblical text to be objective and recover the meaning intended by the author. Because the authors of biblical books are frequently unknown, biblical scholars more often speak of understanding what the text would have meant for the original audience. Thus, someone trained as a biblical scholar might have objected to what I wrote above about thinking like a mountain on the basis that Aldo Leopold did not intend to advocate for the removal of Indigenous people and ranchers from the land. They might object that this is a classic green text and a reading like I have suggested does not fit with Leopold's intent. This idea that the meaning of a passage is what the author intended, however, is part of a nineteenth-century hermeneutic that has been debunked by philosophers and literary critics alike. The philosopher Hans-Georg Gadamer, for instance, has shown that the meaning of something is always created by a dialogue between the text and the presuppositions of the reader.[47] In the 1960s, New Criticism in the United States argued that a reader could not know the intentions of the author and such intentions are irrelevant because the meaning is in the form and structure of the text.[48] Since then, a variety of reader-response criticisms have argued that it is the reader who decides what a text means. The meaning of a text will be influenced by a reader's gender, race, class, religion, politics, and ethics. It is part of the nature of classic texts like the Bible that they have metaphors and narrative patterns that allow them to continue to generate new meanings in successive generations and new contexts.

As someone concerned with climate change, acidification of the oceans, air and water pollution, species extinctions, and the suffering of other animals, I am interested not just in what the Bible meant in its ancient contexts but also in the power of biblical stories to affect change and transform communities today. In this regard, Gale Yee has argued, based on the work of Jane Tompkins, that feminist biblical criticism needs to consider not just the meaning of a text but the social function of an interpretation. Modern criticism with its concern for meaning has lost classical rhetoric's concern with how texts influence society and feminist literary criticism needs to recover a similar concern with social function.[49] In

---

47. Hans-Georg Gadamer, *Truth and Method* (London: Continuum, 1975).

48. William K. Wimsatt and Monroe Beardsley, "The Intentional Fallacy," *Sewanee Review* 54 (1946): 468–88. Revised and republished in William K. Wimsatt, *The Verbal Icon: Studies in the Meaning of Poetry* (Lexington: University of Kentucky Press, 1954), 3–18.

49. Gale A. Yee, "The Author/Text/Reader and Power: Suggestions for a Critical Framework in Biblical Studies," in *Reading from This Place: Social Location and Biblical Interpretation*, ed. Fernando F. Segovia and Mary Ann Tolbert (Minneapolis: Fortress, 1995), 114–15, citing J. P. Tompkins, "The Reader in History: The Changing Shape of Literary Response" in *Reader-Response Criticism: From Formalism to Post-Structuralism*, ed. J. P. Tompkins (Baltimore: Johns Hopkins University Press, 1980), 201–27.

my own thinking about the power of biblical stories to influence contemporary society, I have been influenced by the literary critic, Northrop Frye. Although some aspects of Frye's criticism are out of date, the American Marxist critic Fredric Jameson notes, "The greatness of Frye ... lies in his willingness to raise the issue of community and to draw basic, essentially social, interpretive consequences."[50] Frye's work pervades Jameson's,[51] and, with Frye, he understands literature "as symbolic meditation on the destiny of community."[52] For Frye, the social power of a piece of literature comes from its relation to typical or generic imagery and narrative patterns, which is the types of stories that are told over and over in a society. Horatio Alger, or "rags to riches," stories are a contemporary example. The news media knows such stories are popular with its viewing audience, so stories that fit into this typical pattern appear regularly in the media. In my previous work, I have noted typical narrative patterns and their associated imagery in psalms genres.[53] Because I am interested in the way biblical stories influence contemporary society, this commentary notes typical imagery and stories in the Psalms and the way they interact with contemporary images and stories. The scientific story of coevolution is an example of one such contemporary story.

Coevolution and Niche Construction

Although science has tended to treat other species as objects, the new evolutionary synthesis recognizes other species as agents in mutual and interdependent processes of niche construction and coevolution. Coevolution refers to one or more species influencing the selective pressures on each other and therefore their evolution. This may include various kinds of relationships all the way from mutualism to predator-prey. For example, dogs and humans have coevolved. Genetic and archaeological evidence indicate that the domestication of dogs began as early as 32,000 years ago, and the ancestors of today's dogs (*Canis lupus familiaris*)[54] diverged from European grey wolves (*Canis lupus*) around 18,000–32,000 years ago,[55] thousands

---

50. Fredric Jameson, *The Political Unconscious: Narrative as a Socially Symbolic Act* (Ithaca, NY: Cornell University Press, 1981), 69.

51. Laurence Coupe, *Myth*, ed. John Drakakis (The New Critical Idiom; London: Routledge, 1997), 173.

52. Jameson, *The Political Unconscious*, 69–70.

53. Arthur Walker-Jones, *The Green Psalter: Resources for an Ecological Spirituality* (Minneapolis: Fortress, 2009), 42–51.

54. Biologists debate how to define a species and debate whether dogs are a subspecies of wolf (*Canis lupus familiaris*) or a separate species (*Canis familiaris*). Dogs inhabit a different ecological niche than wolves, but they can interbreed successfully. Gene analysis does not solve the problem as biologists debate *how much* genetic divergence identifies a separate species.

55. Pat Shipman, *The Invaders: How Humans and Their Dogs Drove Neanderthals to Extinction* (Cambridge, MA: Harvard University Press, 2015), 179.

of years before the domestication of any other mammals, during the last ice age while humans were still hunter-gatherers.[56] Western culture tends to assume that humans would be the agents and dogs the objects so that domestication would happen by humans taming wolves. Some scholars imagine this would happen by humans taming wolf pups.[57] This may have been part of the process, but a tame wild animal is much different than a domestic animal, as anyone who has raised a wolf puppy can tell you. It is difficult to imagine hunter-gatherers 25,000 years ago during the last ice age being able to keep the population of about 100 wolves that would be necessary to start a selective breeding program to create domestic dogs, even if they had had the idea.[58]

What is more likely is that some wolves discovered a new ecological niche following bands of human hunter-gatherers around and eating their leftovers and waste. This ecological niche would have created selective pressures that favored smaller and friendlier wolves. Smaller wolves would require fewer calories. Wolves less fearful of humans would waste less energy running away, and friendlier wolves would be less likely to be killed by humans. By contrast, contemporary European grey wolves that have been hunted ruthlessly by humans for centuries have probably developed greater fear of humans and much longer flight distances to survive and are thus different from the wolves of 25,000 years ago. Recent research indicates other ways dogs have adapted to living with humans by learning to track human eye movements[59] and digesting more carbohydrates to better eat human foods high in carbohydrates.[60]

The domestication of other species had a profound effect on the development of human civilization. If dogs gave humans the idea that other species could be domesticated[61] and even helped domesticate them by herding them (sheep and goats were the next mammalian species domesticated), then dogs have had a profound effect on human development. The influence may run the other way, as there is evidence that the selective pressures created by domestication have changed human evolution. Humans also had to adapt to living in close quarters with other species. The paleoanthropologist Pat Shipman argues that those humans who had an ability to understand and work with other species would have had

---

56. Pat Shipman, *The Animal Connection: A New Perspective on What Makes Us Human* (New York: W. W. Norton 2011), 204–20; *The Invaders*, 167–93.

57. Shipman, *The Animal Connection*, 11–13, 270–6.

58. Raymond Coppinger and Lorna Coppinger, *Dogs: A New Understanding of Canine Origin, Behavior, and Evolution* (Chicago: University of Chicago Press, 2002), 39–68.

59. Brian Hare et al., "The Domestication of Social Cognition in Dogs," *Science* 298 (2002): 1634–6.

60. Ewan Callaway, "Dog's Dinner Was Key to Domestication: Genome Study Pinpoints Changes That Turned Wolves into Humanity's Best Friend," *Nature* (2013), doi:10.1038/nature.2013.12280.

61. Xiaoming Wang and Richard H. Tedford, *Dogs: Their Fossil Relatives and Evolutionary History* (New York: Columbia University Press, 2008), 153–4.

an adaptive advantage.[62] A recent study found that lactase persistence in human populations corresponds to dairying areas.[63] Other mammals stop producing the enzyme lactase necessary for digesting milk after they are weaned. Many humans living in areas with domestic sheep, goats, and cattle, however, continue to produce lactase after weaning so that they continue to be able to digest dairy products. Some even argue that domestic species domesticated humans. Yuval Harari provides an extreme and somewhat humorous example of how someone might make the argument that other species domesticated humans. He notes that the domestication of plants and animals did not lead to more leisure or a better diet. Peasants had a poorer diet than hunter-gatherers and worked longer, harder hours for it. He notes that wheat went from being one of many wild grasses in a small area of the Middle East and has managed to spread all around the world and dominate many ecosystems by domesticating humans.

> Within a couple of millennia, humans in many parts of the world were doing little from dawn to dusk other than taking care of wheat plants. It wasn't easy. Wheat demanded a lot of them. Wheat didn't like rocks and pebbles, so Sapiens broke their backs clearing fields. Wheat didn't like sharing its space, water and nutrients with other plants, so men and women laboured long days weeding under the scorching sun. Wheat got sick, so Sapiens had to keep a watch out for worms and blight. Wheat was defenceless against other organisms that liked to eat it, from rabbits to locust swarms, so the farmers had to guard and protect it. Wheat was thirsty, so humans lugged water from springs and streams to water it. Its hunger even impelled Sapiens to collect animal faeces to nourish the ground in which wheat grew.[64]

While this understanding of domestication may overstate the case, it does begin to suggest that humans are interdependent with other species in the process and that other species may benefit and, like dogs, have some agency in the process.

As is already becoming evident in the above discussion, this process of domestication constructs new ecological niches. Niche construction refers to species modifying the environment in ways that change the selective pressures on their descendants. Beavers, for instance, build dams, and this changes the selective pressures on their descendants. The human ability to construct new ecological niches has allowed them to spread into every part of the globe. The creation of tools and the domestication of other species has allowed humans to create new ecological niches. The fossils of early hominids indicate they were often a prey species of large predators, but cooperation and the creation of tools seems to have created a new

---

62. Pat Shipman, "The Animal Connection and Human Evolution," *Current Anthropology* 51 (2010): 525.

63. C. Holden and R. Mace, *Human Biology Phylogenetic Analysis of the Evolution of Lactose Digestion in Adults* (Detroit: Wayne State University Press, 1995) cited in Sasson, *Animal Husbandry in Ancient Israel*, 27.

64. Yuval Noah Harari, *Sapiens: A Brief History of Humankind* (Toronto: Signal, 2014), 80.

ecological niche for humans as a top predator,[65] so successful that they drove other predator and prey species to extinction. In the Levant, the domestication of sheep and goats provided a stable source of dairy products high in fat and protein that could sustain larger human populations. The domestication of cattle for traction provided labor to plow more land and to thresh and transport larger harvests to support larger human populations. The domestication of horses provided the first means of rapid transport and, as students of ancient Near Eastern history know, gave those humans who had them a significant military advantage. Domestication is sometimes viewed as an enslavement of other species, and human objectification and abuse of domestic animals is abhorrent, but they are not mere objects. Cattle and horses are dangerous animals even today and, as Pat Shipman points out, their domestication "is a continually negotiated agreement."[66] The story of human coevolution and niche construction with other species is therefore a story of interrelationship with other species who are subjects, not just objects, in human development.

This commentary will not provide a full argument for the influence of coevolution and niche construction in ancient Israel. It will, however, assume this broader story from biology and animal studies and indicate evidence of it in the Psalms. The ancient writers of the Psalms, of course, would not have had knowledge of modern theories of coevolution and niche construction. The priests who wrote and collected the Psalms lived in Jerusalem, but Jerusalem was a small city in a country where the vast majority of people still lived in villages and practiced a subsistence lifestyle. Even though they lived in a city, they were much closer to an agrarian subsistence lifestyle than modern urbanites living after the urbanization that occurred following the agricultural and industrial revolutions. On the one hand, an ecological hermeneutic is suspicious that those psalms the priests created may reflect the beginnings of urban alienation from the land and legitimate the exploitation of other species and Earth. On the other hand, an ecological hermeneutic is aware the priests lived closer to agrarian, subsistence economies and, therefore, may have had an awareness of human dependence on and interrelationship with other species.

Since humans have evolved with other species, treatments of human history as if ecology and other species were mere background to the human story are an anthropocentric distortion of reality. The writing of history will increasingly need to integrate other species and ecology. One would hope that this would make possible the telling of cultural stories that encourage better lived relationships with other species and Earth.

Canon and Genre

Recent biblical scholarship on the Psalms has argued that the book of Psalms tells a story, though this human story is not usually placed in ecological

---

65. Shipman, *The Invaders*, 48.
66. Shipman, *The Animal Connection*, 245, and *The Invaders*, 5.

context. Historical criticism is the dominant method in biblical scholarship, but individual psalms are difficult to place in historical context or use in the reconstruction of history because of the generic nature of psalms collected and used for generations. For that reason, the main methods that are currently used by Psalms scholars are genre and canonical criticism. Genre criticism identifies types of psalms according to their genre and compares them with other psalms of the same genre and form. Canon criticism examines the way the psalms have been gathered together and ordered in order to persuade, inspire, teach, or tell a story about Israel's life with God. Canon criticism is particularly interested in the superscriptions to the psalms, and the psalms or additions to psalms placed at seams between the five books, because they are evidence of the way those who collected the materials and handed them down, understood them. Psalm 1, for instance, is a "teaching" psalm and so introduces the Psalms as a collection for instruction in faith. At least as far back as the *Midrash Tehillim*, the Psalter was understood to be made up of five books (Pss. 1–41, 42–72, 73–89, 90–106, and 107–150) so that David has five books just as Moses has five books of the Torah.[67] The Psalms are, thus, organized in a way that indicates they can be read as David's instruction in the life of faith.

This commentary treats the second book of the Psalter (Pss. 42–72). The first two books of the Psalter have many psalms with the superscription "of David." The next two books have very few psalms with the superscription "of David." Book Two has the most superscriptions with references to difficulties in David's life and ends with a psalm "of Solomon" and the final line—"the prayers of David are finished." Many of the psalms of Book Two are laments, so the book tends to remember critically the reign of David as part of a movement in the Psalter from lament in these early books toward praise in the final books[68] and from a focus on the failings of the greatest human king of Israel toward an understanding of God as king.[69]

The superscriptions and genres of the Psalms indicate groups of psalms within the Psalter and will be used to organize the discussion into chapters. The way in which the superscriptions and genres indicate these groupings will be discussed in each chapter but by way of preview:

---

67. William G. Braude, *The Midrash on Psalms* (Yale Judaica Series 13; New Haven: Yale University Press, 1954) 1:5.

68. Claus Westermann, *Praise and Lament in the Psalms*, trans. Keith R. Crim and Richard N. Soulen (Atlanta: John Knox, 1981), 257.

69. Brevard Childs, *Introduction to the Old Testament as Scripture* (Philadelphia: Fortress, 1979), 520–1; Peter Ackroyd, *Doors of Perception: A Guide to Reading the Psalms* (London: SCM, 1983), 35; Gerald Sheppard, "Theology and the Book of Psalms," *Int* 46 (1992): 148; James Mays, *The Lord Reigns: A Theological Handbook to the Psalms* (Louisville: Westminster John Knox, 1994), 123–5. For a review of these positions see Harry P. Nasuti, *Defining the Sacred Songs: Genre, Tradition and the Post-Critical Interpretation of the Psalms* (JSOTSup Series, 218; Sheffield: Sheffield Academic, 1999), 138–47.

Chpt.	Title	Superscriptions	Genres
2	As a Doe Groans (Pss. 42–44)	Maskil (2x) of the Korahites (2x)	Laments
3	Urban Empire (Pss. 45–49)	Song (2x) psalm (3x) of the Korahites (5x)	Royal/Zion/Enthronement Wisdom
4	Skies Proclaim (Ps. 50)	A Psalm of Asaph	Oracle
5	Earth as Refuge (Pss. 51–55)	Psalm (1x) Maskil (4x) of David (5x)	Laments
6	Earth as Enemy (Pss. 56–60)	Miktam (5x) of David (5x)	Laments
7	God as Rock (Pss. 61–64)	Of David (4x)	Laments
	Earth's Joy (Pss. 65–68)	Of David (2x) A Song (4x)	Community Thanksgivings
8	Empire's Greenwash (Pss. 69–72)	Of David (2x) Of Solomon (1x)	Laments and a concluding Royal Blessing Prayer

The table shows that repeated terms in the superscriptions and the genres create groups of psalms. Modern scholars created the genre designations such as lament in the column on the right to indicate types of psalms. The meanings of the Hebrew designations "*maskil*" and "*miktam*" in the superscriptions have been lost, but, as the chart above shows, *maskil* and *miktam* seem to have a correspondence with laments.

Book Two begins with two groups of Korahite psalms. The first are laments designated *maskils* that will be discussed in Chapter 2. The second group of Korahite psalms are designated "psalms" or "songs" and have psalms joined by their relationship to Zion and the monarchy. They will be discussed in Chapter 3. Both the superscription to Asaph and the genre of oracle distinguish Psalm 50 from the psalms around it. Psalm 50 also has a unique and ecologically significant understanding of Earth community and warrants separate treatment in Chapter 4. Psalms of David are frequent in the rest of the book. They can be distinguished by the superscriptions and genres that tend to divide them into groups. The first group are laments designated *maskils* and will be treated in Chapter 5. They view Earth as a place of refuge. The next group are laments that are designated as *miktams* and will be treated in Chapter 6. They treat Earth community as enemies and Earth as an object. The next group are laments that are not designated by any term like *miktam* or *maskil* but contain references to God as Rock and will be treated in Chapter 7. The next group are community thanksgivings in which Earth expresses joy and will also be treated in Chapter 7. The next group returns to laments of David and a final Royal Blessing of Solomon. Chapter 8 will discuss the ambiguous relation of empire to Earth.

According to Habel, ecological hermeneutics examines the literary forms and design of the text to discern "whether the narrator or composer designs the material in such a way as to highlight the human characters rather than the non-human dimensions of the text. Or is there a subtle way in which the narrator has empathized with Earth or members of the Earth community by using a particular genre that we, as anthropocentric and Western interpreters, have not discerned? Is the narrator conscious of being an Earth being as well as a human being?"[70] Elsewhere I have argued that the Psalter's genres tend to have typical forms, narratives, and metaphors.[71] These typical narratives and metaphors of the Psalter's genres have typical ecologies that create the Psalter's story of Earth and Earth community. On the one hand, this commentary will show that these genres and their ecologies are bent to the will of empire in ways that are exploitative and anticipate the alienation of humans from Earth of contemporary urban capitalism. On the other hand, the Psalter retains cultural wisdom about human dependence on other species and Earth as subject that coheres both with contemporary understandings of coevolution and niche construction, and the ancient wisdom and values of the story of Turtle Island.

---

70. Habel, *The Birth*, 14.
71. Walker-Jones, *The Green Psalter*, 42–51, 60–73.

Chapter 2

"AS A DOE GROANS" (Pss. 42–44)

The first verse of the second book of the Psalter begins as follows:

> As a doe[1] groans for streams of water,
> thus my being groans for you, O God (Ps. 42:2[1])

This evocative image begins Psalm 42 and the second book of the Psalter. Book Two of the Psalter includes Psalms 42 through 72. Psalm 42 serves as an introduction to Book Two by introducing images that will be elaborated later. Tradition and recent Psalms scholarship associate Book Two with the reigns of David and Solomon[2] and the failure of the covenant with David.[3] A large block of psalms that have the superscription "of David" (Pss. 51–70 and 72) appear in Book Two. The majority are individual laments and are often accompanied with notes that relate them to struggles in David's personal life. Grief and fear tend to narrow human horizons and it is in this rather anthropocentric context of lament and decline and failure of the Davidic monarchy that we hear references to Earth and Earth's creatures.

Psalm 42, however, has a superscription that identifies it not as a psalm of David, but "of the Korahites." Psalm 43 does not have a superscription and scholars suggest that Psalms 42 and 43 were originally one psalm, not least because of the shared refrain, "why is my life cast down" (42:6[5], 12[11]; 43:5). Psalm 42 is the first of a series of psalms whose superscriptions associate them with the Korahites (Pss. 42 and 44–49) and may have circulated as a collection before coming to be included in the Psalter. Another group of Korahite psalms (Pss. 84–85 and 87–88) appears in Book Three of the Psalter, which is usually associated with the divided

---

1. The noun is masculine, but the verb is feminine. Some suggest that a *tav* on the end of deer dropped out by haplography, so doe was the original. Even if the text is not corrected in this way, the male noun could be because of the dominance of the masculine in Hebrew grammar (the use of masculine forms referring to females). Although a (generic) male noun is used, the verb form recognizes that it is a female deer.

2. Nancy deClaissé-Walford, Rolf A. Jacobsen, and Beth LaNeel Tanner, *The Book of Psalms* (NICOT; Grand Rapids, MI: Eerdmans, 2014), 38.

3. J. Clinton McCann, "The Book of Psalms: Introduction, Commentary, and Reflections" in *NIB*, vol. IV, ed. Leander E. Keck et al. (Nashville, TN: Abingdon, 1996), 660.

monarchy, when the Northern tribes had separated from Judah after the death of Solomon.

The Korahites, or more literally "the sons of Korah," were "gatekeepers" in the temple (1 Chron. 26:1, 19) and temple singers (2 Chron. 20:19). This is remembered as an ancient duty dating back to the formation of Israel in the wilderness (1 Chron. 9:19). The two groups of Korahite psalms come before and after the second group of Davidic psalms, bracketing them. This arrangement seems significant. Psalms of David are absent from Book Three, and there are only a few in Book Four until they reappear concentrated at the end of Book Five. This may be part of a "messianic" editing of the Psalter that laments the failures of David's monarchy and looks forward to an ideal David, who will lead the people in worship of God as monarch and Creator.[4] The two groups of Korahite psalms, like the priests themselves, provide a link and continuity between the reign of David and the divided monarch and, perhaps, anticipate the priestly role of David in Book Five. The placement of psalms by the "gatekeepers" before and after the Davidic psalms mirrors their role in the temple.

Deer

Why is this line "as a doe groans for streams of water" so evocative? Cultural and literary criticism helps answer this question by unpacking the range of associations that deer have come to possess in Western art and literature—associations with the mystery of wilderness, fleetness of foot, fertility, and a mixture of grace, timidity, nobility, and courage. The most widely known contemporary examples are Bambi and Rudolph the red-nosed reindeer. The one is a resident of the forest and the other has the magical ability to fly, perhaps an extension of the swiftness of deer.[5] Both also exhibit a combination of timidity and courage. The doe seeking water in Psalm 42 is a good example of this combination of timidity and courage. The doe approaching a watering hole in a dry land must exercise caution because many predators, including humans, may be lying in wait for them, knowing they will eventually come seeking water. If one extends this metaphor through Psalms 42 and 43, then it may evoke just such a situation. The superscription of the psalm associates it with Saul sending people to lie in wait for an opportunity to kill David. And a repeated concern of Psalms 42 and 43 is the enemies and adversaries who "oppress" (42:11[10]; 43:2), "revile" (42:11[10]) and are "deceitful and unjust" (43:2). This fits the image of a deer approaching a wadi. The psalmist identifies with the feelings of a doe who approaches a wadi knowing that enemies may lie in wait to kill her or keep her from life-giving water.

---

4. Arthur Walker-Jones, *The Green Psalter: Resources for an Ecological Spirituality* (Minneapolis: Fortress, 2009), 91–105.

5. John Fletcher, *Deer* (London: Reaktion, 2013).

At the same time, the doe must get water for her fawns. She must overcome fear and show courage to get the water they need to live. As a contemporary reader, I bring many of these associations to the reading of this line. The word *doe* evokes the mixed feelings of vulnerability and determination I may feel approaching God in a time of need.

Contemporary associations with deer may be different than ancient ones. William Brown notes that "the image of the *female* deer, with its head lowered to graze or drink, is a widespread motif" in seventh- and eighth-century Judah and may be distinctively Hebrew.[6] Deer are often pictured in ancient Near Eastern iconography on either side of a tree, perhaps the tree of life, and are taken to represent life and fertility.[7] This association with trees may be based on the fact that the antlers of deer fall off and regrow every year, like the leaves of deciduous trees. Deer antlers thus come to be associated with regeneration and longevity in many cultures.[8]

Deer also have several symbolic associations in the Hebrew Bible. In Western cultures, mountain goats are often associated with firm footing in high places, but in ancient Israel, deer also seem to have been symbolic of firm footing in high places (2 Sam. 22:4; Ps. 18:34[33]; Hab. 3:19). In Prov. 5:19, the deer is either lovely or a loving spouse, or both, and graceful. A reference to deer in Isaiah refers to their ability to "leap" (Isa. 35:6). It is interesting the context connects the deer's leaping with the healing of the lame, singing for joy, and the provision of water in the wilderness. In Isaiah, therefore, the deer is an image for the restoration of the people of God. One of God's questions to Job—"Do you observe the calving of the deer?" (Job 39:1)—may refer to the mystery surrounding wild animals and, perhaps, fertility. Thus, deer in the ancient Near East and the Hebrew Bible may have a broad range of associations including both fleetness of foot and firm footedness on high places, grace, love, fertility, regeneration, and restoration.

Saint Augustine of Hippo (354–430 CE) comments on animals more extensively than many modern commentators, but the way he identifies with other species may not benefit Earth community. In the time of Augustine, catechumens sang Psalm 42 as they approached the baptistery "to arouse in them a longing for the fountain of forgiveness for their sins, like the longing of a deer for the springs of water."[9] In his *Expositions*, Augustine identifies the "springs of water" with both the baptismal font and the understanding of God. He says believers should run like a deer toward the understanding of God because "the deer stands for fleetness of

---

6. William P. Brown, *Seeing the Psalms: A Theology of Metaphor* (Louisville: Westminster John Knox, 2002), 149 and n. 62.

7. Fletcher, *Deer*, 92; I am not sure this is accurate. In my admittedly limited survey, ibexes were more common than deer on either side of the tree representing a goddess.

8. Ibid., 7, 38.

9. Saint Augustine, Bishop of Hippo, *Expositions of the Psalms 33–50*, vol. 2 in *Expositions of the Psalms*, trans. and notes by Maria Boulding, OSB; ed. John E. Rotelle (Hyde Park, NY: New City Press, 2004), 239.

foot."[10] But Augustine does not stop there. He goes on to tell two stories about deer. First, Augustine says, "A hart kills snakes, and after ... burns with a more intense thirst than before; so after dealing with the snakes, he runs to the well-springs even more urgently." He says the snakes represent vices and God will satisfy the thirst of "anyone who comes parched from slaughtering snakes, like a fleet-footed deer."[11] The second story is about deer walking or swimming in single file and resting their heads on the one in front of them. He concludes, "Was it not deer like these that the apostle had in mind? *Bear one another's burdens*, he says, *and so you will fulfill the law of Christ* (Gal 6:2)."[12] These ideas—that deer eat snakes and walk in line with their heads resting on the hindquarters of the one in front of them—go at least as far back as Oppian in his *Cynegetica*, a didactic poem about hunting written in the second century CE.[13] Augustine reasons that "people have seen them doing what I am about to describe; it would not have been recorded about them in writing unless previously observed."[14] People, however, could not have seen this as deer do not do either of these things. Rather this is an example of how an urbanite, whose experience of Earth is mediated by reading, can make other species disappear and become mere metaphors for humans.

This raises the question of whether Psalm 42 is merely using a metaphor to talk about human relations with God or reflects experience of real deer. Can our identification with the deer get beyond anthropocentrism? Can we hear the voice of real deer in it? An indication that Psalm 42 is not just a human cultural metaphor but relates to lived reality is the fact that the doe "groans." As a modern urbanite, I think of deer as mostly silent, but deer actually use a variety of grunts, bleats and wheezes, and a doe may grunt to call her fawns out of hiding or keep them together as they move.[15] Mitchell Dahood follows Ehrlich and Bewer in arguing that *ta'arog* (Ps. 42:2[1]), which the NRSV translates "longing," indicates a vocalization and therefore should be translated "cry."[16] The word occurs only three times in the Hebrew Bible, twice in this verse and once in Joel. That it is followed by *'al*, "over," in Ps. 42:2[1], and by *'eleka*, "to you," in Ps. 42:2[1] and Joel 1:20, seems to indicate more than an internal state like NRSV's "longing," and in Joel 1:19 it is in parallel with *'aleka yhvh 'ekra'*, "to you, O LORD, I cry." In fact, the word appears to be an example of onomatopoeia. Just as the *g* and *r* in the words "grunt"

---

10. Ibid., 241.

11. Ibid., 242.

12. Ibid.

13. Fletcher, *Deer*, 136.

14. Augustine, *Expositions*, 242.

15. "Deer Talk: A Guide to Whitetail Communication," https://www.whitetailsunlimited.com/i/p/bk_deertalk.pdf.

16. Mitchell Dahood, *Psalms 1–50; Introduction, Translation, and Notes* (AB; Garden City, NY: Doubleday, 1966), 255–6, citing A. B. Ehrlich, *Die Psalmen* (Berlin: M. Poppelauer, 1905), 95, and J. A. Bewer in *A Critical and Exegetical Commentary on Obadiah and Joel* (ICC; Edinburgh: T&T Clark, 1912), 92.

and "groan" possess an assonance with the sounds they describe, the *resh* and *gimmel* of *ta'arog* gives it an assonance with the grunting of deer. I would, therefore, translate: "As a doe[17] groans for flowing streams." This is a female voice in Scripture that is often erased by being translated with the generic "deer." Yet one wonders if there is a danger that translating "doe" might support sexist binaries. On the one hand, it associates a female voice with vulnerability, which could reinforce gender stereotypes. On the other hand, leading her fawns to water requires courage and so the doe could be an image of courage. Let the reader decide. In any case, the fact that the deer groans as it searches for water is an indication that Psalm 42 may have the kind of intimate knowledge that comes from living alongside deer.

Furthermore, Psalm 42's use of a deer arises from the long, lived human history with deer. Many people today may not be aware of this history. Archaeologists have found evidence that over five hundred thousand years ago, long before the appearance of *Homo sapiens*, or even Neanderthals, an early hominin ancestor sat with one leg extended and knapped flint using a tool made from an antler. Archaeologists know this from the small pieces of flint still attached to the antler tool found at an archaeological site in Boxgrove, Surrey, and the spray pattern of flint pieces found nearby.[18] The antlers of deer are different than the horns of other animals: "The immense strength and elasticity of antler is far superior to skeletal bone and, until the development of metals, reigned supreme not only as a material for knapping flints, but for weapon tips, sewing needles, making combs and many more tasks."[19]

Not only were deer the source of the tools so central to the development of humans but, for millennia before the rise of agriculture, were also the main source of protein for the majority of humans in Asia, Europe, and North America.[20] North Americans typically distinguish white-tailed deer, and the closely related black-tail and mule deer, from caribou, elk, and moose, but biologically they are

---

17. The MT has a feminine singular verb with a male noun. Dahood mentions that H. L. Ginsberg ("Ugaritic Studies and the Bible," *BA* 8 [1945]: 56) suggested a *tav* has dropped out by haplography, which would make the deer a hind (doe). Dahood (*Psalms 1–50*, 225) prefers to correct the word division, so that the *tav* on the verb is attached to the end of the noun, and understand the verb as an infinitive absolute used as a finite verb. He cites Pss. 17:5 and 35:16 as examples following John Huesman ("Finite Uses of the Infinitive Absolute," *Biblica* 37 [1956]: 290). Ginsburg's solution is preferable, because it is more likely that a letter has been omitted by haplography, than that a scribe divided the words incorrectly. Even if the text is not emended, the verb makes clear that the subject is feminine, and the masculine noun could be due to a preference for the masculine or, in other words, a tendency to use male forms for female subjects.

18. Michael Pitts and Mark Roberts, *Fairweather Eden: Life in Britain Half a Million Years Ago as Revealed by the Excavations at Boxgrove* (London: Arrow, 1998), cited in Fletcher, *Deer*, 38–9.

19. Fletcher, *Deer*, 39.

20. Ibid., 75.

all part of the deer family (*Cervidae*). While tribes on the Great Plains of North America relied on bison, and coastal tribes often depended on mollusks and fish, most tribes in the interior relied on deer. Even in other areas of the world where sheep, goats, and cattle were domesticated and became the main source of meat, deer remained an important supplementary source of meat. This was also the case in ancient Israel. Zooarchaeological finds indicate that deer were a supplementary meat source in all regions and periods.[21]

Archaeologists have wondered why deer were never domesticated. Reindeer may be an exception, though the reindeer of the Sami people are an interesting case because they blur some of the lines between domestic and wild. Domestic animals usually undergo morphological change, but wild and domestic reindeer are morphologically identical. Individuals within a herd may be more or less domesticated and occasionally move between wild and domestic herds. But why have other deer species not been widely domesticated elsewhere? Several reasons have been suggested. Some have suggested humans did not domesticate them because they were so strongly associated with the hunt and the wild that domestication seemed wrong, and certainly such cultural factors have played a role in some areas.[22] Another reason is that stags become extremely dangerous during the rut so that, until the advent of fences, the rut posed a major obstacle to domestication. Fletcher, however, suggests that humans may not have needed to domesticate deer, because humans seem to have learned early that selective burning could increase the browse that helped deer numbers increase and that deer could be attracted by planting foods they liked to eat, like ivy.[23] If active management could increase their numbers and they could be attracted to certain areas, then there was no need to waste time and energy maintaining them all year long like domestic animals. Even after the domestication of other animals, they could provide a supplement to other sources of meat, especially when these were in short supply.

On the other hand, deer often benefit from human agriculture and modification of the environment. They are among the species attracted to the "edge effect" created by the clearing and cultivation of land for agriculture. Humans often attempt to eradicate or drive away animals like wolves that prey on domestic livestock and deer, thus providing an environment for deer that has sources of food and fewer predators (other than humans). Especially in lands prone to drought like Israel, they may be attracted to natural or constructed sources of water for crops and

---

21. Oded Borowski, *Every Living Thing: Daily Use of Animals in Ancient Israel* (Walnut Creek, CA: Altamira, 1998), 187.

22. Jean-Denis Vigne, "Domestication ou appropriation pour la chasse: histoire d'un choix socio-culturel depuis le Neolithique. L'exemple des cerfs (Cervus)," in *Exploitation des Animaux Sauvages à Travers le Temps, xiiie Rencontres Internationales d' Archééet d'Histoire d'Antibes IVe Colloque International de l'Homme et L'Animal, Société de Recherche Interdisciplinaire* (Juan-les-Pins: Editions APCDA, 1993), cited in Fletcher, *Deer*, 80.

23. Fletcher, *Deer*, 76–80.

livestock. Deer may also be the object of "garden hunting."[24] This is the practice in many human cultures of killing for food a few of the wild herbivores and birds that are attracted to gardens.

In this light, reindeer may not be as much of an exception as they seem. Deer may long have been on the boundary between domestic and wild, and this may continue with the growing numbers of deer in many cities. In recent years, urban areas have expanded and the deer populations have increased within these areas. In her study of urban deer populations, Erin McCance showed that people providing artificial feeding sites for deer increased deer-vehicle collisions.[25] Winnipeg is a relatively small city of a little over 700,000, but there are more than a thousand deer living within the Greater Winnipeg area, and Manitoba Public Insurance reported 410 collisions between vehicles and deer in 2006. This is a story repeated in many areas of North America and Europe. Deer may be benefiting from living in urban areas, but human behavior, like creating artificial feed sites, may also be causing suffering.

Behind the image in Psalm 42, therefore, lies real experience with deer that is part of a long history of human-deer interactions, and encounters with deer seeking food and water that continues today, even as deer numbers increase in urban areas.

Spiritual/Material Binary

The previous chapter noted that the English language maintains binaries between human and animal, spirit and matter, and tends to read them into translations of the Hebrew Bible. The Hebrew word *nephesh* appears in v. 1 translated as "being" and appears repeatedly in Psalms 42 and 43. It is translated as "soul" in most major English translations including the KJV, NKJV, NIV, NRSV, and NJPS. "Soul" in English generally refers to the spiritual or immaterial part of a person separate from the body. "Soul" in English thus communicates a binary between spiritual and material. In Genesis, God breathes into dust to create a living "being" (*nephesh*), so the Hebrew word indicates not the spiritual part of a person but the combination of spiritual and material better translated as the whole "being" or "life" of a person. By translating "soul" rather than "life" or "being" in Ps. 42:2[1],

---

24. O. F. Linares, "'Garden Hunting' in the American Tropics," *Human Ecology* 4 (1976): 331–49, cited in Elizabeth J. Reitz and Elizabeth S. Wing, *Zooarchaeology* (Cambridge Manuals in Archaeology; Cambridge: Cambridge University Press, 1999), 287–8, 318.

25. Erin C. McCance, "Understanding Urban White-Tailed Deer (*Odocoileus virginianus*) Movement and Related Social and Ecological Considerations for Management," a dissertation submitted to the University of Manitoba, 2014, https://mspace.lib.umanitoba.ca/bitstream/handle/1993/23573/McCance_Erin.pdf?sequence=1 (accessed January 11, 2018).

major English translations impose a spiritual/material binary that is not present in the Hebrew.

Thus, English readers will tend to read a division between material and spiritual into the passage and assume the doe's longing in v. 2[1] is material and "just a metaphor," whereas the psalmist's "longing for God" is spiritual and the real issue. Similarly, Western readers may not make much of the fact that the same rare verb *ta'arog*, "groan," is used with both "flowing streams" and "God" as objects. Both "flowing streams" and "God" are in parallel lines of poetry. The grammar suggests that the writer and early users of this psalm may not have separated the spiritual and the material. The vocabulary and grammar speak of an arid land where God and water are identified. When God is absent, there is no water. When God is present, there is water.

The psalmist speaks later of remembering going up to festival and singing songs of thanksgiving. Since festivals can be times to give God thanks for the harvest and offer the first fruits, there would have been times in Israel's history when people would not have had a harvest to bring to the temple and give thanks for, because of drought. The temple was understood as the microcosm of the cosmos[26] and identified as the source of water in Ezekiel 47 and Revelation 22. So the psalmist's desire to go up to God's holy hill again would simultaneously be a desire for flowing waters. God is the source of water. Groaning for water would not be just a metaphor for seeking God. Groaning for water would be groaning for God.

If a spiritual/material binary is not read into the psalm, then deer and psalmist, water and God, could be understood as interrelated and interdependent. If there is less of a binary between humans and other animals, then humans can identify with the doe's need for water. The doe might even have her own relationship with God. If there is less of a binary between spiritual and material, then the search for water can be understood as interrelated with a search for God. If God is the source of water, groaning for God and groaning for water may be the same. God provides water and is present in water. Both the doe and the psalmist may be groaning for both water and God.

In Ps. 42:2[1], the psalmist identifies with the doe's need for water in a dry land and the fear and courage involved in seeking water in the presence of enemies. The psalmist's identification with the needs and feelings of a deer may indicate a culture where the human/animal binary is not as strong as in modern culture and animals could be recognized as fellow, embodied creatures.

Water

The human relationship with various forms of water is even more widespread than relationship with deer. Else Holt asks whether the traditional "God as living water"

---

26. Jon D. Levenson, "The Temple and the World," *JR* 64 (1984): 275–98.

interpretation of vv. 2-3[1-2] is too dependent on later Christian intertexts.[27] Holt concludes that "God as living water" is not an accurate interpretation of the psalm from a historical critical perspective but can be from a "literary and theological point of view" because a later Christian interpretation can shine a light on theological potentials in the text.[28] For an ecological reading, however, this shines a light on the potential theological dangers and misuse of the image. The metaphor "God is living water" might spiritualize the metaphor. The adjective "living" needs to be added because water is understood as material and the adjective specifies a special kind of spiritual, nonmaterial water.

The psalm moves from lack of water in v. 2[1] to an overabundance of water in v. 9[8].

> O my God,[29] my being is bowed down,
> > Therefore, I will remember you
> from the land of Jordan and Mount Hermon
> > from Mount Mizar
> Deep calls to deep at the roar of your cataracts,
> > All your breakers and your waves have passed over me.
>
> (vv. 8-9[7-8])

Although v. 9[8] may sound like a reference to ocean currents and waves that are out of place in a dry land, the upper reaches of the Jordan near Hermon is an area where waves could flow over someone's head. Mount Hermon is the area with the highest annual rainfall in Israel, one of the sources of the Jordan, and an area where flash floods and overflowing rivers are possible. On September 15, 2017, the *Times of Israel* reported two teens had been pulled unconscious from the Jordan River between *Sde* Nehemiah and Amir after being swept away by the current.[30] *Sde* Nehemiah and Amir are in an area that is about halfway between Hermon and the Sea of Galilee, not far from where a number of tributaries from the Hermon range converge to form the Jordan River.

This dangerous overabundance of water contrasts with the lack of water in the first verse and alludes to its ambiguous nature. Water is essential for life, but too much water can be deadly. Psalm 42 contains two opposing water metaphors. The first image is of thirst, lack of water, perhaps drought, and the second is of a flash flood overtaking a person. This second image of an individual sinking in mire or under waves is part of a typical narrative in the individual laments that I have

---

27. Else Kragelund Holt, "'… ad fontes aquarum:' God as Water in the Psalms?" in *Metaphors in the Psalms*, ed. Pierre van Hecke and Antji Labahn (Bibliotheca Ephemeridum Theologicarum Lovaniensium; Leuven: Peeters, 2010), 71.

28. Holt, "'… ad fonts aquarum,'" 85.

29. Some Hebrew manuscripts add "my God" to the previous verse, but both direct address to God and God's having forgotten the psalmist are common features of laments, so these two go together well in this verse.

30. "Two Teens Pulled Unconscious from the Jordan," *Times of Israel*, September 15, 2017, https://www.timesofisrael.com/three-teens-swept-away-in-jordan-river/ (accessed March 1, 2018).

noted elsewhere.[31] These are not just metaphors, decorative additions to ideas; these are lived metaphors that come out of a particular ecological setting. They are the experience of people living in a dry land that may experience both water scarcity and flash floods. Although water is essential for human life, either too much water or too little water may be deadly.

Psalm 42 recognizes the complex relationships of humans with water. The imagery would also allow the psalm to be used repeatedly in very different circumstances that involved either too much or two little water.[32] Although the water imagery in the psalm reflects a particular *Sitz im Erde*, the fact that all humans need and experience water means that the psalm will have associations in many other ecological contexts. These associations may be quite different in other ecological contexts. Seafaring communities may associate the "billows" with the billows of the ocean and the dangers of going to sea. It is this ability of the water metaphors to generate associations in many different ecological contexts that contributes to the Psalms being a classic text.[33]

Water and acquiring the water essential for life is a concern that runs through the Bible, from the rivers that flow from Eden and Abraham's dispute with Abimelech's servants over a well, to the waters that flow from the throne of God in the book of Revelation. In Joel 1:20, the only other passage that uses the verb *taʿarog*, "groan," and also includes *ʾelekha*, "to you," and *ʾaphiqe-mayim*, "flowing streams," the situation is one of drought and wildfires, and it is nonhuman animals who cry out to God. Humans and other animals are embodied and rely on water for life.

As someone coming from a country that has an abundance of fresh water, it is difficult for me to appreciate the realities of living in a dry land and to appreciate the extent to which this concern for water is integral to the religion of ancient Israel. Yet even in a country with some of the largest fresh water lakes in the world, the number of Indigenous communities without safe drinking water is a national disgrace. Not far from where I live, 90 percent of the population of the Grassy Narrows First Nation suffers from mercury poisoning because a mining operation dumped mercury upstream in the English-Wabigoon river system they rely on for fish and drinking water. Although governments have long acknowledged the problem, it was not until 2017 that the provincial government promised $85 million to clean up the river system.[34] After decades lobbying for the mercury to be cleaned up, members of the Grassy Narrows community are waiting to

---

31. Walker-Jones, *The Green Psalter*, 49–50.

32. William P. Brown, "Thirsting for God in the Classroom: A Meditation on Psalm 42:1–8," *Teaching Theology and Religion* 6 (2003): 187–8.

33. Sallie McFague, *Metaphorical Theology: Models of God in Religious Language* (Philadelphia: Fortress, 1982).

34. Jody Porter, "Ontario Announces $85M to Clean Up Mercury Near Grassy Narrows, Wabaseemoong First Nations," CBC News/Thunder Bay (http://www.cbc.ca/news/canada/thunder-bay/ontario-mercury-cleanup-1.4180631, accessed February 8, 2017).

see if the money will be spent. This is just one of many cases across Canada and illustrates the intersections of water issues with other justice issues, in this case racism, colonialism, and Indigenous rights. The previous chapter mentioned the case of Shoal Lake First Nation. My experience as a privileged Canadian of an abundance of fresh water is quite different than the experience of many Indigenous people living in the same ecosystems.

In relation to the images in Ps. 42:2[1], God is the source of water in the Hebrew Bible. This is expressed mythically by the four rivers that flow from the Garden of Eden to all the world in Genesis 1, or from the throne of God in the Rev. 22:1. And this is expressed literally elsewhere: "You visit the earth and water it" (Ps. 65:10[9]), "You make springs ... giving drink to every wild animal" (Ps. 104:10-11). And, of course, the story of God giving water from the rock in the wilderness is told and remembered repeatedly in the Hebrew Bible. Animals like the deer also have the spirit of God in them (Ps. 104:29-30) and are cared for by God in the Psalms. God's spirit creates and gives life to all creatures (Ps. 104:30). That there are not even more references that identify God with water, animals, and life, is not surprising. When something is assumed, it does not need to be stated repeatedly. Ancient Hebrews probably only mentioned occasionally what they everywhere assumed: God was the source of water, cared for all creatures, and was the spirit of life present in all Creation.

God, My Rock

> I say to God, my Rock (*selaʿ*), "Why have you forgotten me,
> Why do I walk around in darkness because of[35] oppression by an enemy?"
>
> (Ps. 42:10[9])

Rock is a common metaphor for God in the Psalter, more common than *father*, the metaphor for God that Christians have elevated, if not reified. Michael Knowles argues that the number of times the metaphor appears at the beginning of a psalm (Pss. 18:3[2]; 28:1; 95:1; 144:1), or near the beginning (Pss. 31:3[2], 4[3]; 40:3[2]; 61:3[2]; 62:3[2]; 71:3), or as part of the conclusion (Pss. 18:47[46]; 94:22), indicates the importance of the metaphor.[36] Ithamar Gruenwald argues that God as Rock was an important metaphor for ancient Israelite religion and early Judaism.[37]

---

35. It would also be possible to translate "walk in darkness into oppression by an enemy." In this case, the psalmist would be stumbling in darkness into an enemy. The psalmist's prayer for "light" (Ps. 43:3) would be for light to avoid an enemy in their path.

36. Michael P. Knowles, "'The Rock, His Work Is Perfect': Unusual Imagery for God in Deuteronomy XXXII," *VT* 39 (1989): 307.

37. Ithamar Gruenwald, "God the 'Stone/Rock': Myth, Idolatry, and Cultic Fetishism in Ancient Israel," *JR* 76 (1996): 428-99.

Salvador Fernandes notes that "most scholars who are interested in Biblical Theology only speak of God as a person and often neglect the non-personal (impersonal) metaphors or too quickly translate them into personal language."[38] Translations of the Hebrew Bible tend to capitalize metaphors for God like *father* but do not capitalize metaphors like *rock*. Personal metaphors may be capitalized because they are perceived as more real and sacred than Earth metaphors. This tendency of Western interpreters to focus on human metaphors for God as real and sacred is part of the anthropocentrism of Western cultures and theologies. Just as feminist readers highlight female metaphors for God in the Bible, an ecological reader highlights Earth metaphors for God, such as "God, my Rock."[39]

The emphasis on human metaphors for God reflects the contemporary socioecological setting of a large numbers of humans living in urban areas where they have few significant relationships with Earth and Earth creatures. Most of their relationships are with other humans. In this context, "God, my Rock" may be a meaningless, or dead, metaphor. This is not the case in the Psalms, however, where its prominence and relationship with a whole network of other metaphors for God indicates it is a living metaphor.[40] Ps. 18:2 is a good example of the number of associations:

> The Lord is my Cliff (*selaʻ*), my fortress, and my deliverer,
> my God, my Rock (*tsur*) in whom I take refuge,
> My shield and the horn of my salvation, my lofty refuge *(misgabi)*.

This quote from Psalm 18 shows both the many words that express the basic metaphor— "cliff," "fortress," "rock," "shield," "refuge"—and some of the words that indicate broader associations—"deliverer," "salvation."

God as Rock commonly appears in at least two biblical traditions that are alluded to in Psalm 42. First, Psalm 42 is an individual lament and the metaphor of God as Rock is part of the typical narrative of the individual lament. The prominence of God as Rock in the Psalter, and not elsewhere in the Bible is, in part, because it is part of the typical narrative of the individual lament and related genres, and the individual lament is the most common genre in the Psalter. The imagery of sinking into "mire" or going under "waters" is a common part of this typical narrative pattern of the individual lament:[41]

---

38. Salvador Fernandes, *God as Rock in the Psalter* (European University Studies, Series XXIII Theology, vol. 934; Frankfurt am Main: Peter Lang, 2013), 354.

39. Arthur Walker-Jones, "Honey from the Rock: The Contribution of God as Rock to an Ecological Hermeneutic," in *Exploring Ecological Hermeneutics*, ed. Norman C. Habel and Peter Trudinger (Symposium Series, 46; Atlanta, GA: Society of Biblical Literature, 2008), 91–102.

40. Fernandes, *God as Rock in the Psalter*, 356-7.

41. Walker-Jones, *The Green Psalter*, 50-1.

Save me, O God,
> For the waters have come up to my neck.
> I sink in deep mire, where there is no foothold;
>> I have come into deep waters, and the flood sweeps over me.
>> (Ps. 69:2-3[1-2])

In this context God becomes the rock that provides escape and secure footing. The connection of God as Rock to this imagery is particularly evident in Ps. 40:3[2]:

> He drew me out of the desolate pit,
>> From the muddy clay,
> And put my feet on a rock,
>> Established my steps.

God is the Rock that is able to provide firm footing when "all your breakers and your waves have passed over me" (Ps. 42:8[7]). William Brown identifies Rock as one of a series of concrete images that have to do with the metaphorical domain of God as refuge in the Psalms that represents "both protection and deliverance ... it is a place to which one escapes *and* a place on which one stands firm with feet secured."[42] Or as Othmar Keel says, only God the Rock "is able to provide a sure foundation in 'the mire of the realm of the dead.'"[43]

The second tradition that God as Rock relates to in the context of Psalms 42 and 43 is Zion as the holy mountain and location of the temple. This is part of the ancient Near Eastern belief in a cosmic mountain, abode of the gods and meeting place of heaven and earth,[44] that both holds back the waters of chaos and is the source of fresh waters. God as Rock/cosmic mountain is thus the source of water longed for at the beginning of Psalm 42 and "your holy hill" (Ps. 43:3) that is the psalmist's desired destination.

From an ecological perspective it is also important to note that this Rock is not an inanimate object. It is a relational subject. Rock is conscious, has "forgotten" the psalmist. The Rock is "*my* Rock" who has "forgotten *me*." Brown notes that use of "my" as in "my Rock" indicates an "intensely personal relationship."[45] If spiritual and material are not divided, then the psalmist has an intimate personal relationship with God and the rocks of the temple mount and all rocks of the land of Israel.

The use of this metaphor for God in Psalm 42 and frequently in the Psalms is not accidental or merely decorative. This is a lived, ecological metaphor. A rock

---

42. Brown, *Seeing the Psalms*, 19.

43. Othmar Keel, *The Symbolism of the Biblical World: Ancient Near Eastern Iconography and the Book of Psalms* (Winona Lake, IN: Eisenbrauns, 1997), 72.

44. John D. Levenson, *Sinai & Zion: An Entry into the Jewish Bible* (San Francisco: HarperSanFrancisco, 1985), 111.

45. Brown, *Seeing the Psalms*, 19.

could save a person from a flash flood in a wadi. In the commentary on Psalms 61 and 62 in Chapter 7 we will encounter another major association with God as Rock—protection or refuge in times of war. As Keel puts it, rocks and cliffs "were of paramount importance in a territory beset by military campaigns."[46] Ancient Israelites lived in a rocky land where Rock had many positive associations and possibilities for imaging God.

Sheep and Goats

Sheep and goats, which are adapted to the rocky pastures of the central hill country, appear twice in Psalm 44. While Psalms 42 and 43 are individual laments, Psalm 44 shifts to a national lament over defeat in war. The psalmist twice identifies with sheep and goats. The psalmist complains:

> You have made us like a flock for food,
>   and scattered us among the nations.
> You have sold your people for nothing;
>   You have gained nothing from their sale (44:12-13[11-12]).

A similar complaint comes immediately before the final petitions of the psalm:

> Because of you, we are killed all day long;
>   We are considered a flock for slaughtering (44:23[22]).

This repeated identification with sheep and goats, using slightly different words each time, highlights the importance of the metaphor for the psalm. The Hebrew word here translated as "flock" indicates a mixed flock of sheep and goats (caprines).[47] Sheep and goats were domesticated long before the rise of Israel around 9000 BCE.[48] By about 7000 BCE sheep and goats had become the primary source of meat and other raw materials in the Levant.[49] There is archaeological evidence from 7000 BCE of domestic goats at Jericho and domestic sheep and goats at Ramad and Labweh in what is now Syria and Lebanon.[50] Sheep were the most common domestic

---

46. Keel, *The Symbolism of the Biblical World*, 180.

47. Both domestic sheep (*Ovis aries*) and the domestic goat (*Capra aegagrus hircus*) are part of the Caprini tribe.

48. Michael L. Ryder, *Sheep and Man* (London: Duckworth), 9.

49. Juliet Clutton-Brock, *Domesticated Animals from Early Times* (Austin: University of Texas Press, 1981), 50-1, 56.

50. S. Bökönyi, "Development of Early Stock Rearing in the Near East," *Nature* 264, no. 5581 (1976): 19–23, cited in Clutton-Brock, *Domesticated Animals from Early Times*, 51, fig. 4.4. Sheep bones have been found at Jericho at this time, but it is not clear they are domestic sheep. Clutton-Brock, *Domesticated Animals from Early Times*, 56–7.

animal in ancient Israel. Zooarchaeological studies of Tell Halif show the ratio of sheep to goats in Iron Age Israel was 1.9 to 1 and the ratio of sheep and goats to large cattle was 5.5 to 1.[51] Sheep were thus the most common domestic animal in Iron Age Israel and a fixture of the religion and culture. Abraham, Isaac, Jacob, Moses, and David were all shepherds.

Western culture tends to view humans as the active subjects and animals as the passive objects of domestication. As discussed before, however, contemporary biology is developing an understanding of domestication that reveals more interrelationship and interdependence. An argument can be made that humans, sheep, and goats together constructed a new niche in the Levant and coevolved in that niche. In biology, coevolution is a process where two or more species reciprocally influence each other's evolution. Niche construct is the modification of ecological niches by organisms in ways that change the selective pressures on their descendants.[52] Beavers, for instance, construct lodges, dams, and ponds that change the selection pressures on their descendants. The domestication of plants and animals is another example. "The cultivation and domestication of plants and the breeding of livestock enabled human groups to settle on a long-term basis and, by giving a storable surplus of food, allowed a much larger population, encouraged the accumulation of material possessions and the exchange of goods, stimulated craft specialisation, etc., and hence laid the foundations of modern society."[53]

Sheep and goats would have been particularly helpful in creating an ecological niche in the hill country of ancient Israel and Judah. Sheep and goats can be pastured on land that is considered "marginal" by other agriculturalists.[54] They can make optimal use of pasturage on marginal lands because they can eat different kinds of plants. "Sheep are selective grazers that need areas where grass regenerates at regular intervals. Goats survive on thorny bushes and acadias, but they also eat grass."[55] Caprines are adapted to arid

---

51. J. D. Seger et al., "The Bronze Age Settlements at Tell Halif: Phase II Excavations, 1983-1987," *Bulletin of the American Schools Supplements* 26 (1990), 25-6, cited in Borowski, *Every Living Thing*, 42.

52. F. John Odling-Smee, Kevin N. Laland, and Marcus W. Feldman, *Niche Construction: The Neglected Process in Evolution* (Monographs in Population Biology 37; Princeton, NJ: Princeton University Press, 2003), 44-50; Kevin N. Laland, John Odling-Smee, and Marcus W. Feldman, "Causing A Commotion," *Nature* 429 (2004): 609, https://doi.org/10.1038/429609a.

53. Joris Peters, Angela von den Driesch, and Daniel Helmer, "The Upper Euphrates-Tigris Basin: Cradle of Agro-Pastoralism?" in *The First Steps of Animal Domestication*, ed. J.-D. Vigne, J. Peters, and D. Helmer (Oxford: Oxbow, 2005), 96.

54. Aharon Sasson, *Animal Husbandry in Ancient Israel: A Zooarchaeological Perspective on Livestock Exploitation, Herd Management and Economic Strategies* (Approaches to Anthropological Archaeology; London: Equinox, 2010), 25.

55. Gudrun Dahl and Anders Hjort, *Having Herds: Pastoral Herd Growth and Household Economy* (Stockholm: Department of Anthropology, University of Stockholm, 1976), 251, cited in Sasson, *Animal Husbandry in Ancient Israel*, 34.

conditions[56] and "reproduction rates for both species are relatively high, which ensures stable production of caprine products (e.g., meat, milk, wool, hair) and quick recuperation of herds after periods of stress."[57] Caprines provide dairy products that are a rich source of protein, fat, and calories. Humans can survive in larger numbers in places like the hill country of Israel, because sheep and goats are adapted to arid conditions, able to use marginal lands, and provide a sustainable source of high quality protein.

This new herding ecological niche created new selection pressures that affected sheep, goats, and humans. Domestic animals generally undergo a number of changes in comparison to their wild ancestors including being smaller with smaller brains. The evidence is complex and the interpretation contested, but the body and cranial size of many humans decreased in the transition to agriculture so that some speak of "human domestication." "A key factor in this human-domestication hypothesis is the artificial protective environment created by humans and shared progressively with animals and plants" that "brought about morphological changes similar to those seen in certain domestic animals."[58] A clear example of human adaptation to the new ecological niche would be the continued production of the enzyme lactase into adulthood in order to continue to be able to metabolize milk, unlike most other mammals who cease producing lactase after they are weaned. Holden and Mace found "a strong correlation across cultures between the presence of genes for lactose absorption and a history of dairy farming; this indicates that dairying created the selection pressures that led to genes for lactose absorption becoming common in pastoralist societies."[59] Humans thus coevolved with sheep and goats in this new herding ecological niche.

From an evolutionary perspective, this new ecological niche also benefited sheep and goats. Humans protected them from predators and facilitated their growth in numbers and expansion around the world. Yet this ecological niche caused suffering and death. Sheep and goats suffer from more diseases as a result of domestication and many live short lives. Though how short their lives are depends on whether they are being raised primarily for dairy products or primarily for meat. Sheep and goats were probably originally domesticated for their dairy products, hair, and wool, because in a subsistence situation it does not make sense

---

56. Sasson, *Animal Husbandry in Ancient Israel*, 34, citing M. Evenari et al., *The Negev: The Challenge of a Desert* (Cambridge, MA: Harvard University Press, 1971), 178.

57. Sasson, *Animal Husbandry in Ancient Israel*, 34, citing Dahl and Hjort, *Having Herds*, 103; and K. W. Russell, *After Eden: The Behavioral Ecology of Early Food Production in the Near East and North Africa* (BAR Int. Series 39; Oxford: British Archaeological Reports, 1988), 73–4.

58. H. M. Leach, "Human Domestication Reconsidered," *Current Anthropology* 44 (2003): 360.

59. C. Holden and R. Mace, *Human Biology Phylogenetic Analysis of the Evolution of Lactose Digestion in Adults* (Detroit: Wayne State University Press, 1995) cited in Sasson, *Animal Husbandry in Ancient Israel*, 27.

to kill a sheep or goat for meat and give up an ongoing source of wool and dairy products.

On the one hand, if sheep and goats are raised primarily for meat, then many will be killed after weaning, or at one year. Borowski says, "There are two optimal ages for slaughtering lambs and kids, immediately after weaning and at the age of one year."[60] The first is optimal because, until weaning, the animal has been dependent on its mother's milk and has not required any additional food. The second is optimal because an animal has reached its maximum weight for the minimum food input.[61] After one year they are using forage that could go to other animals and not gaining much more weight. If the agropastoralists are working good land that can provide surpluses for export, most individuals will be killed at 1–3 years (18–30 months) when they reach their maximum weight.[62]

On the other hand, if sheep and goats are raised for dairy products, hair, and wool, some young animals may die of natural causes or may be culled to keep herds within the carrying capacity of the land. More females will be kept alive than males, but females will live until their production of milk and wool begins to decline. Female milking goats, for instance, are usually kept alive for six to eight years.[63] Since ancient Israelites probably raised sheep and goats primarily for dairy products and wool,[64] sheep and goats in ancient Israel would live longer lives.

And, even though ancient Israelites ate meat, they ate far less meat than modern Westerners. Ethnographic and zooarchaeological evidence indicates that livestock products probably provided high quality proteins not otherwise available in the diet,[65] but would have accounted for only about 5 to 17 percent of their calories.[66] Since these livestock products include both meat and dairy products, the amount of meat ancient Israelites ate would be very limited compared to the meat eating of modern Westerners. Meat intake in the United States rose from 114 pounds per person a year in 1950 to 222 pounds per person in 2007, almost forty animals a person per year.[67] The sheep and goats Israelites raised, therefore, lived longer lives

---

60. Borowski, *Every Living Thing*, 57.

61. Ibid.

62. Paula Wapnish, "Archaeozoology: The Integration of Faunal Data with Biblical Archaeology," in *Biblical Archaeology Today, 1990*, ed. A. Biran and J. Aviram (Jerusalem: Israel Exploration Society and Israel Academic of Sciences and Humanities, 1993), 437–8.

63. S. Hirsch, *Sheep and Goats in Ancient Palestine* (Tel Aviv: Palestine Economic Society, 1933), 61, cited in Borowski, *Every Living Thing*, 57; Dahl and Hjort, *Having Herds*, cited in Sasson, *Animal Husbandry in Ancient Israel*, 41.

64. Sasson, *Animal Husbandry in Ancient Israel*, 34–5.

65. Ibid., 116.

66. Ibid., 117.

67. Laura Hobgood-Oster, *The Friends We Keep: Unleashing Christianity's Compassion for Animals* (Waco, TX: Baylor University Press, 2010), 97.

than if they were raised for meat, and Israelites ate much less meat than modern Westerners.

Of course, ancient Israelites would not have had knowledge of the history of domestication, coevolution, and niche construction, but they may have had much different lived relationships with sheep and goats that made them aware of their dependence on caprines and gave them cause to think about the ethics of human relations with them. Cansdale stresses "that these animals are present as an integral part of the life of ordinary people." He points out that "the frequency with which any animal's names occur is some indication of its status. Parallel with this is the range of names given to one species, which can be equally meaningful as an index of its economic and ceremonial importance."[68] Sheep are designated by at least four terms. The most common, general term for sheep is *kebeś* (Exod. 29:39). There are also terms that distinguish a ram, *'ayil* (Gen. 15:9) from a ewe, *rāchēl* (Isa. 53:7), and a young sheep, *śeh* (Exod. 12:5).[69] There are at least seven different terms for goats. There is a word for a female goat, *'ēz* (Gen. 15:9), and several words for a male goat, *tayiš* (Prov. 30:31), *'attūd* (Gen. 31:10), or *tsāpîr* (Dan. 8:21). There is a word for a young female goat, *śĕ'îrat* (Lev. 4:28), and several words for a young male goat, *śā'îr* (Lev. 16:20), or *gĕdî* (Judg. 13:19). And the word *śeh* mentioned above for young sheep can also be used for young goats (Exod. 12:5).[70] These different words for male and female young and old are significant for animal husbandry and the existence of a variety of these names for goats may distinguish different types of goats.

Textual and archaeological evidence indicates that most ancient Israelites kept sheep and goats even in urban areas. There are at least three typical patterns of keeping sheep—nomadic, transhumant, and sedentary.[71] Nomadic herders live in tents and travel continuously to find new pasture for their flocks, often covering longer distances than other herders. A tribe or family may have multiple herds totaling 150,000–200,000 animals.[72] The historicity of the ancestral narratives is debated, but they seem to retain a memory of presettlement ancestors who were nomadic herders, because Abraham wandered continuously over great distances.[73] A few people seem to have continued to follow a nomadic lifestyle throughout the history of Israel as is indicated by the sons of Rechab who continue to follow their ancestor's command to live in tents and not to sow seeds (Jer. 35:1-11),[74] though it should be noted that some nomadic herders do plant and harvest crops

---

68. George Cansdale, *All the Animals of the Bible Lands* (Grand Rapids, MI: Zondervan, 1970), 13.
69. Borowski, *Every Living Thing*, 68–9.
70. Ibid., 62–3.
71. Ibid., 40–5.
72. Ibid., 41.
73. Ibid., 42.
74. Ibid., 39.

and, therefore, may not need to trade with sedentary agriculturalists as is often assumed in biblical archaeology.[75]

The Canaanites, and later Israelites, however, appear to have followed other patterns. While Isaac seems to continue the nomadic tradition, Jacob becomes a transhumant shepherd after his return from Padan Aram.[76] Transhumant shepherds have a home base but move with their herds to find better pasture at various times of year. They tend to have smaller herds of two hundred to five hundred animals.[77] Jacob's father-in-law Laban appears to have been a transhumant herder because his home was close enough to the well for Rachel to run home when she met Jacob, but at other times he kept his herds up to three days' travel away (Gen. 30:36; 31:22), and this gave Jacob time to escape (Gen. 31:19).

Sedentary herders keep their flock in or near a town or village, either in a pen near their home or in their home. The biblical accounts suggest this was a widespread pattern in Canaan and Israel. The stories of the conquest of Canaanite cities includes domestic animals: "Then they devoted to destruction by the edge of the sword all in the city, both men and women, young and old, oxen, sheep, and donkeys" (Josh. 6:21 NRSV). When Saul destroyed the town of Nob, "he put to the sword; men and women, children and infants, oxen, donkeys, and sheep" (1 Sam. 22:19 NRSV). The biblical accounts also assume the Israelites are sedentary herders. Sheep often seem to be close at hand to slaughter for visitors (Judg. 6:19; 13:15). During the time of Hezekiah, sheep seem readily at hand in cities, because "the people of Israel and Judah who lived in the cities of Judah also brought in the tithe of cattle and sheep" (2 Chron. 31:6 NRSV).[78]

Bronze and Iron Age villages had "houses adjacent to each other forming an outer ring, with a wall surrounding an open space with one entrance," which suggests they were constructed by herders to care for sheep and goats.[79] This leads some like Borowski to conclude that most Israelites were sedentary herders. However, the presence of houses in towns and villages does not necessarily indicate sedentary pastoralists as transhumant herders can have a home base where their home is a permanent structure, and they can even have seasonal houses in one or more towns or villages. Thus, Sasson thinks the majority of Israelites may have been transhumant herders.[80] The main point, however, is that Israelites, even those living in towns and cities, would have had extensive and intimate experience with sheep.

---

75. Ibid., 16–17.
76. Ibid., 44.
77. B. C. Yalçin, *Sheep and Goats in Turkey* (Rome: Food and Agriculture Organization, 1986), 11–12.
78. These examples are from Borowski, *Every Living Thing*, 49.
79. Ibid., 41–2, citing A. Mazar, *Archaeology of the Land of the Bible* (New York: Doubleday, 1990), fig. 8.19.
80. Sasson, *Animal Husbandry in Ancient Israel*, 23.

Ancient Israelites may also have had much different cultural associations with sheep and goats. Western culture tends to associate sheep with "stupidity and a failure to stand out from the crowd."[81] The goat tends to have ambivalent associations with being a sacrificial victim or "scapegoat," "goatish" qualities especially smell, as well as associations with lasciviousness and lust.[82] These associations may serve to justify their killing and mistreatment. Sheep and goats, however, have much different associations in other cultures. In China "the image of the sheep/goat/ram signifies (from the Han dynasty onwards) auspiciousness, good fortune, 'renewal and change,' 'happiness and prosperity.'"[83] In other ancient Near Eastern cultures sheep were associated with wealth, status, power, and fertility. In ancient Egypt, for instance, Khnum, the ancient creator god of Upper Egypt, had a ram's head.[84] The "preeminent sacred creature of Amun is the ram with curved horns" and the roads to his temple were flanked by ram-headed lions.[85]

While sheep may not have some of the types of intelligence valued by humans, recent studies have shown them to have types of intelligence appropriate to their kind. "Scientific studies ... show that sheep possess extensive spatial memories, ample capacity to learn from experience and a highly developed ability (beyond that of dogs, and comparable to humans' own) to identify individuals by their faces, even after long periods of separation."[86] This includes recognition and memory of members of their own species and humans,[87] and "forms of emotional and social intelligence equal to or exceeding those of primates."[88] Residents of Marsden in Yorkshire observed how clever sheep can be. The residents installed a cattle grate to keep sheep from coming into the village and eating flowers. They then observed the sheep teaching each other to "commando roll" over the grate so that they could continue to enter the village and eat their favorite flowers.[89]

Armstrong thinks Polyphemous's words in the story of Odysseus may reflect the affection pastoralists come to feel for their sheep. Polyphemous is the cyclops that trapped Odysseus and his men in a cave. In the story they get Polyphemous drunk and then blind him by driving a stake into his eye. Odysseus then ties his men under Polyphemous's sheep as they exit the cave to graze. Odysseus hangs

---

81. Philip Armstrong, *Sheep* (London: Reaktion, 2016), 10.

82. Joy Hinson, *Goat* (London: Reaktion, 2015), 14–15.

83. Patricia Bjaaland Welch, *Chinese Art: A Guide to Motifs and Visual Imagery* (Rutland, VT: 2008), 130–1, cited in Armstrong, *Sheep*, 19.

84. George Hart, ed., *The Routledge Dictionary of Egyptian Gods and Goddesses*, Routledge Dictionaries (2nd ed.; London: Routledge, 2005), 85–6.

85. Ibid., 13–14.

86. Armstrong, *Sheep*, 20.

87. Ibid., 52–3.

88. Ibid., 49–50, citing T. E. Rowell and C. A. Rowell, "The Social Organization of Feral *Ovis aries* Ram Groups in the Pre-rut Period," *Ethology* 95 (1993): 213, 241.

89. Hinson, *Goat*, 47.

under the last sheep to leave the cave, Polyphemous's bellwether. As the bellwether leaves the cave, Polyphemous passes his hand over the back of the ram to make sure no one is riding on it and says,

> Dear old ram, why last of the flock to quit the cave?
> Sick at heart for your master's eye
> That coward gouged out with his wicked crew?

Polyphemous thinks his bellwether is saddened by what has happened to him and this may be an example of affection between shepherds and sheep.

Since many ancient Israelites kept sheep, they too might have had a similar sense of affection for their sheep. Those who keep sheep must identify with them to a greater or lesser extent in order to provide for their needs and keep them healthy. Indeed, one's ability to identify with sheep may correlate with a shepherd's success as a shepherd. In addition, some domestic animals may be kept as pets. After David has Bathsheba's husband killed, the prophet Nathan tells a parable to King David about a rich man who does not want to kill a lamb from his own flock to feed a guest, so he takes the lamb of a poor man.

> But the poor man had nothing but one little ewe lamb, which he had bought. He brought it up, and it grew up with him and with his children; it used to eat of his meager fare, and drink from his cup, and lie in his bosom, and it was like a daughter to him (2 Sam. 12:3 NRSV).

To be plausible, this parable requires that people would sometimes keep domestic animals as pets and might consider them members of the family. While it would be anachronistic to read back contemporary understandings and practices of pet keeping into the biblical text, this passage indicates at least a few people in ancient Israel kept other species as members of their family. This is a prophetic parable, but, for this story to ring true, ancient readers must have found it plausible that people might develop such emotional attachments to their sheep, perhaps even have had that exprience. Indeed, the evidence for humans keeping other species is so ancient and widespread that capacity for cross-species relationships could be considered part of human nature.[90] In any case, the identification with sheep, the metaphor in Psalm 44, would reflect the lived identification with sheep of many ancient Israelites.

Of course, ancient Israelites would not have had any knowledge of coevolution and the history of domestication. But they may have had greater affection for and awareness of their dependence on their domestic animals and that may have resulted in greater care and respect than in modern agriculture. Coevolution and niche construction may be a modern way of understanding the interdependence

---

90. Pat Shipman, *The Animal Connection: A New Perspective on What Makes Us Human* (New York: W. W. Norton, 2011).

and interrelationship of humans with other animals that ancient Israelites would have experienced through close contact and reliance on domestic animals.

Shepherd is a common metaphor for gods and kings in the ancient Near East. Normally, God is considered a good shepherd, but, in this psalm, God seems to be accused of being a bad shepherd. What is God being accused of? Were not sheep regularly slaughtered for food in ancient Israel? The modern reader may read this as a confirmation of the binary between humans and other animals and conclude that the issue is that it is wrong for God to treat humans like animals. Or a modern reader concerned with animal rights might argue that this metaphor assumes violence against animals and, if it is wrong for God to kill sheep, then it should also be wrong for humans to kill sheep. In the end, the answer to this question may depend on one's anthropology and ethics, but I want to suggest below that ancient Israelites were not making a modern distinction between humans and animals; they were identifying with sheep as fellow animals and objecting to the exploitative nature of a market economy and imperialism for both sheep and humans.

Many writers assume that ancient Israel had some form of market economy where agricultural products were either traded or sold to urban elites or to other city-states or empires. Paula Wapnish and Brian Hesse distinguish three models of livestock use that will leave different zooarchaeological records: (1) A "self-contained production/consumption" economy where a community produces and consumes their own livestock products leaves bones from animals of all ages; (2) a "consuming economy" purchases market-age animals from pastoral specialists and leaves more bones of market-age animals (18–30 months or 1–3 years old); (3) a "producing economy" raises animals for export. If production is focused on meat for export, then there would be bones from few market age animals at the site. If production is focused on either dairy or wool, then this might cause different proportions of old or young animal bones at the site.[91] In another article, Wapnish argues that the zooarchaeological record is important for understanding biblical history and argues that the zooarchaeological record at Tel-Dan indicates a transition from dairy and wool to more meat eating as Israelites become more urbanized.[92] In the seventh-century BCE layer of Philistine settlements of Tell Jemmeh and Tel Miqne-Ekron, the majority of bones are from sheep over three years old. She argues that Assyrian markets may have been too attractive or Assyrian tribute demands too great.[93] Local herders sold, or had to send as tribute, young animals and "their own diet included only old animals."[94] These are just two examples of the widespread assumptions that some form of market economy and imperialism were driving forces in ancient Israelite history.

---

91. Paula Wapnish and Brian Hesse, "Urbanization and the Organization of Animal Production at Tell Jemmeh in the Middle Bronze Age Levant," *JNES* 47 (1988): 84.
92. Wapnish, "Archaeozoology," 430–4.
93. Ibid., 439.
94. Borowski, *Every Living Thing*, 61.

Wapnish's argument, however, is based on evidence from only a few sites, two of them Philistine, and one layer or time period. Aharon Sasson compares the zooarchaeological evidence from seventy sites in the southern Levant representing all geographical areas and time periods and types of settlement (rural and urban). He also compares these with ethnographic evidence from other pastoral societies. Sasson goes into detail that I cannot do full justice to here. In general, though, he does not find any difference in the bone profile between urban and rural sites that would indicate a market system that provided meat for urbanites. And he finds no general pattern of bones only from old animals that would indicate trade or tribute to an empire. Instead, he finds that the bones from all sites tend to represent either predominantly young animals or animals of all ages. Moreover, the ratio of sheep to goats indicates herds were being managed for dairy products and wool, not meat. The osteoarchaeological profiles indicate that when animals were killed for meat, all parts of the animal were being used, not just the best parts, indicating a subsistence rather than a market economy. He does an in-depth spatial analysis of Tel Beer-Sheba, a regional, political, administrative, and military center, and finds no evidence of the kind of social stratification that is found in Mesopotamia and Egypt that would indicate a market economy where wealthy elites ate only the choice parts of animals.[95] Sasson, therefore, provides convincing evidence that ancient Israel had a subsistence economy in which caprines were normally kept for dairy products and wool. I think there is some textual and archaeological evidence that from time to time some kings, like Solomon, may have tried to develop a system of tribute that would support a royal hierarchy, and elites may have tried to develop a market economy, but this may have left little evidence in the zooarchaeological record because the majority of Israelites continued to live in a subsistence economy.

Even the word "economy" may be misleading. Subsistence societies may do some trading, but they produce enough to subsist on and do not rely on trade. This is true of nomadic and sedentary populations in both rural and urban areas. The archaeological and textual evidence of people keeping animals even in urban areas is just some of the support for Sasson's contention that, even in urban areas, people were producing enough grains and animal products to subsist without needing to buy food from rural areas. Nomadic, transhumant, and sedentary pastoral subsistence societies have developed practices through trial and error over generations that keep populations of people and animals below the carrying capacity of the land.[96] As Gaulin and Konner say, "non-industrial economies are under producing, maintaining lower than necessary levels of population density, and producing adequate calories and a surplus of protein and leisure most of the time. This is because of periodically occurring shortages to which they are

---

95. Sasson, *Animal Husbandry in Ancient Israel*, 106.
96. Ibid., 10–14.

adapted."⁹⁷ Subsistence societies do not produce more in good years to maximize profit and risk the suffering and death that might occur in poor years, if populations had grown larger than the land could support. Instead, they maintain populations at the capacity of poor years to reduce risk and the suffering that might occur if populations were larger than the land could support during droughts or other hardships.

Among those other hardships would be war and imperial conquest. Records from the great imperial powers of Egypt and Mesopotamia indicate they took large numbers of sheep and goats from the Southern Levant. Even before Israelite times, Pharaoh Thutmoses II (1490–1436 BCE) says that when he was victorious at the battle of Megiddo he received "tribute of silver, gold, lapis lazuli, and turquoise, and . . . grain, wine, and large and small cattle" (the expression translated as "small cattle" refers to sheep and goats). Thutmoses identifies "2,000 goats, and 20,500 sheep" separately in the list of booty he took (*ANET*³, 237).⁹⁸ Similarly, Pharaoh Amenhotep II (1447–1421 BCE) took as booty "all the small cattle," after he was victorious at the battle of Aphek. And, he says he took as booty "all (kinds of) cattle without their limit," after his victory at the battle of Anaharath (*ANET*³, 246–7).⁹⁹

During Israelite times, Assyrian kings say they took large numbers of small cattle as tribute and booty. Tiglath Pileser III (744–727 BCE) records taking "blue-dyed wool, purple-dyed wool, . . . lambs whose stretched hides were dyed purple, . . . small cattle" as booty in a campaign against Syria and Palestine (*ANET*³, 283). After another campaign to Syria, Palestine, and Arabia he says, "I brought away as prisoners 800 (of its) inhabitants with their possessions, . . . their large (and) small cattle" (*ANET*³, 283), and a relief from his palace shows him taking booty that included sheep.¹⁰⁰ Sennacherib (704–681 BCE), in his report of his campaign against Hezekiah of Jerusalem on the Oriental Institute Prism, says, "I drove out . . . 200,150 people, young and old, male and female, horses, mules, donkeys, camels, big and small cattle beyond counting" (*ANET*³, 288). Esarhaddon (680–669 BCE) also had a campaign to Syria and Palestine and says on Prism A of the defeat of Sidon: "I drove to Assyria his teeming people which could not be counted, (also) large and small cattle and donkeys" (*ANET*³, 290). He says on Prism B: "I lead to Assyria his teeming subjects, which could not be counted, (and) large and small cattle and donkeys in great quantities" (*ANET*³, 291).¹⁰¹ I have quoted the inscriptions of several Assyrian rulers at length to show that the taking of people

---

97. S. J. C. Gaulin and M. Konner, "On the Natural Diet of Primates, including Humans," in *Nutrition and the Brain*, vol. 1, ed. R. J. Wurtman and J. J. Wurtman (New York: Raven, 1977), 56, cited in Sasson, *Animal Husbandry in Ancient Israel*, 13.

98. Cited in Borowski, *Every Living Thing*, 65.

99. Ibid., 65.

100. Henri Frankfort, *The Art and Architecture of the Ancient Orient* (Pelican History of Art; Baltimore: Penguin, 1954), 94.

101. Cited in Borowski, *Every Living Thing*, 65, 69.

and sheep by imperial powers was more than an occasional occurrence. The trauma of having family and friends taken captive in war would have been burnt into the collective memory for generations. While the reports distinguish between people and animals, people and animals are all in the same situation—captivity and slavery to imperial powers. In these reports, as in Psalm 44, humans and animals have the same relation to empire.

That imperial powers could take large numbers of sheep may not be an indication that large surpluses were being produced for market, as some modern scholars suggest. Rather, it could indicate the adaptive ability of nomadic and transhumant herders to avoid central governments and wars and the ability of caprine herds to recovery quickly. Mixed herds of sheep and goats can double in size in two to three years.[102] Some nomadic and transhumant herders would be in areas remote from invading armies or could move their flocks there as they approached. Those who had their flocks taken by a conquering army could get new animals from transhumant or nomadic herders to rebuild their flocks. Those who managed to hide most of their flocks could trade or give to others all the young animals that would normally have been culled to keep their flocks within the carrying capacity of the land. These could then be used by those who had lost flocks to regenerate their flocks within a few years. I am speculating on how exactly this would work, but, my point is, that subsistence economies are adapted to bad years and the ability of caprine herds to recover quickly would be part of that adaptation in ancient Israel.

This socioecological background of a subsistence community periodically exposed to imperial conquest and, perhaps, attempts by elites to develop market economies shines new light on Psalm 44's identification with sheep and accusation that God has been a bad shepherd. Psalm 44 may be complaining about the disrespect and exploitation of both humans and animals by market economies and empires. That God has made them "a flock for food" (Ps. 44:12[11]) and a "flock for slaughtering" (Ps. 44:23[22]) refers to marketing the whole flock for meat rather than maintaining the flock for milk and wool. That God has sold them "for

---

102. Sasson, *Animal Husbandry in Ancient Israel*, 21, citing Dahl and Hjort, *Having Herds*, 103; G. Dahl, "Ecology and Equality: The Boran Case," in *Pastoral Production and Society* (Cambridge: Cambridge University Press, 1979), 42; J. Swift, "Disaster and a Sahelian Nomad Economy," in *Drought in Africa: Report of the 1973 Symposium*, ed. D. Alby and R. J. H. Church (London: University of London School of Oriental and African Studies Center for African Studies, 1973), 73; K. W. Russell, *After Eden: The Behavioral Ecology of Early Food Production in the Near East and North Africa* (Oxford: British Archaeological Reports, 1988), 73–74; R. Cribb, *Nomads in Archaeology* (Cambridge: Cambridge University Press, 1991), 29; D. Hopkins, "Pastoralists in Late Bronze Age Palestine: Which Way Did They Go?" *BA* 56 (1993): 207; A. Abu Rabia, *The Negev Bedouin and Livestock Rearing* (Oxford: Berg, 1994), 113; and Ben David, "Stages in the Sedentarization of the Negev Bedouin, a Transition from Former Semi-Nomadic to Settled Population" (PhD dissertation, Hebrew University, 1982), 169.

nothing" and "gained nothing from their sale" (Ps. 44:13[12]) may indicate God is a poor capitalist or, perhaps more likely, that money is considered "nothing" in a subsistence society organized around being secure by having less. Though this also implies that if God had got something for them, then death might have been acceptable. The complaint then is not that they have been sacrificed but that the sacrifice has been exploitative and without respect for the sacrifice.

In contemporary Western societies that emphasize individualism and self-fulfillment, sacrifice for the community is a largely forgotten value. To the extent that it is applied unequally to women, minorities, and the lower classes, it should be rejected. Yet one wonders if this is one of the reasons sheep do not have more positive associations in Judaism and Christianity. They are the archetypical sacrifice in Judaism. The first animal sacrifice includes sheep (Gen. 4:4), God provides a ram in Isaac's place (Gen. 22:13), and the blood of the Passover lamb saves the firstborn of Israel from death (Exod. 12:1-32). The image of vicarious suffering that redeems others in the prophet Isaiah is a sheep (Isa. 53:7). For Christians, Christ is "the lamb of God" (Jn 1:19) who appears at the end of the world in the book of Revelation (5:8).[103] One would think that if Jesus is the Lamb of God, Christians might treat lambs with greater reverence and respect.

---

103. Armstrong, *Sheep*, 13.

Chapter 3

URBAN EMPIRE (Pss. 45–49)

Psalm 45 marks a shift in landscapes. The pastoral, agrarian landscape of Psalms 42–44 covered in the previous chapter shifts to an urban landscape. The references to human identification with deer, sheep, goats, water, and rocks in Psalms 42–44 are replaced by a focus on the city in Psalms 45–49. There are fewer references to Earth community, and they tend to indicate exploitation and alienation from that community.

This shift to an urban landscape is matched by a shift in genres and superscriptions. The genres of Psalms 45 to 50 make them stand out from the laments that precede and follow them in the Psalter. Psalm 50 is distinguished by a superscription to Asaph and a unique genre. The content of Psalm 50 is particularly important for an ecological reading and will receive longer consideration in the next chapter. This chapter treats Psalms 45 to 49. Psalm 45 is a royal wedding song that is a sharp contrast to the laments in the previous songs and creates a transition to Psalms 45–49. In addition to a royal wedding song in Psalm 45, this section includes two songs of Zion, Psalms 46 and 48.[1] These psalms focused on Zion surround Psalm 47, a hymn praising God as King. The final psalm of the sons of Korah, Psalm 49, is a wisdom psalm.

The superscription of Psalm 45 identifies it as a *maskil* and a love *shīr* "song." The title *maskil* connects it with the Korah psalms treated in the previous chapter. The superscription *shīr*, "a song" connects it to the following psalms that are either *shīr*, "a song" (45:1; 46:1), or a *mizmor*, "a psalm" (47:1; 49:1), or both (48:1).

Perfume and Ivory (Ps. 45)

Psalm 45 is a hymn composed for a royal wedding. It is difficult to know which royal wedding, and it was probably used repeatedly. The presence of a royal wedding hymn in the Psalter has puzzled readers, and commentators have often

---

1. The designation "song of Zion" is as much a content designation as a genre. Songs of Zion extol Zion as God's holy city. In terms of genre, Psalm 46 is probably a song of trust and Psalm 48 a hymn.

interpreted it either as referring to the Messiah or as an allegory about Christ and the Church.

Ancient Israel had an ambiguous relationship with the monarchy. On the one hand, the Bible extols David and looks forward to a coming king and Messiah. On the other hand, the prophet Samuel resists the appointment of a king like the nations. God eventually allows Israel a king, but the rest of the Deuteronomistic History[2] can be read as a realization of Samuel's warning about kings and a history of the failure of the Davidic monarchy that ends in exile. The Deuteronomistic History is known as the Former Prophets in Judaism and the Latter Prophets are also well known for their criticisms of kings and the wealthy. J. Clinton McCann argues that Books One through Three trace the failure of the covenant with the Davidic monarchy.[3]

This ambiguous relationship with the monarchy arises out of a particular ecology and has ecological implications. Katherine Newman's study of preindustiral societies correlates certain types of political organizations with certain types of agriculture. She distinguishes between what she calls "wet" and "dry" intensive agriculture. Wet intensive agriculture uses extensive irrigation while dry intensive agriculture does not. "Wet intensive agriculture correlates more highly with state-formation …; dry intensive agriculture, even in cases of class-stratification, is more likely to go along with chieftainship, or with paramount chieftainship."[4] The biblical picture of the pre-monarchic period is of a tribal society with chiefs and paramount chiefs. During the monarchy the kings seem to be struggling to set up a royal social structure akin to the monarchies of the wet intensive agricultural empires of Egypt and Mesopotamia but do not have the land base or agricultural surpluses to sustain royal structures. We may see in Psalms the attempt to merge older ideologies of chieftainship based on subsistence, dry intensive agriculture, with the royal ideologies from wet intensive agricultural areas in Egypt and Mesopotamia. Psalm 45 would be an example of such a royal economic ideology and its ecological implications.

An ecological reader notices evidence in Psalm 45 of the exploitation of women and Earth. Amid the section praising the royal groom are the following lines:

> Myrrh and agar and cassia perfume all your clothes,
>   From palaces of ivory, stringed instruments make you happy.
> Daughters of kings are among your valuables (45:9-10a[8-9a])

---

2. The Deuteronomistic History includes Joshua, Judges, 1 and 2 Samuel, and 1 and 2 Kings.

3. J. Clinton McCann, "The Book of Psalms: Introduction, Commentary, and Reflections," in *NIB*, vol. IV, ed. Leander E. Keck et al. (Nashville: Abingdon, 1996), 660.

4. Katherine S. Newman, *Law and Economic Organization: A Comparative Study of Preindustrial Societies* (Cambridge: Cambridge University Press, 1983), 187–8, cited in David Jobling, "Deconstruction and the Political Analysis of Biblical Texts: A Jamesonian Reading of Psalm 72," *Semeia* 59 (1992): 117.

Myrrh, aloe, and cassia are all fragrances originating in East Asia. In the literary context they indicate the luxury, success, and blessing of the king, but they also speak of a trade in luxury goods and taxes that make the royal court wealthy. The Hebrew word *mor* is usually translated as myrrh. Michael Zohary, who was a professor of botany at Hebrew University, identifies myrrh with *Commiphora abyssinica*, though he says, "further investigation is required to confirm the identification,"[5] and Koops thinks the Hebrew *mor* may include other species of the genus like *myrrha* or *schimperi* and that other types of myrrh may have come from India.[6] *Commiphora abyssinica* is a thorny shrub or small tree that is native to Arabia, Ethiopia, and Somaliland. A fragrant resin exudes naturally from the branches and leaves and larger amounts can be collected by making an incision in the bark. Myrrh was used by the Egyptians as incense in their temples and in the embalming of the dead. In ancient Israel it was an ingredient in the fragrant anointing oil for the tent of the meeting (Exod. 30:23) and a perfume (Est. 2:12; Prov. 7:17; Song 1:13; 3:6; 4:6; 4:14; 5:13; Sir. 24:15). It is among the gifts the Magi from the East are reported to have offered to the child Jesus (Mt. 2:11), and in the book of Revelation it is a precious resin imported from the East (Rev. 18:13).

English translations often have "aloes" here, which the modern reader will associate with *Aloe vera*, but Zohary and Koops both think the best identification of Hebrew *'ahaloth*, Sanskrit *aghal*, and Greek *xylaloe* or *agallochon*, is with the Eaglewood or Agarwood trees (*Aquillaria agallocha Roxb.*) of northern India. These trees grow up to 30 meters, and an expensive perfume can be extracted from their wood.[7] The resin from these trees is sometimes called agar.

English cassia is a cognate of Hebrew *Qetsiah*, and its identification as *Cinnamomum cassia* is fairly certain. Cassia is a "precious perfume" made by steam distillation of the branches and leaves of the tree, which grows up to 10 meters. The tree is native to East Asia and has long been cultivated and its bark, buds, and oil exported.[8] Behind these three perfumes, therefore, lies long-distance trade with the East and hours of labor collecting and distilling fragrance. The resulting perfumes would be costly and probably the result of royalty exploiting the poor.

Further exploitation is hidden in the language of the next line. The king listens to music in "ivory palaces." Carol Adams talks about the "absent referent" that enables "the interweaving of the oppression of women *and* animals."[9] The word "ivory" in the English language is an example of the absent referent. "Ivory"

---

5. Michael Zohary, *Plants of the Bible: A Complete Handbook to All the Plants with 200 Full-Color Plates Taken in the Natural Habitat* (Cambridge: Cambridge University Press, 1982), 200.

6. Robert Koops, *Each According to Its Kind: Plants and Trees in the Bible*, UBS Technical Helps (Redding, UK: United Bible Societies, 2012), 123-4.

7. Zohary, *Plants of the Bible*, 204. Koops, *Each According to its Kind*, 113.

8. Zohary, *Plants of the Bible*, 203.

9. Carol Adams, *The Sexual Politics of Meat: A Feminist-Vegetarian Critical Theory* (20th Anniversary Edition; New York: Continuum, 2010), 13.

translates the Hebrew *shēn*, tooth. The Hebrew thus retains the connection with the teeth or tusks of elephants, while the English obscures the connection. The absent reference in "palaces of ivory" is the large number of dead elephants. The use of elephant tusks for royal palaces was common in the ancient Near East. The Syrian elephant was already rare by biblical times and went extinct in 100 BCE. In the seven years leading up to 2014, the numbers of African elephants declined by 30 percent due to a brutal poaching industry.[10] The word *ivory* in "*ivory palaces*" thus hides the ancient and modern suffering of these highly intelligent and sensitive Earth neighbors. Unlike the previous psalm that identified with deer, sheep, and goats, the only references to Earth community are references to expensive perfumes from fragrant plants and palaces decorated with the tusks of dead elephants.

The exploitation of other animals is often interrelated with the exploitation of women in ancient and modern contexts. The exploitation of women follows immediately on the exploitation of Earth creatures in these verses as they often do in practice. The line following the mention of ivory, translated rather literally, says, "daughters of kings are among your valuables" (v. 10a[9a]). The king may have married a number of daughters of kings to create political alliances with neighboring city states and empires. The section of the psalm that follows tells the new queen to "forget your people," the king will desire her beauty, and she should bow to the king, because he is her lord (vv. 10-11[9-10]). In return she will receive wealth and provide sons for the king. This is the patriarchal model of a woman valued for her beauty and ability to produce children. The empire that objectifies and exploits elephants also objectifies and exploits women.

Urban, Imperial Ideology (Pss. 46–48)

The following three psalms extol the city of God and God as King. Psalm 46 is a Song of Zion that inspired Martin Luther's hymn "A Mighty Fortress is Our God." Although the word "Zion" is not used, the psalm extols the city of God. The words "refuge" and "stronghold" are part of the web of metaphors linked to God as Rock. In the city is "God's holy tabernacle," the temple and, as microcosm of the cosmos, the source of fresh water.

> There is a river whose streams make glad the city of God
>   The holy tabernacle of the Most High (v. 5[4]).

Psalm 46 extols the city of God as a place of refuge and stability:

> God is in the heart of the city, it will not topple
>   God will help it at the break of dawn (v. 6[5]).

---

10. http://www.greatelephantcensus.com/.

From the safety of the city, the community watches God bring wars to an end.

An ecological reader, however, is suspicious of a psalm where Earth outside the city is chaotic and dangerous:

> Therefore we are not afraid when Earth changes,
>   and the mountains topple into the heart of the sea.
> Its waters are a roaring froth
>   Mountains shake from its surf. (vv. 3-4[2-3])

An ecological reader is further disturbed that this chaotic picture of Earth is identified with the enemies of the nation. This is not the kind of identification Earth Bible commentaries seek to foster. The identification of Earth with human enemies is evident in the parallel language used of both in the psalm. Different forms of the same verb (*mvt*) are used for mountains *toppling* into the sea (v. 3[2]) and kingdoms *toppling* (v. 7[6]). Different forms of the same verb (*hmh*) are used when the waters *roar* (v. 3[2]) and when the peoples *roar* (v. 7[6]). The identification of Earth and human enemies is particularly clear in this last verse where kingdoms and Earth appear in parallel poetic lines (in my translation from the Hebrew, I have used italics to highlight the words that I discuss in the text above where they have also been italicized):

> The peoples *roar*, kingdoms *topple*,
>   [God] speaks, Earth melts (v. 7[6]).

This verse highlights another disturbing aspect of the psalm's worldview: God is portrayed as at war with Earth. The title "Lord of Hosts" in the following verse may refer to God as leader of military hosts. Then in v. 9[8], God has brought horrors or desolations on Earth.

It may be significant in this portrayal of God as divine warrior battling Earth that Earth appears without definite articles in Hebrew at the beginning of the psalm but with definite articles toward the end of the psalm. This transition is obscured in English translations that always introduce definite articles even when they are not present in Hebrew. At the beginning of the psalm, there is no article on Earth when the people are not afraid when Earth changes (v. 3[2]). There are also no articles on Mountains and Seas in this verse. I capitalize them to indicate they, along with Earth, may be being understood as subjects. In the middle of the psalm, there is no article on Earth when it melts before God's voice (v. 7[6]). There are, however, articles on Earth toward the end of the psalm when God has "brought desolations on *the* Earth" (v. 10[9]), "makes wars cease to the end of *the* Earth" (v. 10[9]), and is "exalted in *the* Earth" (v. 11[10]). The grammar seems to reflect a devolution of Earth from subject to object. Because the last two have the preposition *bet* prefixed to them, the definite article is represented by the pointing and, therefore, may reflect the assumptions of the Masoretic scribes who added the vowel pointing in the sixth through the ninth centuries of the Common Era and not the understanding of the original authors. In either case, the psalm retains an understanding of Earth as subject but unfortunately a chaotic and threatening subject identified with human enemies, both of which are defeated by God as warrior.

Contemporary culture often identifies human enemies with members of Earth community and uses imagery of being at war with Earth. The reading of this psalm in the context of these contemporary narratives could reinforce ecocidal cultural tendencies.[11]

The next psalm, Psalm 47, is a hymn to God as ruler. It contains no references to nonhuman members of Earth community and is therefore anthropocentric. Furthermore, it uses a definite article on Earth in two of three references. In the first and second references, the psalm calls all peoples to praise God "for the LORD is ... a great ruler over all the earth" (v. 3[2]). "For ruler of all the earth is God" (v. 8a). In these first two references, God's sovereignty seems to make Earth an object. The lack of reference to nonhuman members of Earth community, and the use of definite articles on Earth seem to reflect an anthropocentric, urban socioecology.

Nevertheless, there may be something that can be retrieved for an ecological reading. The third reference to Earth in the psalm—"for to God belong the shields of Earth" (v. 10[9])—has no article on Earth. That the shields of Earth belong to God may indicate Earth as a subject that God protects with shields. It may refer to an understanding of God as Creator and sustainer of Earth. Humans are created in the image of God who protects Earth, so humans should do likewise.

Yet there is another possible interpretation of this phrase. Since "shields" are in parallel with "nobles of the peoples and the people of the God of Abraham," it is possible to interpret the "nobles of the peoples and the people of the God of Abraham" as the "shields," perhaps translating as "guardians of Earth." This might represent an ancient assumption that people of God and their leaders were to be guardians of Earth.

The opening verses of Psalm 48 closely tie them to the previous two psalms. Psalm 48 brings together the main themes of the previous two psalms—the city of Zion and the kingship of God. In fact, the psalm piles up iconic symbols by combining the kingship of God and the city of Zion with the temple and placing them on the cosmic mountain. The iconic or symbolic nature of Mount Zion as the cosmic mountain is evident when Mount Zion is identified as

> Beautiful in elevation, joy of all the earth, Mount Zion,
>   the heights of Zaphon, the city of the great King (v. 3[2]).

---

11. By warning against possible contemporary uses, I am not saying the psalm could not be interpreted ecologically. Ki-Min Bang is right to note the imagery of God as warrior (*chaoskampf*) may have been understood in the ancient Near East not as battling Earth but the elements of Earth that threatened the stability necessary for the fertility and flourishing of all creatures ("Psalm 46: A Missing Key to Understanding Psalm 46: Revisiting the Chaoskampf," *Conversations with the Biblical World* 37 (2017): 68–89).

The heights of Zaphon can be translated as "in the far north" (NRSV), but Jerusalem is not in the far north. Mount Zaphon is the highest mountain in Syria and sacred as the mountain of Baal. The expression "beautiful in elevation" also seems more appropriate to Zaphon than Zion. Thus, the psalm appropriates the symbolism of Canaan's most sacred mountain for Mount Zion. The cosmic mountain is combined with the temple when, later in the psalm, the people meditate on the temple as a symbol of God's faithfulness (v. 10[9]). Clinton McCann notes that Psalm 48 "recalls" Exodus 15, the Song of the Sea, which celebrates the defeat of Pharaoh and his army.[12] The kings gathered in force against the city in Psalm 48 were "in panic" (*nevhalu*; Ps. 48:6[5]; Exod. 15:15), seized with "trembling" (*ra'adah* Ps. 48:7[6]; *ra'ad* Exod. 15:15) and in "pain" (*khil*; Ps. 48:7[6]; Exod. 15:14). The references to the "east wind" (v. 8[7]) recall the "east wind" that drove back the sea in Exod. 14:21. Moreover, Psalm 48 and Exodus both end with God on the holy mountain. Exodus 15 uses language and imagery from a common ancient Near Eastern creation story to praise the mythic significance of God's defeat of the Egyptians. That creation story is also present in a number of psalms. In this common ancient Near Eastern creation story, God defeats the forces of chaos represented by Sea in order to establish order and then ascends the divine mountain to the temple and is proclaimed king of the gods.[13] The "trembling" and "pain" of God's enemies cited above is typical of this pattern as is the verb used for God's "establishing" (*kwn*) Zion in v. 9[8]. Another reference to Creation may be present in the reference to the temple in v. 10[9], since the temple was understood as a microcosm of the cosmos. This piling up of metaphors, appropriation of a Canaanite sacred mountain, the temple, and allusions to the formation of Israel, combined with an ancient Near Eastern creation story, make this psalm a powerful symbolic statement.

The psalm identifies Zion as "the city of the great ruler" (v. 3[2]), but there may be some ambiguity as ruler could refer to either God or the human king. The human king is unlikely as the psalm later refers to "the city of our God" (v. 9[8]). Though the distinction may not make much difference for royal ideology. Belief in God as ruler can sometimes delegitimize human kings, as it sometimes did in Israel, but the fact that Zion is elsewhere the city of David would tend to mean that extolling the presence of God in Jerusalem would tend to provide ideological support for the Davidic monarchy. McCann notes that "verse 3 is apparent testimony to the belief in Zion's indestructibility, a conviction upon which Isaiah's advice to King Ahaz seems to be based (see Isa. 7:1-16) and that Jeremiah later opposed (see Jer. 7:1-15)."[14] Psalm 48, therefore, is deeply ambiguous, capable either of subverting or supporting empire.

---

12. McCann, "The Book of Psalms," 872.

13. Frank Moore Cross, *Canaanite Myth and Hebrew Epic: Essays in the History of the Religion of Israel* (Cambridge, MA: Harvard University Press, 1973), 162-3; Patrick D. Miller Jr., *The Divine Warrior in Early Israel*, HSM 5 (Cambridge, MA: Harvard University Press, 1973); Arthur Walker-Jones, "Alternative Cosmogonies in the Psalms" (PhD dissertation, Princeton Theological Seminary, 1991), 65-6.

14. McCann, "The Book of Psalms," 872.

An ecological reader notices that amid the use of all this iconic, possibly ideological language for the holy city, the human relationship to Earth and Earth community recedes in the background. Mount Zion is portrayed as a holy mountain, but, unlike the mountains that totter in Ps. 46:3[2], Mount Zion is a docile mountain owned by God as the personal pronoun in the first verse makes clear. There seems to be some awareness of Earth as subject, as Earth appears without a definite article in v. 11[10]. But the other reference to Earth in the psalm appears with a definite article. This may be evidence of a middle stage in the objectification of Earth in an urban socioecology. Such symbolism easily becomes justification for human monarchy and ownership of land and resources to the benefit of some humans at the expense of other humans and other species.

Although an ecological reader is suspicious of the urban, imperial ideology of Psalm 48 and how it might function today, there may be elements of the psalm that could be retrieved for an ecological reading. The reference to Earth without an article in v. 11[10]—God's name reaches "the ends of Earth"—may recall an ancient and widespread understanding evident elsewhere in the Psalter of Earth as a subject. The portrayal of Zion as a sacred mountain could engender appreciation for all hills and mountains as sacred sources of refuge and strength. Zion as God's creation, and the temple as the microcosm of the cosmos, could engender appreciation for all Creation as sacred.

Embodiment (Ps. 49)

Psalm 49 provides an important corrective to the dangers of the imperial symbolism of the previous psalms and the powerful and wealthy royal court it might serve to support. The psalm begins with an announcement in the style of wisdom literature that the psalmist will "speak wisdom" and solve a "riddle" (vv. 1-5[1-4]). It then proceeds to critique trust in wealth on the basis that humans die like all other animals.

> Why should I fear . . .
> Those who trust in wealth,
>   who boast of great riches.
> It certainly cannot redeem a person,
>   or pay to God their ransom
> The redemption of their life is too precious,
>   so they will perish forever (vv. 6-9[5-8])
> Like a flock for Sheol they are appointed,
>   with death as their shepherd they go down. (v. 15a[14a])

In the context of this psalm, the point is not that humans are different than sheep and goats. The point is that they are like sheep and goats. Just as humans appoint sheep for slaughter, God decides when humans die. The wealthy will die like everyone else. Death is the great leveler.

Yet another verse in the psalm could support a Christian theological claim that sometimes functions to deny the shared mortality of humans and other animals.

> Surely God will redeem my life from the hand of Sheol,
> for [God] will receive me. (v. 16[15])

This expression uses the same verb as God's receiving of Enoch in Gen. 5:24, which would support the idea that this is a reference to an afterlife. But the psalm itself contradicts this interpretation. The Hebrew of v. 11[10] is difficult but it seems to emphasize that all people, even the wise, will die.

> When one considers the wise, they die
> fool and brute die together,
> and leave their wealth to others.

David Pleins points out that the use of this expression elsewhere in the Psalms and the Bible generally refers to deliverance from evil in this life.[15] "The psalmist is not being promised eternal life after death, as some commentators suggest, but life in this life. When all has been said and done, God will shield the psalmist from the oppression of those who boast in their wealth and allow the psalmist to live peacefully in the presence of God."[16]

The expression "hand of Sheol" instead of simply "Sheol" may be significant. The "hand of Sheol" could refer to the power of death in this life. Deliverance from the hand of Sheol could mean deliverance from persecution, illness, or a life cut short, rather than eternal life. In the context of this psalm about fear of people who trust in wealth and boast in riches, it could refer to the deadly power of trust in wealth. Being received by God would then mean being delivered from the power of money in order to live life with God.

In addition to the identification with sheep, Psalm 49 contains a refrain that identifies humans with other animals. The wording in the Hebrew is slightly different in each version of the refrain.

> But a human cannot abide in wealth.
>   They are like animals that perish. (v. 13[12])
> A human has wealth but does not understand.
>   They are like animals that perish (v. 21[20]).

---

15. Pss. 18:17; 30; 55:13-20; 86:12-13; 88:4-16; 116:1-6, 8-10, 15; 139:7-10; 141:7-10 and Jon. 2:3-10. J. David Pleins, "Death and Endurance: Reassessing the Literary Structure and Theology of Psalm 49," *JSOT* 69 (1996): 23.

16. Nancy deClaissé-Walford, Rolf A. Jacobsen, and Beth LaNeel Tanner, *The Book of Psalms* (NICOT; Grand Rapids, MI: Eerdmans, 2014), 445.

The word translated as "perish" is from a Hebrew root that can have several different meanings. Pleins translates "are silenced" rather than "perish." He understands this repeated and final word of the psalm to be emphasizing the "attentive silence" that is essential for wisdom.[17] Although Pleins does not make this point, his translation makes animals models of wisdom. I do not, however, find this translation entirely convincing, because mortality seems to me the dominant theme of the psalm and "perish" seems more likely. Nevertheless, that this is another meaning of the root makes the word multivalent and could lead to appreciation of the wisdom of animals.

The word translated as "wealth," *yeqar*, is also multivalent. It could be translated as "riches" as the New International Version does or as "honor" as the New Jewish Publication Society Tanakh does. The New Revised Standard Version translation "pomp" may bring out some of its multivalence in the English translation. A few manuscripts have the same verb "abide" in v. 21[20] as in v. 13[12] rather than "understand." Similarly, a few Hebrew manuscripts add a "but" at the beginning of v. 21[20] as in v. 13[12]. I think, however, that the different verbs and grammar are more difficult and therefore more likely original. The use of "understand" in the final refrain that ends the psalm serves to emphasize the "understanding" that is the central concern of this wisdom psalm.

The understanding of this psalm that all creatures perish could play an important role in environmental ethics. Richard Twine argues that "the humility of acknowledging both vulnerability and agency in relation to all human embodiment undermines the socio-historical Western moral imperative to deny and control our bodies."[18] This psalm could undermine the Western assumption that humans should deny and control their bodies. It argues that understanding the fragility of life and God's control of life is wisdom. Christians need to be wary of a belief in resurrection that denies the material world, rather than understanding it as an affirmation of God's commitment to the body and the material world in all its fragility and dependence on the Creator.

---

17. Pleins, "Death and Endurance," 26, 27.
18. Richard T. Twine, "Ma(r)king Essence-Ecofeminism and Embodiment." *Ethics and the Environment* 6 (2001): 51.

Chapter 4

SKIES PROCLAIM (Ps. 50)

Psalm 50 stands out for a number of reasons, including a relationship with Earth that is much different than the psalms that come before and after it. The urban landscape of the preceding psalms gives way to a landscape inclusive of pastures and wilderness areas (vv. 10-13). In contrast to the absence of Earth community and objectification of Earth in the preceding psalms, this psalm mentions many members of Earth community—"a young bull" and "goats" (v. 9), "every wild animal of the field ... the cattle on a thousand hills" (v. 10), "all the birds of the air, and all the bugs[1] of the field" (v. 11), and "bulls" (v. 13). In addition, the psalm addresses Earth as a subject (v. 1). This chapter suggests that the Psalter portrays Asaph as an ideal priest who maintains right relations not just between Israel and God but also between God, Israel, and all Creation.

Asaph

The first reason the psalm stands out is because of the ascription to Asaph. This may not at first seem terribly significant, but Asaph is the only individual other than David who has a collection of psalms ascribed to him. There are psalms ascribed to other individuals, and there are collections ascribed to the sons of Korah, but they are a group named after their ancestor, not an individual. Scholars have wondered why this one psalm appears separate from the rest of the psalms ascribed to Asaph (Pss. 50 and 73–83). I would suggest this places the Asaph psalms in locations that reflect Asaph's role the book of Chronicles ascribes to him as the chief priest under King David. First, it creates a ring structure in the final form of the Psalter so that a collection of psalms of David (Pss. 51–65 and 68–70) that have superscriptions relating them to difficulties in his personal life have psalms of Asaph before and after them. Two groups of psalms of the sons of Korah (Pss. 42–49 and 84–88) stand before the first Asaph psalm and after the last Asaph psalm. In the book of Chronicles, Asaph is appointed by David as Chief Priest in Jerusalem (1 Chron.

---

1. Richard Whitekettle, "Bugs, Bunny, or Boar?: Identifying *Ziz* Animals of Psalms 50 and 80," *CBQ* 67 (2005): 250–64, especially 264 n. 33.

16:5) and the leader of singing (1 Chron. 16:7). Chronicles also seems to remember him along with David as a writer of psalms (1 Chron. 29:30). Thus the structure of the Psalter reflects Asaph's role in Chronicles as chief priest under David and composer of psalms alongside David.

Psalm 50 also stands out because of its genre. The group of Korahite psalms before it were characterized by a variety of genres, and it is followed by the psalms of David in which personal laments predominate. Scholars debate the genre of Psalm 50 but generally recognize the prophetic elements. Psalm 51, the next psalm, has a superscription that says, "when the prophet Nathan came to him after he had gone in to Bathsheba." This means the editors of the Psalter have placed a "prophetic" psalm of Asaph before David's repentance for sexually assaulting Bathsheba and murdering her husband Uriah. This psalm stands in the Psalter in the position of Nathan's prophecy. This gives Asaph a major role in the reader's movement through the Psalter following the development of David.

Psalms scholars recognize the progress of the righteous person as a major theme of the final form of the Psalter[2] and that David plays the role of the ideal righteous person who goes from being king to leading Israel in worship of God as King.[3] I have argued elsewhere that David also leads all Creation in worship of God as Creator because God's kingship is based on Creation and Creation is a common theme, especially towards the end of the Psalter.[4] What has not been recognized is that Asaph plays a role in David's progress as a righteous person. He is an ancient, ideal priest, who plays a central role in David's repentance and eventual transformation.

Just as we learn about a singer by the songs they sing, the reader of the Psalter learns about Asaph from the psalms ascribed to him. Or, perhaps more accurately, we learn about the editors of the Psalter's understanding of Asaph as an ideal figure. Psalms scholars identify a number of unique features of the Asaph collection, and several of these are present in Psalm 50. First, Asaph is a priest. Perhaps it goes without saying that Asaph speaks as a priest, because Asaph is identified by the Chronicler as the chief Levite appointed by David. Nevertheless, the content of the songs of Asaph reinforce his identity as a priest. Buss notes that the Asaph psalms contain several expressions of closeness to God that are also closely connected

---

2. Jerome F. D. Creach, *The Destiny of the Righteous in the Psalms* (St. Louis, MO: Chalice, 2008).

3. Brevard Childs, *Introduction to the Old Testament as Scripture* (Philadelphia: Fortress, 1979), 520–1; Peter Ackroyd, *Doors of Perception: A Guide to Reading the Psalms* (London: SCM, 1983), 35; Gerald Sheppard, "Theology and the Book of Psalms," *Int* 46 (1992): 148; James Mays, *The Lord Reigns: A Theological Handbook to the Psalms* (Louisville: Westminster John Knox, 1994), 123–5. For a review of these positions see Harry P. Nasuti, *Defining the Sacred Songs: Genre, Tradition and the Post-Critical Interpretation of the Psalms* (JSOTSup Series, 218; Sheffield: Sheffield Academic, 1999), 138–47.

4. Arthur Walker-Jones, *The Green Psalter: Resources for an Ecological Spirituality* (Minneapolis, MN: Fortress Press, 2009), 81–110.

to the temple.⁵ A major concern of Psalm 50 is a priestly concern with correct sacrifice to God.

Second, Asaph is prophetic.⁶ Nasuti shows that Asaph has ties to what he, following Robert Wilson, calls the Ephraimite tradition represented by northern prophets like Amos and Hosea, the Elohist source of the Pentateuch, and Deuteronomy.⁷ In addition to these ties to prophets, the Asaph collection has a high number of prophetic oracles of judgment with direct divine speech in the first person (Pss. 50, 75, 81, and 82).⁸ Verses 2-6 contain imagery typical of God's appearance (theophany) in the Hebrew Bible, and the remainder of the psalm is the longest direct speech from God in the Psalter. Accordingly, Nasuti notes that, while there are other "prophetic" psalms, Psalm 50 is the only "pure theophany" in the Psalter, being "almost completely dominated by the theophanic aspect."⁹ Thus, Asaph appears as a prophet of divine judgment.

Third, Asaph is wise. Tradition critics note the wisdom elements of the collection. The most striking is the contrast between the wicked and the righteous in Psalms 50 and 73. Psalm 50 mentions "those who are loyal" (v. 6) and has a lengthy description of the "wicked" in typical wisdom style (vv. 16-22). This contrast between the wicked and the righteous connects Asaph both to wisdom literature and to a major theme of the Psalter. The words of Asaph thus contribute to a portrayal of him as an ancient, wise, and prophetic figure who plays a key role in David's progress through the Psalter as an ideal righteous person.

Sun, Earth, and Skies

In addition to priestly, prophetic, and wisdom elements, Karl Johan Illman identified Creation as a theme of the Asaph psalms.¹⁰ What Illman identifies as Creation is the imagery of God appearing in a storm to battle the waters of chaos and establish order on Earth (Pss. 74:12-17; 75:4[3]; 76:9[8]; 77:17[16]). Although fire and wind (v. 3) do not accompany God's appearance in other Asaph psalms, they do accompany God's appearance to battle chaos elsewhere in the Psalter (Pss. 29:7; 104:4). Thus, Psalm 50 begins with language alluding to God as Creator similar to other psalms of Asaph. God as Creator addresses Earth as a subject:

---

5. Martin Buss, "The Psalms of Asaph and Korah," *JBL* 82 (1963): 382. Buss also thinks there are Levitical connections (386).

6. The Chronicler refers to Asaph as a "seer" (2 Chron. 29:30).

7. Harry P. Nasuti, *Tradition History and the Psalms of Asaph* (Atlanta: Scholars, 1988), 115.

8. Nasuti, *Tradition History*, 127–33.

9. Nasuti, *Asaph*, 147.

10. Karl-Johan Illman, *Thema und Tradition in den Asaf-Psalmen* (Abo: Abo Akademi, 1976), 17–19, cited in Christine Danette Brown Jones, "The Psalms of Asaph: A Study of the Function of a Psalm Collection" (PhD dissertation, Baylor University, 2009), 159.

> God, God the LORD, speaks and calls Earth,
>> from the rising of Sun to his setting.
> From Zion, perfection of beauty,
>> God shines forth.
> Our God comes and does not keep silent
>> a devouring fire in front
>> and wind swirling around.[11]
> God calls to the skies above
>> and to the Earth to judge God's people.
> "Gather to me my loyal ones,
>> who made a covenant with me by sacrifice."
> Skies declare God's righteousness
>> when God judges. Selah. (vv. 1-6)

The use of definite articles gives mixed signals about whether Sun, Earth, and Skies are subjects or objects. Skies and Earth have definite articles on them in v. 4 as the translation indicates. Earth and Sun do not have definite articles in v. 1 and Skies do not have an article on them in v. 6. In ancient Near Eastern covenants, it was customary to call gods as witnesses. Sun and Earth were gods in ancient Near Eastern pantheons. While the development of monotheism in Israel meant Sun and Earth were no longer gods, and perhaps began to sometimes have definite articles attached to them, they continue to be spoken of as subjects rather than as objects. Not only do they appear without definite articles, but Earth and Skies appear to have active roles calling the people and acting as witnesses of the righteousness of God's judgment, as they do elsewhere in the Bible. In Psalm 50, Earth can hear God's call and gather God's people. Sun is a subject moving through the skies during the day. Skies are able to declare God's righteousness.

I am not suggesting that contemporary readers need to take this language literally. The chemist James Lovelock proposed that the biosphere is a complex, self-regulating system that can be thought of as a single organism. He called this the Gaia hypothesis after the Greek goddess, Earth.[12] The philosopher of science, Michael Ruse, examines why this hypothesis created a furor among scientists, especially biologists, yet was widely embraced by the public. He traces the long history of the idea in Western culture and philosophy. He notes that scientists recognize that it resulted in better understanding of the role of feedback loops (important for understanding climate change), yet the metaphor has largely "failed as science" because the metaphor implies things anathema to scientists—teleology, purpose, and values. But for those same reasons it has had "success as philosophy."[13] For science, evolution does not have some necessary end that is

---

11. I have omitted the masculine pronouns in order to create an inclusive translation.

12. James E. Lovelock, *Gaia: A New Look at Life on Earth* (New York: Oxford University Press, 1987).

13. Michael Ruse, *The Gaia Hypothesis: Science on a Pagan Planet* (Chicago: University of Chicago Press, 2013), 223.

better than other ends. But thinking about the best future and the values that lead there are the realm of philosophy, ethics, and theology. The modern treatment of Earth as an object appears to threaten the future of humans and many other species, so it may be important to find ways to recover some of the wisdom for philosophy and ethics of thinking and speaking of Earth as a subject.

Sacrifice

God's case against Israel in the central part of the psalm (vv. 8-15) has to do with their sacrifices, though what God is saying about sacrifice is debated.

> [8] I do not make an argument against you on account of your sacrifices,
>   and your burnt offerings that are before me daily.
> [9] I will not take a young bull from your house,
>   from your pens male goats.
> [10] For every animal of the forest belongs to me,
>   the cattle on a thousand hills.
> [11] I know every bird of the mountains,
>   and the bugs of the field[14] are with me.
> [12] If I were hungry, I would not tell you,
>   for the world and all that is in it is mine.
> [13] Do I eat the flesh of mighty bulls,
>   and the blood of male goats do I drink?
> [14] Sacrifice to God a thank offering,
>   and fulfill your vows to the Most High.
> [15] Call on me in the day of need;
>   I will rescue you and you will honor me.

Many modern readers will come to this debate with an assumption that animal sacrifice is an abhorrent and outdated practice. Christians see Christ's sacrifice as having done away with the need for sacrifice. Jonathan Klawans points out that Reformed, Conservative, and Reconstructionist Jews also assume that animal sacrifice is "hopelessly outmoded and meaningless." While Christian and Jewish presuppositions differ on many points, they assume animal sacrifice is "a morally and spiritually incomplete ritual."[15] Animal rights activists see the sacrifice of animals as abhorrent because it causes suffering and death to other animals who, like humans, think, feel, and want to live. Klawans adds that many scholars

---

14. Whitekettle, "Bugs, Bunny, or Boar?," 264 n. 33.

15. Jonathan Klawans, "Sacrifice in Ancient Israel: Pure Bodies, Domesticated Animals, and the Divine Shepherd," in *A Communion of Subjects: Animals in Religion, Science, and Ethics*, ed. Paul Waldau and Kimberley Patton (New York: Columbia University Press, 2006), 66.

work out of this assumption and fail to understand the meaning of sacrifice in its historical and cultural context.[16]

Mary Douglas points out that modern slaughter houses and laboratories cause more animal suffering and death than sacrifice in ancient Israel did and deprives the animals "of the privilege of dying with meaning and dignity."[17] The book of Leviticus seems to allow only the eating of meat from animals properly sacrificed to God in the temple,[18] limits the species that can be sacrificed, and further limits sacrifice to a few individuals from among these species. What is more, meat was a very small part of the diet of an ancient Israelite.[19] While the following statistics were mentioned in the discussion of the quality of life of sheep and goats in Chapter 3, they may bear repeating in the context of sacrifice. By contrast to the small amounts of meat ancient Israelites ate, USDA figures indicate that in the United States "meat eating escalated dramatically in the last fifty years" from 144 pounds per person in 1950 to 222 pounds per person in 2007. This represents almost forty animals per person for a total of over ten billion animals killed in one year in one country.[20] As Klawans points out, discontinuing animal sacrifice has not improved the situation of animals or reduced interhuman violence, moderns have just separated the refrigerator from the temple.[21] Actually, if we consider the number of humans that die in car accidents, workplace accidents, war, or gun violence in schools, then a case could be made that we have developed cultural legitimations for the sacrifice of human bodies. Before rushing to judge on the basis of modern assumptions that sacrifice is outdated, meaningless, and abhorrent, it may be worth pausing to consider whether ancient Israelites had better relationships with other species. Perhaps modern humans could learn something from ancient Israelites about how to relate to other species.

The anthropologist Tim Ingold suggests that there may be something to be learned from hunter-gatherers who spend far more of their lives with other

---

16. Ibid., 65.

17. Mary Douglas, *Leviticus as Literature* (Oxford: Oxford University Press, 2001), 67, citing Jean-Louis Durand, "La Bête Grècque, Propositions pour un Topologie des Corps à Manger," in *La Cuisine du Sacrifice en Pays Grec*, ed. M. Detienne and J.-P. Vernant (Paris: Gallimard, 1979), 134.

18. Robert Seesengood, "What Would Jesus Eat? Ethical Vegetarianism in Nascent Christianity," in *The Bible and Posthumanism*, ed. Jennifer L. Koosed (Atlanta: Society of Biblical Literature, 2014), 233–4, citing Baruch J. Schwartz, "Leviticus," pp. 203–80, in *The Jewish Study Bible*, ed. Adele Berlin and Marc Zvi Brettler (New York: Oxford, 2004), 248.

19. Aharon Sasson, *Animal Husbandry in Ancient Israel: A Zooarchaeological Perspective on Livestock Exploitation, Herd Management and Economic Strategies* (Approaches to Anthropological Archaeology; London: Equinox, 2010), 117.

20. Laura Hobgood-Oster, *The Friends We Keep: Unleashing Christianity's Compassion for Animals* (Waco, TX: Baylor University Press, 2010), 97.

21. Klawans, "Sacrifice in Ancient Israel," 65.

species than most modern humans do.[22] He argues that hunter-gatherers have a relationship of trust with the species they hunt.[23] For example, the Cree of Canada

> suppose that animals intentionally present themselves to the hunter to be killed. The hunter consumes the meat, but the soul of the animal is released to be reclothed with flesh. Hunting here, as among many northern peoples, is conceived as a rite of regeneration: consumption follows killing as birth follows intercourse, and both acts are integral to the reproductive cycles, respectively, of animals and humans. However, animals will not return to hunters who have treated them badly in the past. One treats an animal badly by failing to observe the proper, respectful procedures in the processes of butchering, consumption and disposal of the bones, or by causing undue pain and suffering to the animal in killing it. Above all, animals are offended by *unnecessary* killing: that is, by killing as an end in itself rather than to satisfy genuine consumption needs. They are offended, too, if the meat is not properly shared around [to] all those in the community who need it.[24]

As the quote indicates, this relationship of trust often has a conservation function. Ingold contrasts the hunter-gather's relationship of trust with what he labels the pastoralist's relationship of domination.

Pastoralists, like the ancient Israelites, however, may also have relations of trust. Rane Willerslev et al. examine the cosmologies of Indigenous groups in Russia some of whom herd reindeer and some of whom remain hunter-gatherers. They argue that pastoralists also have a relationship of trust with domestic animals.[25] Even if hunter-gatherers have a relationship of trust, it still involves killing, and herders may have domesticated reindeer in order to more clearly model the ideal relationship of trust, though their cosmology would also show why some hunter-gatherers resisted domestication, because they might perceive confining animals as violating trust.[26] Thus, a cosmology that included respect for other species might explain both domestication and the resistance of some hunter-gatherers to domestication. In response, Ingold acknowledges that

---

22. Tim Ingold, *The Perception of the Environment: Essays on Livelihood, Dwelling, and Skill* (London: Routledge, 2000), 76.

23. Ibid., 69–76.

24. Ibid., 67.

25. Rane Willerslev, Piers Vitebsky, and Anatoly Alekseyev, "Sacrifice as the Ideal Hunt: A Cosmological Explanation of the Origin of the Reindeer," *Journal of the Royal Anthropological Institute* 21 (2014): 1–23.

26. Rane Willerslev, Piers Vitebsky, and Anatoly Alekseyev, "Response: Defending the Thesis on the 'Hunter's Double Bind,'" *Journal of the Royal Anthropological Institute* 21 (2015): 29–30.

early pastoralists could have had relationships of trust with animals, but later pastoralists like the Israelites understood themselves as rulers over domestic animals.[27]

The argument Ingold makes and the evidence Ingold cites for a hunter-gather's relationship of trust have analogies in Israelite culture. While the Bible does understand humans as having dominion over other species (Gen. 1:26-28), and thus acting as rulers, it also contains evidence similar to the evidence Ingold presents for a relationship of trust and the evidence that Willerslev et al. provide for this relationship motivating domestication. Just as the Cree hunter may understand the life of the animal they have killed as being transferred to life in another realm, the Hebrew Bible may understand sacrifice as transferring the life of the sacrificial victim to another realm and the elaborate rituals for sacrifice may indicate respect. Kosher regulations specify that Israelites are not to eat the blood of an animal because the life of the animal is in the blood (Gen. 9:4; Lev. 17:14). Mary Douglas quotes Jacob Milgrom's statement that the "offering is not destroyed but transformed into smoke, etherealized" and concludes that "the act of sacrifice is less a killing than a transformation from one kind of existence to another."[28] Jonathan Klawans argues convincingly that, although Israelites understood themselves as in a hierarchical relationship with their domestic animals, that relationship was one of identity and empathy. Klawans argues that the sacrificial system was understood in the context of an understanding of God as their shepherd. "The key to understanding ancient Israelite sacrifice is to remember the analogy: as God is to Israel, so is Israel to its flocks and herds."[29] He cites examples from the Psalms and the prophets of God as a shepherd caring for Israel (Pss. 23:1-2; Isa. 40:11; Ezek. 34:15-16).[30] "The sacrificial animal must be birthed, protected, fed, and guided—all things that Israel wished for themselves from God."[31] He concludes, "If placing oneself in the position of another constitutes the essence of empathy, then ancient Israel had empathy to spare for their own domesticated animals, even when—or perhaps, especially when—they carefully guided them to the altar to sacrifice them to their own divine shepherd."[32] Perhaps the dividing line between respect and lack of respect for other species should be drawn not between hunter-gathering and pastoralism but between pastoralism and factory farming. The Bible may reflect more respectful relations with domestic animals and may have wisdom still relevant for modern societies.

27. Tim Ingold, "From the Master's Point of View: Hunting *is* Sacrifice." *Journal of the Royal Anthropological Institute* 21 (2015): 26-7.
28. Douglas, *Leviticus as Literature*, 69.
29. Klawans, "Sacrifice in Ancient Israel," 74.
30. Ibid., 75.
31. Ibid., 74.
32. Ibid., 75.

Bulls and Goats

Of all the sacrifices that could be mentioned, why a young bull, and male goats (v. 9)? When I read "young bulls" in Psalm 50, my associations with those words as a modern urbanite are limited because I have limited experience with real bulls. I have seen cattle in fields on drives in the country and came closer to a few on visits to farms, but most of my ideas about bulls are mediated by a few cultural images—Texas longhorns, bull fights, and Disney's Ferdinand the Bull. Hannah Velten adds, "In a media-informed age, you may see the cow as a staggering BSE-infected 'mad cow,' an exploited 'poor cow,' an environment-polluting 'hoofed locust,' or an esteemed 'sacred cow.'"[33] Peoples in ancient Israel and many contemporary peoples in Asia and Africa who live with bulls daily would have much greater lived experiences and richer cultural associations. They would have seen them "as fearsome adversaries, mythical beings, mobile wealth, and respected companion."[34]

Bulls and cows have come to have quite distinct cultural associations, which reflect and reinforce patriarchal culture. Cows have come to be associated with dairy products and fecundity. By contrast, bulls are associated with courage, power, and, by extension, royalty, and divinity. The bull as a symbol of power, courage, royalty and divinity is ancient and widespread. The wild ancestor of domestic cattle, the Aurochs[35] or Wild Ox (*Bos Primigenius*), was a massive and impressive creature. The bull was comparable in size and weight to an American Bison, standing one and a half to almost two meters at the shoulder and weighing around 700 kg (1,500 lb). The Aurochs did not become extinct until the last recorded individual was killed in a game park in Poland in 1672, and were once widespread in Europe and Asia, and known by biblical writers.[36] The hunting of an Aurochs was challenging and dangerous, and, in many cultures, the killing of an Auroch came to symbolize manhood and the power and majesty of kings. Julius Caesar (100–44 BCE) encountered them in Germany and says they were "slightly smaller than elephants ... extremely fierce and swift-footed, and attack people and animals on sight. The Germans carefully trap them in pits, and then slaughter them. Such tasks make the young German men tough." He says they mount the horns and those who have killed the most gain "considerable acclaim" (*Gallic Wars*, 6:28).[37] Tiglath Pilesar I (1115–1076 BCE) says, "Under the auspices of Hercules ... four wild bulls ... with my long arrows tipped with iron, and with heavy blows I took their lives." Rameses III (1186–1155 BCE) is shown hunting Aurochs in the marshes along the banks of the Nile on a stone relief at Medinet Habu. Amenhotep III

---

33. Hannah Velten, *Cow* (London: Reaktion, 2007), 8.
34. Ibid., 9.
35. The Aurochs is distinct from the Oryx, which is a genus of large antelopes.
36. Num. 23:22; 24:8; Deut. 33:17; Job 39:9; Pss. 29:6; 92:11[10].
37. Cited in Velten, *Cow*, 16.

(1417–1379 BCE) reports killing ninety-six bulls by driving them into an enclosure with a ditch.[38]

The domestic bull shares with the Aurochs these associations with power, royalty, and divinity. The Hebrew word used for "bulls" in verse 13 (*'abîr*) can also be used as an adjective meaning "mighty, valiant." A number of ancient Near Eastern gods are portrayed as bulls. Even Israel's God is sometimes portrayed as a bull. It is the same word (*'abîr*) that is used when God is portrayed as "Bull of Jacob" (Gen. 49:24; Isa. 49:26) or "Bull of Israel" (Isa. 1:24).

In many cultures cattle represent wealth. As nomadic peoples settled and became farmers, cattle became a form of wealth that contributed to the early stratification of society.[39] Thus the Roman scholar Marcus Terentius Varro (116–127 BCE) could say, "The very word for money is derived from them, for cattle are the basis of all wealth." The Latin word for wealth, *pecunia*, is derived from the Latin word for cattle, sheep, and goats, *pecus* (Varro, *Res Rusticae*, 1.11). Similarly, the English word "cattle" is derived from Anglo-French, *catel*, "property," Old French *chattel*, which are from Medieval Latin, *capitale*, "property, stock."[40] So the English words "cattle" and "capital" are related. In the Bible, sheep, goats, and cattle represent wealth. Abraham, for instance, is said to have acquired "sheep and cattle" in Egypt (Gen. 12:16) and be "rich in livestock" when he left (Gen. 13:2), and Lot who accompanied him had "sheep and cattle" (Gen. 13:5).[41] After the development of a monarchy, rulers appear to have maintained large herds of cattle (1 Chron. 27:29).

Cattle were domesticated around 7000 BCE. Since Aurochs are large and can be dangerous, anthropologists wonder how domestication occurred. Many early cultures sacrificed bulls and Eduard Hahn thinks the need for more docile animals to sacrifice may have motivated domestication.[42] Others think people tamed calves and then used them to lure wild cattle into herds as cattle are naturally herd animals.[43] While anthropologists do not know how they were domesticated, scholars generally agree that cattle were originally domesticated for traction (to pull things), not for meat or milk as modern Europeans might assume. In ancient

---

38. Ibid., 14–15.

39. Ibid., 22.

40. Online Etymology Dictionary, http://www.etymonline.com/index.php?term=cattle (accessed December 30, 2014).

41. See also Gen. 20:14; 24:35; 26:14. The Hebrew phrase in each of these cases is *z'on ubaqar*, except Deut. 8:13, which has them in reverse order, and 26:14, which has *miqneh ts'on umiqneh baqar*. Since Abraham's flocks are referred to generally as *miqneh* in 13:2, this word seems to indicate the collection of all his various domestic animals, and *z'on ubaqar* seems to refer to "sheep and cattle."

42. Eduard Hahn, *Die Haustiere und ihre Beziehungen zur Wirtschaft des Menschen* (Leipzig: Duncker & Humblot, 1896), cited by Velten, *Cow*, 19.

43. F. E. Zeuner, "The History of the Domestication of Cattle," in *Man and Cattle: Proceedings of a Symposium on Domestication*, ed. A. E. Mourant and F. E. Zeuner (Royal Anthropological Institute Occasional Paper no. 18; 1963), 10, cited in Velten, *Cow*, 19–20.

Israel, as in many parts of the world today, cattle would have been "raised primarily for traction and for their milk and dung, and secondarily for meat, hide, and other by-products."[44] That cows were used as draft animals in biblical times is evident from a number of biblical references (1 Sam. 6:7; Num. 19:2). Clutton-Brock says,

> To many peasant farmers throughout the rest of the world, today, as in the past, a cow (or an ox) is a draught animal whose primary function in life is to draw a cart or plough. The cow may also provide a little milk and it will be killed and eaten when it becomes too old to work and breed any longer. Every part of the carcase [sic] is used, the meat and marrow for eating, the horns, bones, and hide for artefacts, weapons, and clothing, the fat for tallow (for lighting), the hooves for gelatin and glue; whilst from the living animal the manure is an essential part of the farming cycle and in some countries it is used as a fuel, and even as a building material. There is no other animal that provides such a versatile range of resources as domestic cattle.[45]

What is more, cattle provided labor for plowing and threshing that made it possible to support a larger human population in ancient Israel. Cattle, however, use a lot of water and pasture. The number of cattle, therefore, would be kept low relative to the number of sheep and goats, which need less water and pasture.[46]

Bodenheimer says that of the primitive cattle breeds, the Baladi[47] is best adapted to the semiarid ecology, able to live off native vegetation, somewhat like goats, and graze alongside other sheep and goats.[48] That Baladi are well adapted to the ecology make it likely that this type has survived with little change into modern times and thus is similar to the cattle of ancient Israel. The Arabic word *baladi* means "rural" or "indigenous." The Baladi are small cattle, though males can be almost twice the size of females. Currently, Israeli government researchers are trying to revive the breed because they are so efficient. Baladi cattle had almost disappeared because of the introduction of breeds developed to produce more milk and meat, but, with the rise in feed costs because of climate change, breeders have come to appreciate the efficiency of the Baladi. They produce more for the amount they are fed.[49]

---

44. Oded Borowski, *Every Living Thing: Daily Use of Animals in Ancient Israel* (Walnut Creek, CA: Altamira, 1998), 74.

45. Juliet Clutton-Brock, *Domesticated Animals from Early Times* (Austin: University of Texas Press, 1981), 62.

46. Sasson, *Animal Husbandry in Ancient Israel*, 56.

47. He and Borowski call it the Arab cow, but Sasson calls it the Baladi, which is the contemporary breed name (I. L. Mason, *A World Dictionary of Livestock Breeds, Types and Varieties* [4th ed.; Wallingford: CABI Publishing, 1996], 273).

48. F. S. Bodenheimer, *Animal Life in Palestine: An Introduction to the Problems of Animal Ecology and Zoogeography* (Jerusalem: Mayer, 1935), 120.

49. Eli Ashkenazi, "Saving the Sturdy Little Cow that Fed Israel's Founders," Haartez.com, May 28, 2013, https://www.haaretz.com/.premium-saving-the-sturdy-little-cow-that-fed-israel-s-founders-1.5270529 (accessed December 29, 2014).

Returning to why bulls and goats are the two animals mentioned in Psalm 50, at least two possible reasons suggest themselves. The first is because these two animals would be the most frequently culled in this particular socioecology. Agrarian societies carefully monitor the size of their herds and the grazing capacity of the land. They regularly cull their herds in order to maintain them within the carrying capacity of the land. Typically they will keep more females than males. Cattle were domesticated for traction and provided important labor to make dryland farming more productive but required far more water and pasture than goats. Just enough cattle would be kept for traction. Some males would need to be kept for stud, and some would be castrated to make them more manageable, but more females would probably be kept alive longer, because they are easier to manage in the harness and provide milk and more cattle. Males would be killed either after weaning, before they began to use pasture, or after one year when they had gained the most weight for the amount of pasture needed. The "young bulls" and "male goats" that Psalm 50 specifies, therefore, are the ones most likely to be culled.[50] Therefore, the Israelite religion and its sacrificial practices are a part of constructing a particular ecological niche.

A modern reader might question the metaphor, God as shepherd, because it implies that God sacrifices human lives. But pastoralists who thought about herd size and the carrying capacity of the land may have had a different perspective on this metaphor. The Israelites' experience as pastoralists may have lead them to understand that some individuals needed to die to maintain the carrying capacity of the land and understood God as making those decisions for humans, just as they made those decisions for their sheep. God was criticized as a bad shepherd not because God chose when people died but if death came in ways that were unnecessary, disrespectful, unjust, or purposeless. While no individual wants to die, their perspective as pastoralists may have helped them understand death as making way for future generations and contributing to the long-term well-being of the community. As moderns, we seem to have forgotten that death is part of life and that exceeding the carrying capacity of Earth may cause untold suffering and death.

The second reason bulls and goats are specified may have to do with the economics of sacrifice and one of the main concerns of the psalm. Because bulls represented wealth, one can imagine that different classes in ancient Israel might have reacted differently to God's rejection of the sacrifice of bulls and goats in Psalm 50. For a wealthy individual or community that had large herds, offering young bulls and goats might not be difficult. Wealthy families would typically have a number of bulls they needed to cull. Poorer families, however, might only be able to afford one cow that they depended on to plough their fields, tread their grain, and provide milk. The wealthy might feel that the sacrifice of bulls would fulfill their obligations, whereas the poor might be relieved that God was rejecting

---

50. I do not know why male sheep are not mentioned. This might be worth more research.

those sacrifices and calling for ethical behavior and relationship with God. In the context of the Psalms, where the wealthy are often criticized, this psalm may allude to the wealthy whose piety involves animal sacrifices but not ethical behavior and relationship with God.

Right Relations

The naming of bulls and goats may imply a critique of the wealthy and their reliance on sacrifice. The verses that refer to sacrifice, vv. 8-9 and vv. 14-15, surround vv. 10-13:

> For every animal of the forest belongs to me,
>   the cattle on a thousand hills.
> I know every bird of the mountains,
>   and the bugs[51] of the field are with me.
> If I were hungry, I would not tell you,
>   for the world and all that is in it is mine.

Verses 10-13 make the point that God does not need sacrifices because everything is already God's. But they elaborate on this point at length and in detail. They emphasize that not only do all the types of creatures in every habitat belong to God but that God has a relationship with them. The language emphasizes diversity inclusive of all geographies—every animal of the forest, the cattle on a thousand hills, every bird of the mountains, the bugs of the field—culminating in "all the world." The poetry creates concentric circles. The verses about sacrifice are the outer circle. The verses about God's ownership of everything are inside them. Verse 11 is in the center of the circles:

> I know every bird of the mountains,
>   and the bugs of the field are with me.

Birds and bugs are both kinds of creatures that are numerous, diverse, and wonderful. Here the emphasis is not on God's ownership but on God's knowledge and relationship. The Hebrew verb translated "know" ($yd‘$) is a common one with a broad range of meaning. It includes both knowledge and intimate relationship. Some English translations make the second line into one about God's ownership, but the Hebrew just says "with me" (‘$imadi$). In contemporary culture, these lines might be read through the lens of scientific rationality and have to do with knowing facts about these species, but the language is expansive enough to include intimate knowledge and presence with birds and insects as subjects, not objects. This would conform to God's relationship with creatures elsewhere in the Psalms

---

51. Whitekettle, "Bugs, Bunny, or Boar?," 264 n. 33.

and the Hebrew Bible where God provides food for them (Ps. 104:14, 21, 27; Mt. 6:26) and enjoys them (Ps. 104:26, 31).

As was mentioned at the beginning of this chapter, scholars debate what Psalm 50 is saying about sacrifice. The debate hinges on the first line of v. 14. It could be translated as either "sacrifice to God thanksgiving" or "sacrifice to God a thank offering." The verse begins with an imperative form of the verb sacrifice (*zevakh*) with a word as its object *tôdāh* that can refer either to the act of thanksgiving or a type of offering. The NRSV seems to leave the question open with the ambiguous: "Offer to God a sacrifice of thanksgiving." Those Christians and Jews who consider sacrifice outmoded are attracted to the first translation and a reading of the psalm that understands it as rejecting sacrifice and advocating the act of thanksgiving as a replacement. In its historical and literary context, however, the second translation seems more likely. The following lines refer to a practice that seems to be assumed by many psalms of lament and thanksgiving in the Psalter. A person in distress would call out to God for help. They might make a vow that they would promise to fulfill after they were delivered from trouble. Either as an expression of certainty that God would deliver them, or after they had been delivered, they would fulfill their vows and come to the temple to sacrifice a thank offering. Thus the psalm is not rejecting sacrifice but rejecting a type of sacrifice that the wealthy are susceptible to that offers bulls and goats, without being in a relationship with, and depending on, God for blessing and salvation. The Psalms often describe the wicked as those who have no need for God and the righteous as those who depend on God.[52] Thus God rejects sacrifice that occurs outside a relationship of dependence and calls for sacrifice that is part of a relationship with God.

Ancient Israelite sacrifice occurs within the context of a purity system. In order to sacrifice, the worshipper must purify themselves and their offering. The purity system seems to be based on the idea that humans are created in the image of God. Since God does not die or have sex, worshippers must separate themselves from things connected or associated with sex and death to purify themselves and be more fully in the image of God in order to approach God. Since God is portrayed in Psalm 50 as in relationship with all creatures, even birds and bugs, then humans should also be in relationship to other creatures. This is why the creation of humans in the image of God in Genesis is immediately followed by the command to have dominion. The image of God in humanity is understood as in relationship with other species.[53] The language of dominion is hierarchical and problematic because it has been used to justify exploitation, but it also includes the idea that the true nature of humans is to be in relationship with other creatures. Like the relationship of a shepherd with sheep, this relationship is not about the

---

52. J. Clinton McCann, "The Book of Psalms: Introduction, Commentary, and Reflections," in *NIB*, vol. IV, ed. Leander E. Keck et al. (Nashville, TN: Abingdon, 1996), 667.

53. Arthur Walker-Jones, "Naming the Human Animal: Genesis 1–3 and Other Animals in Human Becoming," *Zygon: Journal of Religion and Science* 52 (2017): 1005–28.

exploitation of objects but relationship with subjects who are also creatures of God known and cared for by God.

This psalm only spends time describing the wicked, so the reader is left to infer the behavior of the righteous. The wicked associate with thieves and adulterers, lie, and slander their relatives. The righteous person would presumably not do these things or do the opposite. There may be an allusion to humans bearing the image of God when God says to the wicked, "You were sure you were like me." In any case, the righteous person should be in the image of God, and God is portrayed in the psalm as speaking to Earth and Skies, and in relationship with other creatures. The righteous person then would be in right relationship not only with other humans and God but also with all of Earth community and Earth.

A psalm with the authority of the ancient and wise chief priest of David sings a song of prophetic judgment that portrays God as in relationship with all creatures and the wicked person as neither being in relationship with God or having right relations with other humans. While the righteous person is not described, the implication is that they should depend on God and be in right relation with Earth and Earth community.

This section began by noting that animal sacrifice seems abhorrent and outdated to many moderns. The immediate preference of many Jews, Christians, and animal rights activists would be to read Psalm 50 as rejecting animal sacrifice in favor of a thankful attitude. Although the psalm read in its historical and literary context does not advocate doing away with animal sacrifice, its meaning in ancient contexts does not prevent it from coming to have other meanings in contemporary contexts.

At least two readings of the psalm could be used to argue against violence toward other species. Although Psalm 50 does not advocate replacing animal sacrifice with thanksgiving, it could be read that way in contemporary contexts, because it does indicate that relationship with God is fundamental to ritual activity and thus would remain fundamental when new ritual activities develop in new contexts. Jews and Christians no longer practice animal sacrifice, but relationship with God should remain central to new forms of worship. The relationship in Psalm 50 includes not just an attitude of thanksgiving but also a relationship of dependence that includes actions (fulfilling vows) and worship.

Second, the portrayal of God in relationship with Earth and Earth community provides a model for the righteous person. In Psalm 50, the wicked person who does not have this relationship engages in unjust behavior that is destructive to family and community. By contrast, God is in right relationship with Earth and Earth community. Presumably, the righteous person who depends on God, and seeks to be a bearer of the image of God, should seek to be in right relationships with Earth and Earth community. In this way a contemporary reading of this psalm would support just and caring treatment of Earth and members of Earth community. Imaging the Creator who owns and is intimately related to even the smallest creatures might mean working to end the suffering and death of those creatures, whether that be by killing for food or by destruction of their habitats.

In summary, Psalm 50 presents God as addressing Earth, Sun, and Skies as subjects capable of calling the people and witnessing to righteousness. Many modern readers may find sacrifice abhorrent and might argue that the beliefs and rituals surrounding sacrifice are merely designed to alleviate the guilt the person sacrificing rightly feels for killing another sentient being. Modern slaughter houses and laboratories, however, cause more suffering and death, and sacrifice as set forth in the Bible has the advantage of treating the sacrificial animals as subjects worthy of respect. God's criticism of the people's sacrifice is that it lacks relationship with and dependence on God implied in a thank offering. If God is portrayed as addressing Earth, Sun and Skies, and is in relationship with all species, even bugs, then the righteous person should treat Earth as subject and be in solidarity with Earth community. In the contemporary world, this dependence on God who is in relationship with all creatures might involve working against the exploitation of Earth and Earth community.

Chapter 5

EARTH AS REFUGE (Pss. 51-55)

Psalm 50, a prophetic oracle ascribed to Asaph, is followed by a collection of psalms ascribed to David. Franz-Lothar Hossfeld and Erich Zenger note a pattern to the genres in this collection: "For the collection Psalms 51–72 (the so-called second Davidic Psalter), from a form-critical point of view, we find the following sequence: Petition (Psalm 51)—Lament (Psalms 52–55)—Petition (Psalm 56–60)—Confidence (Psalm 61–64)—Praise/Thanksgiving (Psalms 65–68)—Lament (Psalm 69–71)—Petition (Psalm 72)."[1] Scholars generally hold that these modern genre designations do not correspond to designations in the superscriptions of the psalms and are uncertain what terms like *maskil* and *miktam* mean. In this collection, however, *maskil* and *miktam* do seem to have some correspondence with modern genre designations. Hossfeld and Zenger designate Psalms 52–55 as laments and their superscriptions indicate they are *maskils*. They designate Psalms 56–60 as petitions and their superscriptions indicate they are *miktams*. What is significant for our purposes is that these different genre designations and superscriptions also correspond to different portrayals of Earth and Earth community. Psalms 52–55 portray Earth as a refuge. Psalms 56–60 portray Earth as dangerous. This chapter discusses the first of these clusters, Psalms 51–55, and its portrayal of Earth as a place of refuge and grounding.

Frederick Gaiser recognizes a number of links between Psalm 51 and the previous psalm that identify it in the final form of the Psalter as David's response to God's judgment in Psalm 50.[2] In Ps. 50:9 God rejects the people's sacrifice: "I will not take a young bull from your house, or goats from your folds." In Ps. 51:18[16] David agrees that "you do not desire a sacrifice and were I to give you a burnt offering, you would not be pleased." God will not accept a "young bull" in Ps. 50:9, but in Psalm 51 the psalmist believes that God will accept a "broken breath and a broken and crushed heart" (v. 19[17]), and then "young bulls will be offered on your altar" (v. 21[19]). Even if this last verse is a later addition to make the psalm

---

1. Frank-Lothar Hossfeld and Erich Zenger, *Psalms 2: A Commentary on Psalms 51–100*, trans. Linda M. Maloney, in *Hermeneia: A Critical and Historical Commentary on the Bible*, ed. Klaus Baltzer (Minneapolis: Fortress, 2005), 2.

2. Frederick J. Gaiser, "The David of Psalm 51: Reading Psalm 51 in Light of Psalm 50," *Word & World* 23 (2003): 382–94.

conform to traditional understandings of the importance of sacrifice, the final editors understand it as David responding to the judgment in the previous psalm. Within the broader story of the Psalter, this makes Psalm 51 a key transition in the transformation of David that continues through the David collection and from there through the rest of the Psalter.

Za'atar

Take away my sin with za'atar and purify me;
Wash me and I will be whiter than snow (Ps. 51:9[7])

Botanists debate what plant is referred to by the Hebrew word *'ezov* in this verse. The traditional translation in English coming through Greek versions is hyssop. There is general agreement, however, that this is not the European hyssop (*Hyssopus*), because it does not grow in Israel. Some botanists propose the caper bush (*Capparis spinosa*), because it fits the description of a plant growing on a wall in 1 Kgs 5:33[4:33].[3] It seems unlikely, however, that the caper bush would fit the reference to hyssop in Jn 19:29. The same plant seems to be in view because the Hebrew *'ezov* is translated using *hussopos* "hyssop" in Kings, and that is the Greek word used in Jn 19:29. The caper bush, however, would probably not produce a stick substantial enough to lift a sponge to the lips of Jesus.[4] Therefore, many scholars identify the plant as *Origanum syriacum*. It seldom grows in cracks in cliffs or walls as in 1 Kgs 5:13[4:33] but might grow large enough to produce a stick long enough to lift a sponge to the lips of Jesus (Jn 19:29). The Samaritans use *Origanum* to sprinkle the Passover sacrifice, and the "small flowers grouped in dense spikes" and "wooly bracts as long as the calyx"[5] would make a bunch of several stems good for this purpose. Michael Zohary follows a number of botanists in calling this plant "Syrian hyssop" to distinguish it from "European hyssop," but Koops thinks "marjoram" would be better because *Majorana syriaca* is a synonym for *Origanum syriacum*.[6] Marjoram, however, usually refers specifically to *Origanum vulgare* in English. *Origanum syriacum* is called *za'atar* in Arabic and is one of the main ingredients in the spice mixture *za'atar* to which it gives its name and which is becoming known among English speakers. I have, therefore,

---

3. Robert Koops, *Each According to Its Kind: Plants and Trees in the Bible* (UBS Technical Helps; Redding, UK: United Bible Societies, 2012), 97.

4. "Stick" or "branch" is added by English translations. The Greek just has *hussopos*. It is possible the *hussopos* is being put with the sour wine and something else is being used to offer them to Jesus.

5. Michael Zohary, *Plants of the Bible: A Complete Handbook to All the Plants with 200 Full-Color Plates Taken in the Natural Habitat* (London: Cambridge University Press, 1982), 97.

6. Koops, *Each According to Its Kind*, 156-7.

translated za'atar, though this perhaps has the disadvantage of sounding like a spice mixture to English speakers.

Although its botanical identification is debated, za'atar's association with religious rites of purification in the Bible is clear. Moses told the Israelites to dip a clump of za'atar into the blood of the Passover lamb and put it on the lintel and doorposts of their homes to protect themselves from the plague (Exod. 12:21-22). It was used in a similar manner when a house was cleansed of leprosy (Lev. 14:2-53) and was used both as part of the sacrifice and to sprinkle the mixture of water and ashes from the sacrifice to purify people who had come in contact with a dead body (Num. 19). Thus, za'atar is associated with purification rites. While commentaries typically take this psalm's use of za'atar as a "spiritual" extension of za'atar's use in purification, it could also be understood as indicating a spirituality that integrates the material into the spiritual, such that common plants of the material world and their use in rituals are part of spirituality, not separate from it.

The English language imposes a spiritual/material dualism on this psalm by translating *ruakh* as "spirit" rather than as "wind" or "breath." If *ruakh* were translated as breath or wind instead of spirit, the verses in question would read as follows:

Create (*bara'*) in me a pure heart, O God,
   a steady (*kwn*) breath/wind renew in me.
Do not cast me away from you,
   and your holy wind/breath do not take from me.
Return me to the joy of your salvation,
   And a noble breath/wind support me. (vv. 12-14[10-12])

In this translation, the "spirit" is not some non-corporeal essence inside a person or non-corporeal divine essence from a heavenly realm. The wind that caresses our faces and ruffles our hair is the breath of God, the spirit of God. Every breath we take is a breathing in and out of the breath of God. The word translated "create" is the verb used only for God's creation in the Hebrew Bible, so breathing is the ongoing creation of God that connects us with the creation of the world. The breath that creates us is the breath that creates all other creatures. God is present in this world in every wind and breath. A divine breath sweeps over Creation and is breathed by all creatures. Our breathing is the breathing of Creation. Creation's breathing is our breathing.

A Green Olive Tree

Psalm 52 is another lament that continues the theme of those who trust in their wealth rather than in God (v. 9[7]). By contrast, the psalmist is "like a green olive tree in the house of God" (v. 10[8]). This image of a tree connects this psalm with Ps. 1:3 where the righteous person is "a tree planted by streams of water," Ps. 80:11[10] where Israel is a "cedar of God," and Ps. 92:13[12] where the righteous is "like a palm tree, like a cedar in Lebanon." The psalms look forward to a time when "trees of the forest shall shout for joy" (Ps. 96:12) and both humans and "fruit trees and all cedars" will praise God (Ps. 148:9). The Psalms, therefore, identify trees and humans as dependent on God and destined for praise of God.

Trees have a rich and extensive symbolism in the ancient Near East and in the Bible that can only be hinted at here.[7] Trees were common in temples in the ancient Near East and were often identified with goddesses.[8] The prophets condemned the worship of foreign gods "under every green tree" (Ezek. 6:13), but the temple included the imagery of trees and may have included gardens and trees in its courts. The Garden of Eden with its tree of life seems to be an "archetype for the temple."[9] In Psalm 52 it is not a goddess but the righteous person who is a tree in the temple.

But why an *olive* tree? The olive tree's relationship with humans on the eastern edge of the Mediterranean Basin is an ancient one. The domestic olive tree *Olea Europaea sativa* is a variant of the wild olive tree *Olea Europaea sylvestris*, which is native to the Eastern Mediterranean Basin. Archaeological evidence from a site in Galilee indicates humans began using olives as early as the Upper Paleolithic twenty thousand years ago.[10] The olive seems to have been domesticated by six thousand years ago. Genetic analysis indicates that it may have been domesticated at several locations and continued to mix with the wild variant.[11]

The olive tree is indigenous to the Eastern Mediterranean Basin and thus adapted to living "among the rocks and poor soil ... on the mountain slopes of Galilee, Samaria, and Judea."[12] It is a modest yet highly productive and long-lived, evergreen tree. It grows to a height of 5 to 10 meters and has a trunk that may grow to a meter in width and become hollow and gnarled with age. "It is richly branched and abundantly covered with oblong-lanceolate evergreen leaves, gray below and blue-green above. Its clusters of small, white flowers appear in spring."[13] There are olive groves in Israel that may be more than a thousand years old.[14] One

---

7. See William P. Brown, *Seeing the Psalms: A Theology of Metaphor* (Louisville: Westminster John Knox, 2002), 55–79.

8. Othmar Keel, *The Symbolism of the Biblical World: Ancient Near Eastern Iconography and the Book of Psalms* (Winona Lake, IN: Eisenbrauns, 1997), 125 fig. 162a and 186–7.

9. Dexter E. Callender, Jr., *Adam in Myth and History: Ancient Israelite Perspectives on the Primal Human* (Harvard Semitic Studies 48; Winona Lake, IN: Eisenbraous, 2000), 50–4.

10. Ehud Weiss et al., "The Broad Spectrum Revisited: Evidence from Plant Remains," *Proceedings of the National Academy of Sciences* 101 (2004): 9551.

11. Concepcion M. Diez et al., "Olive Domestication and Diversification in the Mediterranean Basin," *New Phytologist* 206 (2015): 436.

12. Zohary, *Plants of the Bible*, 56.

13. Ibid., 57.

14. Ibid., 56.

mature olive tree can produce 10–20 kilograms (22–44 pounds) of fruit that can be processed to yield 1.3–2.6 kilograms (3–6 pounds) of oil.[15]

The socioecological importance of the tree is reflected in Israelite religion and culture. "People ate olive fruits, but more importantly, they squeezed the oil from the fruits, and used it for cooking, for lamps, for rubbing on the body, for medicine and in religion."[16] "So popular were the tree and its fruit that, apart from the daily diet, the oil was used in holy ointments of kings and priests, and for anointing the sick, for lighting at home and in the Temple, and as a solvent of various spices, incenses and aromatics used as perfumes and in cosmetics."[17]

"Its agricultural significance during biblical times is evident from the many scriptural references to olive groves, olive trees and olive oil."[18] The second dove returns to Noah's ark with an olive leaf in its beak. (The presence of a dove and an olive leaf in this story about the origins of humanity, the same species mentioned in these psalms, indicates the significance of both in this ecological niche.) In the parable of the trees, the olive tree declines the offer to be king, because he recognizes his role is to provide oil for God and people (Judg. 9:9). The main agricultural trees of ancient Israel, the olive, the fig, and the vine all decline to be monarch, and the trees appoint the bramble. In this parable the righteous are humble and produce fruit for others.

This metaphor—the psalmist as an olive tree—is not mere decoration. It arises out of a particular ecological niche that informs human identification with it. The olive is an important agricultural crop in this ecological niche. It is rich in good oils that are dense in calories to fuel the human body. The meaning of the metaphor may not be merely spiritual. That is, it may not only have a message about spiritual dependence on God. This commentary has been suggesting that ancient Israelites may not have maintained as strong binaries between the material and the spiritual, Earth and humans, and in our contemporary context it may be worth considering what it would mean to read in ways that blur those binaries. In this case, humans, like trees, are embodied. Just as the water in Psalm 42 came from God and seeking water was seeking God, both trees and humans depend on water. Both trees and humans are rooted in and adapted to a particular ecological niche. And in that ecological niche, both trees and humans have value and purpose in Earth community as they provide habitat and food for others.

---

15. Koops, *Each According to Its Kind*, 61, citing Nigel Hepper, *Baker Encyclopedia of Bible Plants: Flowers and Trees, Fruits and Vegetables, Ecology* (Grand Rapids, MI: Baker, 1992), 107.

16. Koops, *Each According to Its Kind*, 61.

17. Zohary, *Plants of the Bible*, 56.

18. Ibid., 56.

The Wings of a Dove

The psalmist identifies with a dove in Ps. 55:7[6] by wishing to have wings like a dove. But why a *dove*? Why not a songbird or an eagle? If the psalmist wants to escape, does it matter what wings they fly away with? Part of the answer to this question has to do with the choice most translators make in translating into English. Dove could have been translated as pigeon, because the same word in Hebrew (*yonah*) is used for both. In English translations, pigeon tends to be used for sacrifices, often prefixed with "young", and dove tends to be used for all literal and figurative uses.[19] There is, however, no zoological distinction between them, and the two words are sometimes used interchangeably in English. Pigeon used to refer to young birds, especially young doves. Currently, *pigeon* has come to be "the term that is usually applied to the larger species, and *dove* to the smaller ones, but they are of the same family, the family Columbidae."[20] Domestic pigeons are a subspecies of the wild rock pigeon (*Columbia livia*), and the white doves used by magicians and sometimes released at ceremonies are albino domestic pigeons. (Turtledove translates a different Hebrew word, and, although similar looking, they are from a different genus, *Streptopelia turtur*.) Translators may choose *dove* rather than *pigeon* in Psalm 52 because dove has come to have positive connotations and pigeon negative connotations. Woody Allen calls pigeons "rats with wings" in *Stardust Memories* (1980). "In 2000 London's Mayor, Ken Livingstone, described pigeons as 'rats with wings' and declared war on the world-famous Trafalgar Square pigeons."[21]

Yet the negative connotations associated with pigeons are relatively recent. In England, the pigeon was considered a culinary delicacy among the landed gentry, and having a dovecote and raising pigeons was an indicator of class. Laws were passed allowing only landed gentry to raise pigeons.[22] Until the invention of the telegraph and the telephone, homing pigeons were the fastest way to send messages and, until very recently, continued to be valued when other methods were not available or failed, especially at sea or during war. Barbara Allen tells the story of one such pigeon during the First World War.

> One of the most remarkable pigeons was named Cher Ami ("Dear Friend"), a blue chequered cock, who saved the members of the "Lost Battalion" of New York's 77th Division of the US Army. On 27 October 1918 at Grand Pré, the soldiers were under heavy attack, and there was only one bird left to be released, the others having perished due to enemy gunfire. Cher Ami was released, and then was hit by enemy fire. But he managed to reach his loft at Rampont, a

---

19. George Cansdale, *All the Animals of the Bible Lands* (Grand Rapids, MI: Zondervan, 1970), 170.
20. Barbara Allen, *Pigeon* (Animal Series; London: Reaktion, 2009), 20.
21. Ibid., 160.
22. Ibid., 94.

distance of 40 miles in 25 minutes close to death. The message cylinder was still attached to his wounded leg, which was hanging together by a few strips of sinew. Thanks to his bravery, the battalion was quickly rescued. Cher Ami was awarded the French Croix de Guerre.[23]

There is a monument to him at Verdun. The work of pigeons was so important and valued during the war that there are also monuments to pigeons killed in the war at Lille, Belgium, and Berlin.[24] Messenger pigeons continued to be the most reliable method of communication when other methods failed even during the Second World War. A pigeon named Winkie is a good example. "In 1942 a British Beaufort was forced down into the North Sea. Winkie was thrown from her container and, against the odds, made worse by the oily water clogging her wing feathers, managed to fly 120 miles to the Scottish coast to get help. A rescue team located the crew, clinging to a dinghy, and they were brought to safety."[25]

This positive regard for pigeons is an ancient one. In the ancient Near East, pigeons were associated with gods and were a preferred sacrifice in some cultures. They had been domesticated in Egypt by 3000 BCE. The earliest record of them as food comes from around 2500 BCE. "More than 57,000 pigeons were sacrificed to the god Ammon at Thebes in the twelfth century BCE" during the reign of Rameses II.[26] Domestication may go back even earlier in Mesopotamia, if a terra cotta dove from 4500 BCE is any indication.[27] They were also commonly used by the Hittites and Mesopotamians as sacrifices.[28] Doves were associated with the leading goddess of the Semitic pantheon variously called Innana in Sumerian, Ishtar in Akkadian, Astoreth in West Semitic, or Astarte in Greek.[29] Among the Canaanites, "the goddess Anath counted doves as one of her favourite animals."[30] Cyrus the Great in the sixth century BCE set up a network of pigeons to carry messages that covered the Achaemenid Persian Empire.[31]

In Israel, pigeons were considered clean because they eat seeds and therefore could be eaten and used for sacrifice. Abraham sacrificed a pigeon and a turtledove (Gen. 15:9), and they were the only acceptable sacrificial birds (Lev. 5:11; 12:8). They were included in both burnt offerings and purification offerings. Poor people who could not afford to sacrifice a larger animal could sacrifice pigeons. By Roman times, pigeons seem to have been being used mostly for

---

23. Ibid., 114.
24. Ibid., 111–12.
25. Ibid., 119.
26. Ibid., 59.
27. Cansdale, *All the Animals of the Bible Lands*, 171.
28. Allen, *Pigeon* 58.
29. Ibid., 60.
30. Ibid., 59.
31. Ibid., 102, citing Peter and Jean Hansell, *Doves and Dovecotes* (Bath, UK: Millstream, 1988), 17.

sacrificial purposes and not for food.³² That they were sacrificial birds indicates that they were valued and considered sacred, though one doubts the pigeon being sacrificed would appreciate this sort of honor. The fact that they were part of the burnt offering may be why they come to be associated in film and literature with people who are persecuted.³³

In terms of why a dove in Psalm 55, there are some fairly simple reasons why a pigeon may have been chosen. The Hebrew word for pigeon comes from a root meaning "to moan." This may be because the calls of pigeons sound like moaning and thus the choice of a moaning pigeon may have been appropriate for a lament. Pigeons are associated with lament and petition elsewhere in the Hebrew Bible (Isa. 38:14; 59:11; Ezek. 7:16; Nah. 2:8[7]). While pigeon wings are not very large, the ancients may have known that they had strong wings, either by observation or because they were already being used to carry messages. Pigeons are capable of flying up to 70 miles per hour³⁴ and will sometimes use their speed and agility to evade hawks.

The deeper reasons for the choice of a pigeon, however, may be the role of a pigeon in this particular ecological niche and the associations that role would create. First, the pigeon is a domestic animal, yet they blur the line between domestic and wild. The keeping of pigeons often relies on providing them with attractive lodgings and relying on their social nature and homing instincts rather than caging them. The naturalist George-Louis Leclerc, Comte de Buffon, writing in the eighteenth century, says:

> To induce the Pigeons to settle we must erect a lofty building, well-covered without and fitted with numerous cells. They really are not domestics like dogs and horses; or prisoners like fowls: they are rather voluntary captives, transient guests who continue to reside in the dwellings assigned them only because they like it and are pleased with the situation which affords abundance of food, and all the conveniences and comforts of life.³⁵

This suggests interesting parallels between the domestic pigeon and the urban human. The person who comes to live in an urban area may be attracted by the safety provided by walls and the convenience and services available living close to others. Yet living in urban areas requires a certain domestication of humans. The psalmist may feel like a pigeon that has been attracted by the conveniences of

---

32. Abra Spiciarich, Yuval Gadot, and Lidar Sapir-Hen, "The Faunal Evidence from Early Roman Jerusalem: The People behind the Garbage," *Journal of the Institute of Archaeology of Tel Aviv University* 44 (2017): 98–117.

33. Bernard Lazare, *Le Fumier de Job* (Paris: Honoré Champion, 1928), cited in Miriam Rothschild, *Butterfly Cooing like a Dove* (New York: Doubleday, 1991), 156, cited in Allen, *Pigeon*, 66.

34. Allen, *Pigeon*, 105.

35. Allen, *Pigeon*, 94, citing Hansell and Hansell, *Doves and Dovecotes*, 39.

urban life, only to be disturbed by the violence of humans and wish to escape to the wilderness

Second, the choice of a pigeon fits well with the psalm's frequent imagery of God as rock, cliff, stronghold, and refuge. Pigeons nest on ledges on cliff faces. This is why they have so easily adapted to cities with their tall cliff-like buildings. In the Psalter, God is often pictured as a rocky mountain or cliff that serves as a sure defense and refuge against enemies. Thus a bird that nests in ledges and holes in cliffs is particularly suited to the theological geography of the Psalms.

Third, the use of pigeons in burnt or "holocaust" offerings has led to their association with people who are persecuted. Thus, Bernard Lazar says, "Look in the literature, there is no bird so persecuted as the Dove: nevertheless it was she that God chose to be sacrificed on his altar. God said: Offer me in holocaust not those who persecute but those who are persecuted."[36] Books and movies thus associate Jews during the Second World War with doves and pigeons. For instance, the main character in Isaac Bashevis Singer's short story "Pigeons," Professor Vladislav Eibeschutz, loves and feeds pigeons and is killed by Antisemites.[37] Or in Bohumil Hrabel's *I Served the King of England*, the main character is eventually jailed but while in jail finds daily joy and salvation in feeding abandoned courier pigeons.[38]

In addition to these ancient connotations, doves and pigeons have developed many associations in Western culture, any of which might enrich contemporary readings of Psalm 55. Western culture often associates pigeons with the lower classes. Pigeon racing is considered a blue-collar sport. In the movie *On the Waterfront* (1954), Marlon Brando plays Terry Malloy who keeps pigeons and runs errands for the corrupt head of the Union. Various scenes and the dialogues identify him with the pigeons he keeps. He witnesses a mob hit and struggles with whether to be an informant. In one scene his description of his pigeons is also a description of his own life: "This city is full of hawks, that's a fact ... they hang around on top of big hotels and they spot a pigeon in the park and fly down on them." In the movie *Mary Poppins* (1964), a woman sitting on the steps of St. Paul's Cathedral in London, surrounded by pigeons, sings, "Feed the birds, tuppence a bag." The lyricists Robert B. and Richard M. Sherman said, "The song was about caring for the lowliest, the insignificant."[39] Barbara Allen notes that the pigeons who surround Bert the chimney sweep as he draws pictures on the sidewalk are "of his own class (the streets), unnoticed by the well-to-do, but there nonetheless."[40] Given that the Psalms often complain about the wealthy, this association of pigeons

---

36. Allen, *Pigeon*, 66, citing Lazare, *Le Fumier de Job*, cited in Rothschild, *Butterfly Cooing like a Dove*, 156.

37. In *A Friend of Kafka and Other Stories* (London: Jonathan Cape, 1972).

38. Bohumil Hrabel, *I Served the King of England*, trans. Paul Wilson (New York: New Directions, 2007).

39. Allen, *Pigeon*, 147.

40. Ibid.

with lower classes would be an appropriate modern extension of the meaning of Psalm 55.

The psalmist wants to fly to the "wilderness." This word "wilderness" has become freighted with meaning in English. The meaning of "wilderness" and its implications are hotly contested in contemporary society. Nature writing often portrays wilderness areas as sacred places of refuge, renewal, and healing, a sentiment that may go back to biblical passages like Psalm 55. Yet among other groups in contemporary society, wilderness is a dangerous place that needs to be conquered, or wilderness may be a source of natural resources (lumber, minerals) that need to be extracted. White industrialists may promise Indigenous peoples jobs and revenue from resource extraction projects. Environmentalism may intersect with Indigenous rights and colonialism. White environmentalists may either want Indigenous rights extinguished in areas they designate wilderness or attempt to enlist Indigenous peoples to protect "wilderness" areas.

In the contemporary world, mention of pigeons might remind one of the many pigeon species that Europeans drove to extinction. The Dodo bird, a large, flightless, pigeon went extinct in 1680 shortly after the arrival of Europeans on the island of Mauritius. It is one of a number of lesser known flightless pigeons that went extinct after Europeans and their companion animals arrived on islands where the pigeons lived. In North America, passenger pigeons were once so numerous they darkened the skies. Historians and biologists estimate that there were three to five billion passenger pigeons that made up 25 to 40 percent of all birds in what became the United States.[41] Passenger pigeons were an important food source on the frontier. Then in the 1800s hunters began traveling in large numbers on the new railroads to passenger-pigeon-nesting colonies and killing astonishing numbers of pigeons and shipping them to major cities. In 1851, hunters killed and shipped 1.8 million passenger pigeons from the nesting colony at Plattsburgh, New York. In 1883, hunters killed two million passenger pigeons in Monroe County, Wisconsin.[42] Passenger pigeons were also trapped for use in trap shooting. Here the numbers are also astonishing. "In one competition, a participant had to kill 30,000 birds just to be considered for a prize."[43] Not only were large numbers of pigeons killed for sport, but the individuals were often maimed before release to make them more "flighty." The last documented passenger pigeon in the wild was shot in 1900. The last passenger pigeon in captivity was named Martha. She died in Cincinnati Zoo in 1914.[44]

Can religion promote a better human relationship with pigeons? Allen makes an interesting suggestion that the religious associations people in Venice make

---

41. Richard Ellis, *No Turning Back: The Life and Death of Animal Species* (New York: Harper, 2004), 73, cited in Allen, *Pigeon*, 170.

42. Christopher Cokinos, *Hope is the Thing with Feathers* (Jeremy P. Tarcher/Penguin, 2000), 217, cited in Allen, *Pigeon*, 175.

43. Ellis, *No Turning Back*, 173, cited in Allen, *Pigeon*, 177.

44. Allen, *Pigeon*, 181–4.

with pigeons may have led to more acceptance of pigeons than in London. As mentioned above, a mayor of London declared war on the pigeons of Trafalgar Square. He banned the selling of corn, introduced hawks, and used water hoses and industrial vacuums to rid the Square of pigeons.[45] By contrast, "pigeons have become one of Venice's mascots and are highly protected and treasured." Allen wonders if this is "because of the flight of white doves around Piazza di San Marco during Holy Week (representing the Holy Spirit)."[46] She wonders if pigeons would be better treated in London if pigeons represented the Holy Spirit and Trafalgar Square were a sacred site.[47] Pigeons are treated with respect in Hinduism and Sikhism. "In Hinduism the pigeon is a messenger of the god of death and justice, Yama" and "thousands of pigeons are fed daily in Hindu temples."[48] "Sikhs feed pigeons to honour the high priest and warrior Guru Govind Singh, who was a known friend of the pigeon ... [T]hey believe that when they are reincarnated they will never know hunger if they have fed pigeons in their previous life."[49] In Christianity, a dove represents the Holy Spirit, as has already been mentioned, and a dove can represent the church or a person's soul in its journey toward God. A strong spiritual/material binary in Western Christianity can make the dove a spiritual symbol with no relation to real pigeons, and rob them of any intrinsic value or respect as images of God. The binaries, however, were evidently not so strong in Venice as to prevent a belief that doves represented the Holy Spirit from leading to better relations. Perhaps if the spiritual/material binary was reduced, then real pigeons could be seen as imaging the divine and worthy of care and respect.

In conclusion, this chapter has examined a group of individual laments that begins the Davidic collection. It has shown that English translations often impose a spiritual/material binary on the Hebrew text that is not present in the original. Thus the same Hebrew word is translated as both *spirit* and *wind* or *breath*. In the original Hebrew, however, the spirit of God is the wind that blows over the face of Creation and the breath of God that gives life and breath to every creature. The use of za'atar in a purification ritual combines spiritual purification with a ritual with a plant. The spiritual/material binary may also be imposed on the naming of species. Members of the same species tend to be called *doves* when they image the divine, but *pigeons* in other contexts. These psalms, therefore, exhibit a far greater integration of the spiritual and the material in the original Hebrew than in English translation.

This chapter has also shown that in the midst of lamenting sin, David longs for reintegration into Earth and Earth community. David longs to be a green olive tree adapted to his environment and rooted in Earth and provided with water

---

45. Ibid., 160.
46. Ibid.
47. Ibid., 161.
48. Ibid., 79–80.
49. Ibid., 80.

from God. David identifies with a harmless pigeon who has been domesticated by urban life but experiences violence from companions and wants to return to the wilderness. Before David and the reader of the Psalms can begin the long journey into reintegration with Earth and Earth community, their relationship with Earth takes a negative turn in the next group of psalms.

Chapter 6

EARTH AS ENEMY (Pss. 56-60)

While the previous psalms treated Earth as a refuge, these psalms treat members of Earth community and Earth as enemies. They are also part of a Davidic collection with superscriptions referring to events in David's life, and they could be categorized as individual laments, like the previous groups. But these psalms have more petition in them than the previous group. And, whereas the superscriptions of the previous group of Davidic psalms identified them as *maskils*, these are *miktams*. Thus the superscription *miktam*, the emphasis on petition, and the changed attitude toward Earth community separates these psalms from what comes before and after. The discussion that follows will focus on the references to the wings of God (Ps. 57:2[1]), lions (Pss. 57:5[4]; 58:7[6]), dogs in Ps. 59:7[6], 15[14], and finally the reference to Earth in Ps. 60:4[2].

Wings

Psalm 57 begins with the psalmist's prayer for mercy and expression of faith in refuge under the shadow of God's wings. Joel LeMon says the metaphor of God's wings is *multistable* because so many varieties of images of winged gods and goddesses occur in the iconography of the ancient Near East.[1] Multistable perception refers to the rapid changing of visual associations. The ancient readers could simultaneously associate the image with a variety of different types of the wing imagery they might have seen in iconography. LeMon's method controls for the images that show up in the archaeology of the Levant and are closest to a psalm's text. While these scholarly controls may show what associations might have been more likely for more ancient Israelites, I would argue that it is part of the nature of reading that imagery is multivalent.

Biblical scholars have generally discussed several possible origins for the imagery of God's wings in the ancient Near Eastern context. According to G. Kwakkel, scholars have made three types of suggestions for the origin of the expression: First, birds protecting their young as in Deut. 32:11 and Mt. 23:37;

---

1. Joel M. LeMon, *Yahweh's Winged Form in the Psalms: Exploring Congruent Iconography and Texts* (Orbis Biblicus et Orientalis 242; Fribourg: Academic Press, 2010), 111–12, 192–3.

second, the wings of the cherubim; or third, winged solar discs or images of winged goddesses and gods in ancient Near Eastern iconography.[2] The wings of the cherubim are unlikely as their wings are never identified as God's wings in the Hebrew Bible, people would not be able to enter the Holy of Holies, and are never portrayed as seeking protection under them in the Hebrew Bible.[3]

Kwakkel is to be commended for using ornithological information to investigate what real bird might lie behind the metaphors. He argues that the image refers to chickens because they are known to gather their chicks under their wings. Some have thought this unlikely as chickens were domesticated in India and are not mentioned in the Hebrew Bible. He counters that chicken bones have been found in Late Bronze and Iron Age sites in ancient Israel,[4] though he too thinks the language is so formulaic that the metaphor had probably become "conventionalised"[5] and, along with LeMon, thinks the primary reference was probably to winged gods and goddesses. Moreover, LeMon notes that the iconography of the sun disc has more anthropomorphic and military elements as it moves from Egypt into Syria and Mesopotamia.[6] The images of gods and goddesses tend to have more human features than they did in Egypt.

Animal studies scholars sometimes point to the mixing of the features of humans with other animals in religious stories and imagery as evidence of less distinct human/animal and divine/animal binaries that might indicate a positive form of human identification with other animals. Although the metaphor may have become anthropomorphic and ossified, it is still present in the biblical text for recovery. The image of God with wings, possibly the wings of a mother bird, could blur the lines between divinity and animals. At a minimum, birds might be of intrinsic value because they image the divine.

Since the psalmist wished to have "wings like a pigeon/dove" in Psalm 55, and Psalm 56 has a pigeon/dove in the superscription, perhaps the nearest association for the canonical reader of Psalm 57 is the wings of a pigeon/dove. Pigeons are unique in having young that remain in the nest until they are almost the size of adults. Male and female pigeons take turns sitting on the nest with them. In addition to sitting on the nest with them, they will protect their young by striking

---

2. G. Kwakkel, "Under Y<small>HWH</small>'s Wings," in Pierre van Hecke and Antji Labahn, eds. *Metaphors in the Psalms* (Bibliotheca Ephemeridum Theologicarum Lovaniensium; Leuven: Uitgeveru Peeters, 2010), 141. See also LeMon, *Yahweh's Winged Form*, 1–2, who breaks the categories down into a little more detail.

3. Kwakkel, "Under Y<small>HWH</small>'s Wings," 154–5; LeMon, *Yahweh's Winged Form*, 94.

4. Kwakkel, "Under Y<small>HWH</small>'s Wings," 151.

5. Ibid., 142, 164–5.

6. Tallay Ornan, "A Complex System of Religious Symbols: The Case of the Winged Disk in Near Eastern Imagery of the First Millennium BCE," in *Crafts and Images in Contact: Studies on Eastern Mediterranean Art of the First* Millennium, ed. Claudia E. Suter and Christoph Uehlinger (Fribourg: University Press, 2005), 206–41, cited in LeMon, *Yahweh's Winged Form*, 96.

out with their wings. Since ancient Israelites raised pigeons to eat and sacrifice in the temple, they would be intimately aware of these behaviors.

Since several goddesses in the ancient Near East are associated with pigeons/doves, this metaphor might also blur gender binaries. This imagery is well represented in ancient Israel. LeMon notes that "a terra cotta cult stand from twelfth-century Beth Shean depicts a goddess holding a dove under each of her arms" and a terra cotta shrine from Transjordan in the eighth or the ninth century features a dove.[7] Many Samaritan ivories include winged female deities, including one that shows two female deities kneeling with wings outstretched in protection and blessing.[8] In addition, small terra cotta doves suspended on pillars with wings spread "have also been found in large numbers" in seventh-century Judah, often in homes and tombs.[9] Othmar Keel and Uehlinger argue that, in the Middle and Late Bronze Ages, the dove is a messenger of the goddess or can appear in place of the goddess. As messengers of the goddess they would bring messages of blessing and love from survivors to the deceased.[10] LeMon thinks that while "the wings of the Horus falcon surely indicate his protection, the spread wings of the dove seem to convey something different."[11] Yet pigeon wings could indicate other types of protection, the ability to fly away from danger, the ability to ascend to the heavens, or a mother hen's protective wings. The wings of God might, therefore, be an image that blurs the boundaries between male and female, animal and divine.

Lions

Psalm 57 also contains imagery of the enemies as lions that continues into the following psalm:

> My life I lay down among lions who burn for human children,
> > Their teeth are spears and arrows, and their tongues a sharpened sword.
> > > (Ps. 57:5[4])

> God, smash their teeth in their mouths,
> > The fangs[12] of young lions crush, LORD. (Ps. 58:7[6])

---

7. LeMon, *Yahweh's Winged Form*, 34.
8. Ibid., 56.
9. Ibid., 34–5.
10. Othmar Keel and Christopher Uehlinger, *Gods, Goddesses and Images of God in Ancient Israel*, trans. Thomas H. Trapp (Minneapolis: Fortress, 1998), 323–5.
11. LeMon, *Yahweh's Winged Form*, 36.
12. Mitchell Dahood, "The Etymology of *Malta'ot* (Ps 58,7)," *CBQ* 17 (1955): 300–3; Jo Ann Hackett and John Huehnergard, "On Breaking Teeth," *HTR* 77 (1984): 259–75.

Brent Strawn, in his extensive study of lions in the Hebrew Bible and the ancient Near East, says that the lion is a polyvalent symbol, but the many literal and metaphorical references "seem to be dependent on the primary aspects of *threat* and *power*."[13] Among the literal references to lions in the Hebrew Bible "the emphasis on the fearsome aspects of the lion—its roar, killing, rending, devouring, and so forth—demonstrates that these were the characteristics of lions that were 'uppermost in people's minds.'"[14] Psalms 57 and 58 thus make use of what is "uppermost in people's minds" when they point to the lions' tongues, teeth and fangs. Commentators generally point out that the focus on the mouth of the enemies is appropriate as the psalmist accuses them of lying.

The Hebrew Bible uses lions as metaphors for God, the king, the righteous, and frequently for enemies and the wicked.[15] The portrayal of the wicked as lions is common to other ancient Near Eastern cultures. For instance, the sufferer in the Babylonian Theodicy says the wicked is like "the savage lion who devoured the choicest flesh."[16] Later his friend responds, "Come, consider the lion that you mentioned, the enemy of the cattle. For the crime which the lion committed the pit awaits him."[17] Strawn concludes after surveying the ancient Near Eastern parallels that the Hebrew Bible, and especially the Psalter, uses this enemy as lion metaphor "more extensively, consistently, and personally than does the broader Near Eastern context."[18]

Psalm 57 seems to me to be combining the lion as enemy with another type of lion metaphor that Strawn traces—lion hunting—that is also present in the quote in the previous paragraph from the Babylonian Theodicy. Both Psalm 57 and the Babylonian Theodicy mention a lion falling into a pit.

> They prepared a net for my feet to trap me,[19]
> > The dug in front of me a pit.
> > They fell into it themselves. (Ps. 57:7[6])

---

13. Brent Strawn, *What Is Stronger than a Lion? Leonine Image and Metaphor in the Hebrew Bible and the Ancient Near East* (Orbis Biblicus et Orientalis 212; Fribourg: Academic Press, 2005), 26–7.

14. Ibid., 45. The quote within the quote is from Paul Henle, "Metaphor," in *Language, Thought, Culture*, ed. Paul Henle (Ann Arbor: University of Michigan Press, 1965), 185–6.

15. Strawn, *What Is Stronger than a Lion?*, 50.

16. W. G. Lambert, *Babylonian Wisdom Literature*, vol. 75 (Oxford: Clarendon, 1967), 50.

17. Ibid., 75:61–2.

18. Strawn, *What Is Stronger than a Lion?*, 274.

19. Here I follow the suggestion of the New Jewish Publication Society translation and understand the root *kpp* not as a verb meaning "bend," thus the NRSV translation "my soul was bowed down," but related to a noun preserved in Mishnaic Hebrew referring to a wicker trap for fish.

The metaphor is mixed here as the enemies are both the lions and hunters who set the net and dig the pit, but this kind of mixed metaphor is common in the Psalms. The sense of divine justice is clear. It is also clear that Psalm 58 combines references to lions with a reference to a method of hunting lions.

The hunting of lions is attested early in the iconographic record and becomes widely attached to royal ideology. The earliest record showing a lion hunt has no royal figure. The Hunters Palette from Predynastic Egypt shows a line of hunters hunting a lion.[20] Later iconography and inscriptions attach lion hunting to the king in Mesopotamia and the Pharaoah in Egypt. From Mesopotamia, the Uruk/Warka Stela from around 3000 BCE shows royal figures killing lions, one with a spear and one with a bow.[21] This motif is developed extensively in later periods. Tiglath-Pileser (1114–1076 BCE) says, "By the command of the god Ninurta, who loves me, I killed on foot 120 lions with my wildly outstanding assault. In addition, 800 lions I felled from my light chariot."[22] Subsequent rulers made similar claims in rather formulaic language. Elnathan Weissert shows that the ruler's lion hunt had a religious dimension: "the king was believed to be following in the footsteps of his divine patrons" who defeated the mythical forces of chaos. As the ruler of humankind, the king was "expected to subdue the incarnate hosts of chaos, that is, the lions."[23]

Similarly, in Egypt, Amenhotep II (1390–1352 BCE) issued scarabs and inscriptions that advertised the "lions which His Majesty brought (down) with his own arrows from Year 1 to year 10: fierce lions, 102."[24] Tutankhamun (1336–1327 BCE) is portrayed on two panels on his coffin. In one he is riding in a chariot with bow drawn ready to kill lions. In the other panel he is in the identical pose, bow drawn ready to kill Nubians.[25] This is a particularly striking example of what is generally the case that, in addition to animals being identified with enemies, hunting is understood as analogous to war. As is generally the case to this day, animals, hunting, war, and race intersect.

The idea of enmity between humans and lions goes way back in human evolutionary history. The predator tooth marks on the fossils of early hominids indicate that they were often a prey species of large predators.[26] According to

---

20. Strawn, *What Is Stronger than a Lion?*, 161, 448, fig. 4.111.

21. Ibid., 134, 418, fig. 4.1.

22. Ibid., 163.

23. Elnathan Weissert, "Royal Hunt and Royal Triumph in a Prism Fragment of Ashurbanipal (82-5-22,2)," *Assyria 1995: Proceedings of the 10th Anniversary Symposium of the Neo-Assyrian Text Corpus Project, Helsinki, September 7–11, 1995* (Helsinki: Neo-Assyrian Text Corpus Project, 1997): 349, cited in Strawn, *What Is Stronger than a Lion?*, 170.

24. William C. Hayes, *The Sceptre of Egypt* (Cambridge: Harvard University Press, 1959) 2:232, cited in Strawn, *What Is Stronger than a Lion?*, 162.

25. Strawn, *What Is Stronger than a Lion?*, 162, 448, figs. 4.113 and 4.114.

26. Pat Shipman, *The Animal Connection: A New Perspective on What Makes Us Human* (New York and London: W. W. Norton, 2011), 22.

the paleoanthropologist, Pat Shipman, the discovery of tools and cooperating in hunting changed the dynamics. Humans created a new predator ecological niche and began spreading around the world.[27] A human cultural adaptation to this new predator ecological niche may have been to treat competitors like lions as enemies and cooperate in hunting them. The royal lion hunt would then be a hierarchical form of cooperation making use of an ancient cultural adaptation to a predator ecological niche.

From Earth's perspective, the problem with using lions as a metaphor for human enemies is that metaphors are interactive. As Max Black puts it, "If to call a man a wolf is to put him in a special light, we must not forget that the metaphor makes the wolf seem more human than he otherwise would."[28] Similarly, feminists note that when father is used as a metaphor for God, human fathers seem more divine. In the case of lions, when enemies are called lions, lions seem more like enemies.

The problem with the metaphor of enemies as lions in contemporary contexts is that lions have been treated as if they were enemies by humans for so long that they are now extinct in many areas and driven to threatened or endangered status in the remaining areas they inhabit. Lions once ranged from sub-Saharan Africa into Northern Africa and Southwest Asia, east into Europe and west to India. The lion went extinct in Europe about 2,000 years ago and disappeared from the other countries outside sub-Saharan Africa over the last 150 years. Only one small, isolated population remains in Gir National Forest in India. Even within sub-Saharan Africa, lion numbers declined by 43 percent from 1993 to 2014.[29] I do not know if biblical imagery of lions as enemies has been directly cited to legitimate the killing of lions. This would be worthy of further study. But it is part of a broader pattern of destruction of Earth and Earth community that has been justified by interpretations of the Bible. What is more, European "over-hunting and colonial expansion had a devastating impact" on lions in the nineteenth century.[30] Colonialism and environmental exploitation go hand in hand. "In the 1890s, as European farmers and ranchers settled in East Africa, protecting domestic animals from predation by lions led to hunting on a large scale.[31] John A. Hunter, a Scottish safari guide ... single-handedly killed several hundred lions in the Ngorongoro crater." Traditionally, hunters do not kill females or young animals, but these lion hunters did not hesitate to kill pregnant females and females with cubs. One hunter, Frederick Courteney Selous (1851–1917), writes: "The one killed by my friend carried in her womb three cubs (two males and a female) that would

---

27. Pat Shipman, "The Animal Connection and Human Evolution," *Current Anthropology* 51 (2010): 522; *The Animal Connection*, 47–55. 48–50.

28. Max Black, *Models and Metaphors: Studies in Language and Philosophy* (Ithaca: Cornell University Press, 1962), 44.

29. P. Henschel et al., "*Panthera leo* West Africa Subpopulation," The IUCN Red List of Threatened Species 2015 (https://www.iucnredlist.org/species/68933833/54067639).

30. Deirdre Jackson, *Lion* (London: Reaktion, 2010), 185.

31. Ibid., 166.

probably have seen the light a few hours later."[32] The *New York Times* reporting on the exploits of Paul Rainey said, "Lions are being slaughtered like American rabbits."[33] Rainey killed seventy-four lions, and the movie about the hunt, *Paul J. Rainey's African Hunt* (1912), ran for fifteen months in New York and grossed $500,000. The American Museum of Natural History endorsed it saying the picture was "simultaneously entertaining [and] educationally and morally uplifting."[34] It is difficult for me to understand how a museum of natural history could consider a movie about slaughtering large numbers of lions "morally uplifting."

In the modern world, royalty is replaced by wealthy people who can afford to play "great white hunter" on an African safari. Formulaic language and imagery on monuments and inscriptions is replaced with photographs of hunters in stereotypical poses over dead lions.

Another problem with the contemporary use of the lions-as-enemies metaphor is that it distorts reality by the psychological displacement involved. The enemy is called a lion because the lion is a dangerous predator and symbolic representative of the forces of chaos. But humans are far more dangerous to lions than lions are to humans. What is more, humans are far more likely to be injured or killed by other humans than by lions. The metaphor of human enemies as lions displaces and denies the reality that humans are far more dangerous to other humans than lions.

Treating lions as enemies, however, may not have been the only possible human cultural adaptation to predation by lions. Elizabeth Marshall Thomas says that in the 1950s when she lived with the !Kung Bushmen of the Kalahari, they seemed to have a truce with lions. She remembers sleeping on the ground one night and awaking in the morning to find lion tracks right beside her. She says in retrospect she wishes she had studied the relationship of the Bushmen with lions, but, in those days, anthropologists did not study human relationships with other species.[35]

Thomas makes these comments in the preface to a book by Marcus Baynes-Rock, *Among the Bone Eaters: Encounters with the Hyenas of Harar*. Baynes-Rock is an anthropologist who was interested in predation and learned that unlike other areas of Africa where hyenas were feared and vilified, the people of Harar allowed hyenas into the city and humans and hyenas had adapted to living together. I cannot do justice to the book here but, to make a long story short, he begins to follow hyenas around the city at night and is eventually accepted by the younger members and then the older members of a family of hyenas. In the process, he learns a great deal about hyenas and their adaptation to living in a city. Toward the end of the book, Baynes-Rock visits a famous and long running hyena research project. Although he does not describe it this way, that research project carefully

32. Ibid., 167.
33. Ibid., 168.
34. Ibid., 168.
35. Elizabeth Marshall Thomas, "Foreword," in Marcus Baynes-Rock, *Among the Bone Eaters: Encounters with Hyenas in Harar* (University Park: Pennsylvania State University Press, 2015), x.

maintains the human/animal divide with hyenas as objects. Researchers in trucks use radio collars to follow and observe hyenas in a park for wildlife. He struggles with thinking their methodology is superior to his because they are gathering extensive quantitative data and these "wild" hyenas are the "real" hyenas. Toward the end of the book he realizes that he has come to know hyenas as subjects rather than as objects, that wildlife parks are not so "wild," and the hyenas of Harar may represent the future of hyenas. Given growing human populations, hyenas need to learn to live alongside humans and vice versa. The hyenas of Harar may indeed model the future of hyena-human relations.[36]

The same may be said of lion-human relations. While hunting was the main threat to lions in the nineteenth and early twentieth centuries, the threat to lions in the late twentieth and early twenty-first centuries is an exploding human population with shrinking habitat for lions. While overhunting decimated lion populations in Asia and Africa in the nineteenth century, the growth and spread of human populations threatens them in the twentieth and twenty-first centuries. The population of India grew from 376.3 million in 1950 to 1.31 billion in 2015. The population of sub-Saharan Africa grew from 179.6 million in 1950 to 969.2 million in 2015.[37] This population growth reduces lion habitat and brings lions into more frequent contact with humans so that, in the twenty-first century, "the main threats to lions are indiscriminate killing (primarily as a result of retaliatory or pre-emptive killing to protect human life and livestock) and prey base depletion."[38] Maybe there is something to be learned from the hyenas of Harar about how to live alongside other members of Earth community rather than being at war with them. One can only hope that humans will find better ways of living with this magnificent creature who is used not only as a metaphor for enemies but also as a metaphor for the righteous and for God in the Hebrew Bible.

Dogs

Contemporary readers accustomed to thinking of dogs as humanity's "best friend" may be surprised and a little disturbed that they are also used as metaphors for enemies in the Psalms, though Western culture also uses dogs as metaphors for enemies as when Saddam Hussein was portrayed as a wild or mad dog by the international media.[39] Dogs are so ubiquitous in human culture that they sometimes go unnoticed, as they often go unnoticed in biblical commentaries on Psalm 59. Major commentators consider "fortress" the organizing metaphor of

---

36. Baynes-Rock, *Among the Bone Eaters*, esp. 157–8.

37. Rounded numbers from an online database query of United Nations 2017 Review of World Population Prospects, https://esa.un.org/unpd/wpp/.

38. Henschel, "*Panthera leo* West Africa Subpopulation," The IUCN Red List of Threatened Species 2015 (https://www.iucnredlist.org/species/68933833/54067639).

39. Susan McHugh, *Dog* (London: Reaktion, 2004), 193–6.

Psalm 59, yet Brian Doyle has shown that dogs are an important structural and metaphorical part of the psalm.[40] Good cases can be made for both *fortress* and *dogs* as organizing metaphors, but I will argue below that, an Earth being should be suspicious of the way they work together in this psalm. After the translation of the psalm below, I will explain why *summit* is a better translation than *fortress*. Both summit and fortress are italicized in the translation to highlight their place in the psalm and prepare for the discussion of them that follows (in my translation from the Hebrew, I have used italics to highlight the words that I discuss in the text above where they have also been italicized).

¹To the Leader. Do not Destroy. For David. A *Miktam*, when Saul sent and had his house watched to kill him.
²Deliver me from my enemies, My God,
    away from those who rise against me, lift me to a *summit* (*těsaggěvenî*)
³Deliver me from those who do evil,
    and from men of blood save me.
⁴For, look, they lie in wait for my life.
    The strong[41] quarrel with me,
    for no offense of mine
    and no transgression, O Lord.
⁵Without cause they run and make ready.
    Get up at my call and look!
⁶But you, Lord God of Hosts, God of Israel,
awake to visit[42] the nations.
Do not show mercy on any whose treachery brought sorrow. Selah
⁷They return at evening.
    They whine like *dogs*,
    and go around a city.[43]
⁸Look, they spew[44] at the mouth,

---

40. Brian Doyle, "Howling like Dogs: Metaphorical Language in Psalm 59," *VT* 49 (2004): 61–82.

41. The root is the same as for "strength" elsewhere in the psalm, so I have translated it as "strong."

42. NRSV has "to punish." The Hebrew word is widely used to mean visit, attend, muster, or review.

43. Many translations have "the city," but the Hebrew has "a city."

44. Commentators debate whether this verb refers to the dogs or the enemies and, therefore, how it should be translated. Hermann Gunkel, *Einleitung in die Psalmen* (Göttingen: Vandenhoeck & Ruprecht, 1926), 254; Hans-Joachim Kraus, *Psalms 1-59* (Minneapolis: Fortress, 1993), 542-3; Marvin Tate, *Psalms 51-100 in Word Biblical Commentary*, vol. 20 (Dallas, TX: Word, 1990), 93; and others, take it as referring to the dogs. Brian Doyle rightly notes the ambiguity of the word ("Howling like Dogs," 62, n. 7).

daggers[45] on their lips,
for "Who hears?"
⁹But you, O Lord, should laugh at them;
You could mock all nations.
¹⁰My Strength, for you I will watch,[46]
for God is my *Summit* (*misgabbî*).
¹¹My loyal[47] God will go before me,
God will let me see those who spy on me.[48]
¹²Do not kill them, or my people might forget.
Make them totter[49] by your power,
and bring them down,
Our Shield, My Lord.
¹³Because of the sin in their mouth, the word on their lips,
may they be captured in their pride,
and because a curse and a lie they recount,
¹⁴Finish them with anger,
finish them and they will be no more,
that they may know to the ends of Earth,
that God rules in Jacob. Selah.
¹⁵They return at evening.
They whine like *dogs*,
and go around a city.
¹⁶As for them,[50] they toss about for food;

---

45. Some find "swords" difficult and suggest the *bet* has been corrupted from *peh*, so that the original text read "insults." Far from difficult, the image is related to frequent references in the Hebrew Bible to words as swords.

46. Doyle and Baetgen translate "I will sing" based on the Syriac. This would imply a confusion of *mem* and *yod* at an early period. The text has "his strength," but it is difficult to make any sense of that reading, and *yod* and *vav* are easily confused, so it is likely that the original reading was "my strength," and most translators agree.

47. Reading "my loyalty" with the Qere, rather than the Kethib "his loyalty." The difference in Hebrew is between a suffixed *yod* or *vav*. The two letters are easily confused in some scripts. Because there is little difference in meaning, I have chosen to translate with the Qere for the sake of English style, rather than the Kethib, which is more difficult and therefore more likely original.

48. The word is a participial form used as a noun that BDB defines as "(insidious) watcher" with a 1 cs pronoun. Thus, TNK has "my watchful foes." I have translated "those who spy on me." Some commentaries and translations have "slander me" (TNIV), or "my enemies" (NRSV). Doyle is right that this misses the contrast with the immediately preceding verb: God lets or causes the psalmist to see those who are looking at him ("Howling like Dogs," 63, n. 11).

49. The same verbal root appears in v. 15 below where I have translated it as "toss about."

50. Verses 15 and 16 begin with independent pronouns—they and I—emphasizing the contrast. In order to bring out this contrast in English, where independent pronouns are

> If they are not satisfied, they remain.⁵¹
> ¹⁷But as for me, I will sing of your strength,
>   and cry for joy in the morning at your loyalty.
> For you are a *Summit*(*misgabbî*) for me,
>   and a Refuge (*mānōs*) when I am in trouble.
> ¹⁸My strength, for you I will make music,
>   for God is my *Summit* (*misgabbî*),
>   my loyal God.

A few words are in order about this translation of Psalm 59, because unexamined, contemporary, cultural assumptions may have influenced translations at several points, including the two main metaphors in the psalm. As mentioned above, the translation of a Hebrew word (*misgabbî*) that refers to a *high place* or *summit* as "fortress" in most modern translations changes a part of Earth, a rocky summit, into a feat of human military engineering, a fortress. Several other Hebrew words and phrases can be translated fortress, but the Hebrew root of this word (*misgabbî*) refers to height and has frequent associations with refuge and security.⁵² In the translation above, I have translated the word more literally as *summit* in order to emphasize the geographical and ecological source of the metaphor. The Hebrew word, therefore, alludes to the socioecological location of ancient Israelites living in a land where the rocky, central hill country provided security and protection from human and animal attacks.

Similarly, English translators may have made the dogs sound aggressive and dangerous by translating the verb *yehĕmū* (vv. 7[6] and 15[14]) as "howling" (NRSV), "growling" (TNK), or "snarling" (TNIV). Sometimes the Hebrew root implies a fairly loud or aggressive sound, but other times the sound does not seem loud, or aggressive, and may even be internal. On the one hand, the word might imply a fairly loud sound when it is used of the "roar" of waves (Ps. 46:4[3]; Isa. 51:5; Jer. 31:35; 50:42; 51:55) and the "uproar" of many peoples (1Kgs 1:41; Ps. 46:7[6]; Isa. 17:12; 22:2). These two appear in parallel in Isa. 17:12.

On the other hand, the verb *yehĕmū* (vv. 7[6] and 15[14]) that some translate as "howling," "growling," or "snarling" comes from the root *hmh* that is used in ways

---

the norm rather than the exception, I have translated "As for them, they …" and "As for me, I …"

51. The Hebrew root is a homonym that can be translated as either "lodge overnight" or "grumble." The difference in translation may imply a slight change in pointing of the MT, though no change in the consonantal text. Most commentators choose the later and translate it in relation to dogs as growl, howl, whine, or the like. Doyle thinks the fact that the dogs "return" means they could not stay overnight. But staying overnight does not mean they stay through the following day, and, in any case, this analysis may be getting a little too literal. The enemies in the psalm lie in wait and watch, so "remain" fits with the behavior of the enemies in the rest of the psalm. Dogs might also remain until they find food.

52. BDB; *HALOT*.

that do not seem to imply a loud or aggressive sound. NRSV translates "*growl* like a bear" in Isa. 59:11, but it is in parallel with "like doves we moan mournfully," which presumably is not very loud. Bears can make a moaning sound, which would fit the sense of discouragement in the context. Elsewhere, the sound can be compared to the cooing of doves (Ezek. 7:16). The root can apply to a "murmur" or "moan" of discouragement (Pss. 42:6[5]; 42:12[11]; 43:6[5]) and complaint in prayer (Pss. 55:18[17]; 77:4[3]).[53] It can refer to the sound of internal emotions (Jer. 4:19; 31:20) that, although strong, are presumably not loud as they are compared to the sound of the strumming of a lyre (Isa. 16:11) or a flute (Jer. 48:36). Linguists have documented the relationship of some words to the sounds they describe, and if this is the case with the Hebrew root *hmh*, then it may be a word for "humming" or "murmuring" sounds. The examples in the previous paragraph when the sound appears loud may be because of large numbers of people or waves murmuring.

In the case of Psalm 59, if they are lying in wait (v. 4[3]), spying on the psalmist, and think their words will not be heard (v. 9[8]), then one would not expect loud and overtly aggressive sounds. If the dogs are waiting for food, then they would be more likely to whine. Rather than "growling" or "snarling," therefore, I have translated "whine." The image is still a negative one, but an image of subservience rather than aggression. The words for *summit* and *dogs* are in italics in the translation to highlight the number of verses dedicated to dogs and the repetition of words from the Hebrew root for summit at key points in the psalm. As will become evident, the translation "whine" is important for understanding the real dogs behind this metaphor.

For a contemporary reader like myself accustomed to thinking of dogs as humanity's "best friend," and concerned to develop better lived relationships with the many threatened and endangered Earth creatures, Psalm 59's repeated statements that the enemies are "like dogs" (vv. 7[6] and 14) is deeply disturbing. The simile requires, and perhaps perpetuates, an assumption that dogs are by their *nature* suitable to say something derogatory about human enemies. It is akin to saying the enemies are "like women." Contemporary culture is beginning to tell very different stories about dogs and their intrinsic value as subjects with their own agency. Thirty-seven percent of households in the United States have a dog and 70 percent of these owners consider their dog a member of the family.[54] Recently, anthropologists and evolutionary ecologists have uncovered evidence of the importance of dogs for human development and have begun to reconstruct a story of the coevolution of dogs and humans.[55] Because dogs are the species

---

53. BDB.

54. American Veterinary Medicine Association, *US Pet Ownership & Demographics Source Book (2012)*, cited in the American Veterinary Medicine Association Website (https://www.avma.org/KB/Resources/Statistics/Pages/Market-research-statistics-US-pet-ownership.aspx) accessed August 7, 2013.

55. Raymond Coppinger and Lorna Coppinger, *Dogs: A New Understanding of Canine Origin, Behavior, and Evolution* (Chicago: University of Chicago Press, 2002); Ádám Miklósi,

that humans have some of the closest relationships with and, for this reason, have become liminal figures mediating between humans and other species, some have suggested that dogs would be a good place to begin developing better lived symbolic relationships with other species and Earth. What is disturbing for an ecological hermeneutic, however, is that not only Psalm 59 but the Bible as a whole has a generally negative attitude toward dogs. Why does the Bible have such a negative view of dogs? Can Jewish and Christian communities who base their life and worship on these texts construct better lived relationships with dogs, other species, and Earth?

It needs to be acknowledged that the contrast in the previous paragraphs between the largely negative attitude of the Bible toward dogs and more positive contemporary attitudes as humanity's "best friend" is an oversimplification. Contemporary attitudes are actually deeply contested and ambiguous. People's positive attitudes toward their pets are often not extended to other species[56] or even other members of the same species. Dogs are the most common pet and often treated as members of the family; yet dogs are also the most common research animal and often treated as objects and endure untold suffering. The Coppingers argue on the basis of biology that some human relationships like those with working dogs are mutual, but in the case of other relationships, like those with purebred dogs and dogs used in research, humans are far from a dog's best friend.[57] At the same time, the discussion below will show that more positive attitudes may have existed in Ancient Israel, and suggest that the negative attitudes that came to be expressed in the Hebrew Bible come from a particular socioecological context.

Unfortunately, the depiction of enemies as dogs in Psalm 59 reflects a generally negative view of dogs in the Hebrew Bible. For instance, Jehuda Feliks says in *Encyclopedia Judaica* that "the dog is usually spoken of disparagingly."[58] If one looks at the way "dog" is used in the Hebrew Bible, there are two frequent uses, and then several less frequent uses. Among the most frequent uses of "dog," the first appears in several similar passages in the Deuteronomistic History where dog is used as a symbol of low status and subservience. Typical is Mephibosheth's response to David's kindness in 2 Sam. 9:8—"He did obeisance and said, 'What is your servant that you should look upon a dead dog such as I?'" In this passage Mephibosheth does "obeisance" and identifies himself as David's "servant." This is

---

Dog Behaviour, Evolution, and Cognition (Oxford Biology; Oxford: Oxford University Press, 2007); Xiaoming Wang and Richard H. Tedford, *Dogs: Their Fossil Relatives and Evolutionary History* (New York: Columbia University Press, 2008).

56. Marc Shell, "The Family Pet," *Representations* 15 (1986): 126, cited in Erica Fudge, *Animal* (London: Reaktion, 2002), 32.

57. Coppinger and Coppinger, *Dogs*, 227–52.

58. Jehuda Feliks, "Dog," p. 733, in *Encyclopaedia Judaica*, ed. Michael Berenbaum and Fred Skolnik (vol. 5, 2nd ed.; Detroit, MI: Macmillan Reference USA, 2007).

just one of several uses of "dog," "dead dog," or "dog's head" with fairly stereotypical language to express subservience.[59]

Other passages in this group also associate "dog" with "loyalty" (2 Sam. 3:8) and being a "servant" (2 Kgs 8:13). In some cases, as in the above quote, it is an expression of humility. In other cases, the speaker objects to being treated as subservient or insignificant, as in Goliath's initial reaction to having to fight a boy with a slingshot (1 Sam. 17:43). Similar uses of dog as symbolic of low status continue in the Intertestamental Literature (Sir. 26:25) and the Christian Bible (Mt. 7:6; 15:26-27 // Mk 7:27-28; Lk. 16:21).

This use of "dog" seems to have been ancient and widespread among Semitic peoples. Semitic vassals of Pharoah frequently use "dog" as an expression of humility in their correspondence with him in the Amarna letters written in Akkadian and dating from the fourteenth century BCE.[60] The Lachish letters written in Hebrew in the sixth century also use "dog" as an expression of humility.[61] From the same period, Neo-Babylonian letters use "dead dog" in a similar way.[62]

This use of dogs to symbolize low social status may be related to some of the less frequent uses of "dog." Proverbs compares dogs eating their vomit to fools and their folly (Prov. 26:11). Although disgusting to humans, the ability to get nutrition from vomit and feces is an advantageous adaptation for a scavenger. The association with low status may also help explain the peculiar passage in Judg. 7:5 where Gideon separates troops according to who laps water from the river like dogs, rather than cupping it in their hands. The emphasis is on the small number of people God needs for victory, but an added connotation may be the low status of those God needs for victory.

The second frequent use of "dog" is the references, particularly in the Deuteronomistic History to people's dead bodies being eaten by dogs as an expression of disgrace and divine judgment. The most familiar examples are Ahab and Jezebel (1 Kgs 21:19; 21:23-24; 22:38; 2 Kgs 9:10, 36). But prophets announced the same judgment on Jeroboam (1 Kgs 14:11) and Baasha (1 Kgs 16:4). There are also references to dogs eating dead bodies in Ps. 68:24[23] and Jer. 15:3. Greek and Roman literature also refers to it.[63] This gruesome reality for humans continues to be a contemporary reality. ITV news reporters filmed dogs eating the corpses of Iraqi people during the 1991 Gulf War. The images were archived and never

---

59. 1 Sam. 17:43; 24:14; 2 Sam. 3:8; 9:8; 16:9; 2 Kgs 8:13; Job 30:1.

60. EA 60, 6-7; 61, 2-3; 201, 15; 202, 13; 247, 15; cf. also 320, 22; 322, 17; 319, 19, cited in G. Botterweck, "Keleb," *TDOT*, VII:150.

61. *KAI* 192, 4; 195, 4; 196, 3, cited in Botterweck, "Keleb," VII:150.

62. *ABL* 521, 6; 721, 5; 831, 5; 1285, 12; *CAD*, VII, 72, cited in Botterweck, "Keleb," VII:150.

63. Homer, *Iliad*, XV: 579; Sophocles, *Antigone*, 206; Euripides, *Hecuba*, 1077, cited in Sophia Menache, "Dogs: God's Worst Enemies?" *Society and Animals: Journal of Human-Animal Studies* 5 (1997): 2.

released.[64] This ancient and widespread reality may contribute to a negative view of dogs and lie behind the symbolic association of dogs with the boundary between life and death.

There are some references in the Bible to the positive roles dogs play in human society, but even these often occur in disparaging contexts. Dogs provide a service in many human societies by keeping camps and villages clear of waste and some of the vermin and diseases the waste might attract. While the fact that dogs would eat dead bodies mentioned in the previous paragraph would have been gruesome to humans, the dogs were providing a disposal service that might have reduced the transmission of parasites and diseases. Similarly, dogs are recommended as the way to dispose of unclean meat in Exod. 22:31, though, by eating unclean meat, dogs would become unclean and this may have contributed to negative attitudes to them.

Several passages refer to dogs warning of intruders. This role appears to be the allusion in references to no dog barking at the Israelites when they leave Egypt (Exod. 11:7; Jdt. 11:19). There is a reference to the use of dogs to herd sheep in Job 30:1 though they are being used to indicate low social status. Isaiah refers to the role of dogs as sentinels but in the context of making a point about bad human sentinels (Isa. 56:10-11). This role of dogs may be the source of Sir. 13:18: "What peace is there between a dog and a hyena? And what peace between the rich and the poor?" The comparison to the rich and poor might be merely coincidental, if not for the fact that dogs are used symbolically in many cultures to reinforce the boundaries between classes, as they are in Job 30:1.

There is also some evidence for dogs as companions. From a later period,[65] the book of Tobit refers to a dog accompanying his master on his travels (6:2; 11:4). Additional evidence for dogs in domestic settings is the unnamed Canaanite woman's observation in the gospel of Matthew that "even the dogs eat from the crumbs from their master's table" (15:27). In the society of the time, a Canaanite probably would have had higher status than a Jew like Jesus, so the woman is using the comparison to dogs to turn the tables and express humility and respect for Jesus. This then is another example of the use of dogs to symbolize humility. The Bible, therefore, shows some awareness of the positive roles dogs can play in human society, but even these may appear in disparaging contexts.

In contrast to the attitudes of ancient Israelites and Babylonians, Egyptians may have had a different attitude toward dogs. Botterweck claims ancient Egyptians could use "dog" metaphorically to mean "slave" or "servant" like Semitic peoples but provides no evidence.[66] Dogs appear on Egyptian iconography in a variety

---

64. Robert Fisk, "The Human Cost: 'Does Tony Have any Idea what the Flies Are Like that Feed Off the Dead?" *Independent*, online edition, January 26, 2003, cited in McHugh, *Dog*, 195 (the URL she cites is no longer available).

65. The story is set in the eighth century BCE, but it appears to have been written in the second century BCE.

66. Botterweck, "Keleb," VII:148.

of working roles and in domestic settings. In Egyptian literature, they are given endearing names that suggest affectionate relationships with their human companions. Some dogs are even named after their owners.[67] Cultural critics have noticed the development from generic names like "Spot" to more affectionate names and even human names as evidence of the development of contemporary attitudes towards dogs as family members and companions.[68] Ancient Egyptians, therefore, appear to have had more positive attitudes toward dogs with similarities to contemporary attitudes and lived relationships.

There may also be biblical evidence of more positive attitudes within ancient Israel society than the dominant, "disparaging" attitude. There are many examples of cultures having complex relationships with dogs that may include both positive and negative attitudes. Different cultures or different groups within cultures may have differing attitudes toward dogs, often depending on their relationships with power. Dogs most often carry associations with faithfulness or ferociousness, but either of these characteristics can be viewed positively or negatively. The ferociousness of dogs and their association with wolves can occasion either fear or admiration. The faithfulness and loyalty of dogs can occasion either admiration for their loyalty or, as we have seen in the ancient Near East, denigration for their subservience. While there is no conclusive evidence, the fact that one group in Israel went by a name that had the same root as the root for dog suggests there may have been more positive attitudes toward dogs in ancient Israel that are not fully represented in the final form of the Bible. The name Caleb comes from the root for dog and is the name both of a group and their eponymous ancestor. Caleb is remembered as one of two people in the wilderness generation who remained faithful to God. Joshua and Caleb are remembered as the only two who argued for obeying God's promise and entering the land. Many cultures associate dogs with faithfulness, so it is suggestive that the eponymous ancestor of this group is remembered as faithful to God. While the evidence is not conclusive, it does suggest that at least one group in Israel may either have had a positive relationship with dogs, or a positive symbolic association with the faithfulness of dogs, or both.

Some of the more positive contemporary attitudes toward dogs mentioned earlier are the result of developments within Christianity during the Middle Ages[69]

---

67. Botterweck, "Keleb," VII:148.

68. This has come to be part of what is meant by "pet," but I find myself avoiding that word for contemporary relationships with dogs, in part, because humans have always kept pets, but the meaning of that practice has changed over time, and, in part, because contemporary understandings of "pet" as applied to breed dogs can be exploitative and I want to use language of "family" and "companion" that can suggest better relationships to dogs and all Earth's creatures.

69. Popular medieval, Christian bestiaries told stories of the loyalty and faithfulness of dogs as examples of Christian values. These Christian bestiaries often quoted the first-century Roman Pliny's collection of stories about the faithfulness of dogs, thus building on earlier Greek and Roman attitudes toward them. The loyalty of dogs could still have

and the rise of the middle class and urbanization after the industrial revolution. These more positive attitudes are coupled with negative attitudes that make "dog" a highly ambiguous reference. While some things, like the Egyptian's attitudes toward their dogs or the name Caleb, suggest some people in ancient Israel could have had positive attitudes toward dogs, the dominant view in the founding documents of Judaism and Christianity is largely negative.

Of Wild Dogs and Mad Humans

What little commentators have to say about the use of dogs in Psalm 59 tends to reinforce cultural stereotypes about dogs as ferocious and frightening. They do not analyze either the historical or scientific accuracy of the metaphor or its ancient and contemporary social symbolic function. For an ecological interpretation, however, the historic and social symbolic roles of dogs are important, because the metaphor of dogs as enemies continues to this day and plays negative ideological roles in the structuring of human societies and their relationship to other species.

Commentators seem generally content to reinforce cultural ideas about dogs as wild and frightening without asking about the scientific accuracy or ideological functions of the metaphor. They usually characterize them as "wild dogs"[70] or "wild dogs or jackals."[71] McCann calls them "aggressive dogs." Keel even argues that the

---

negative associations with subservience, but positive associations with Christian values, contributed to their more often being honored and valued for their faithfulness. The legend of the holy greyhound St. Guinefort is a prime example. A Church inquisitor documented the story in the mid-thirteenth century. A French knight left the dog guarding his infant son. While the knight was away, a huge serpent entered the room. In the ensuing struggle the dog killed the serpent, but the boy fell out of his crib, and both dog and boy became covered in blood. On returning, and seeing the blood, the knight mistaking his sleeping son for dead, and thinking Guinefort had killed him, killed the dog. The inquisitor reports that when he found the dead serpent, he "deeply regretting having killed so useful a dog," buried the dog in a well, covered it with stones, and planted trees to commemorate the event. The martyrdom was rejected by the Roman Catholic Church, but Guinefort continued to be worshipped locally into the nineteenth century as a healing saint. Jean-Claude Schmitt, *The Holy Greyhound: Guinefort, Healer of Children since the Thirteenth Century* (Cambridge: Cambridge University Press, 1983) 124–5, cited in McHugh, *Dog*, 70.

70. Kraus, *Psalms 1–50*, 541; Zenger specifies "masses of wild dogs, not domestic animals" (Frank-Lothar Hossfeld and Erich Zenger, *Psalms 2: A Commentary on Psalms 51–100*, ed. Klaus Baltzer, trans. Linda M. Maloney, in *Hermeneia: A Critical and Historical Commentary on the Bible* (Minneapolis: Fortress, 2005), 90; James Mays, *The Lord Reigns: A Theological Handbook to the Psalms* (Louisville: Westminster John Knox, 1994), 213.

71. Mitchell Dahood, *Psalms 1–50* (Anchor Bible; Garden City, NY: Doubleday, 1966), 69.

dogs in Psalm 59 are understood as demon possessed.[72] Kraus and McCann repeat Nötscher's judgment that the dogs are "a picture of disgusting, self-seeking, and hateful activity."[73] Tate quotes Kirkpatrick's description of the dogs in Ps. 22: 17[16] as "a troop of savage and hungry dogs."[74] Zenger emphasizes the dogs as a wild and menacing threat:

> Here are masses of wild dogs, not domestic animals … most of the day they lie about, sleeping; … as night is falling, they begin their hunting forays and move in packs from garbage heap to garbage heap; their menacing howls can be heard throughout the city. Ordinarily the closed gates of the city prevent them from entering, something that is altogether possible and represents a special threat.[75]

While one could say that Zenger accurately captures the function of this metaphor in contemporary and ancient societies, he does not inquire about its social and ecological functions. Nötscher, Kirpatrick, and Zenger's dramatic descriptions play on human fears but are accompanied by little ideological analysis or discussion of historical or scientific evidence about dogs. They appear to read the text through the cultural lens of the dog as ferocious wolf and, therefore, go well beyond the evidence of the text and emphasize a contemporary, cultural stereotype. Among the exceptions are James Anderson, who added a rather lengthy footnote to Calvin's *Commentary* with a fairly accurate description of village dogs from Harmer's *Observations* from travels in the Near East.[76] Another exception is Tate who gives a concise summary of evidence of positive and negative perceptions of dogs in the ancient Near East.[77] He does not, however, inquire about historical and scientific accuracy, or the ancient or contemporary socioecological function of the metaphor.

The psalm itself provides limited information about who the dogs are. The clearest description is in the two refrains and the verse following the second refrain:

> They return at evening,
> They whine like dogs,

---

72. Othmar Keel, *The Symbolism of the Biblical World: Ancient Near Eastern Iconography and the Book of Psalms* (Winona Lake, IN: Eisenbrauns, 1997), 85–7.

73. Kraus, *Psalms 1–50*, 541; J. Clinton McCann, "The Book of Psalms: Introduction, Commentary, and Reflections," in *NIB*, vol. IV, ed. Leander E. Keck et al. (Nashville, TN: Abingdon, 1996), 914.

74. A. F. Kirkpatrick, *The Book of Psalms* (Cambridge: Cambridge University Press, 1902), 334, cited in Tate, *Psalms 51–100*, 97.

75. Hossfeld and Zenger, *Psalms 2*, 90.

76. John Calvin, *Commentary on the Book of Psalms*, trans. and ed. James Anderson (Edinburgh: Calvin Translation Society, 1846), II, 391–2, n. 2.

77. Tate, *Psalms 51–100*, 97.

And go around a city (vv. 7[6], 15[14])
As for them, they toss about for food;
If they are not satisfied, they remain. (v. 16[15])

All the text explicitly tells the reader is that the dogs go around cities at night whining and, if they do not find food, they remain. I have already argued that the word normally translated "howl" or "snarl" is probably better translated "whine." *Canids* have some behaviors that may be considered "disgusting" by humans, but these may be adaptive for dogs and, in any case, are not mentioned here. To say, as Nötscher does, that they are "self-seeking and hateful" projects human intentions on dogs who are, after all, just looking for food. It is actually the human enemies who are bloodthirsty and seek to kill the psalmist. The greatest danger to the psalmist is from humans, not dogs.

The word *dogs* is in the plural, but saying they are packs or "masses" implies large groups of dogs acting together, which moves beyond the evidence of the text. Moreover, the word used for the dogs in the refrains, *keleb*, seems to refer to domestic dogs rather than jackals or wolves.[78] Classical Hebrew has other words to specify jackals and wolves. It is possible that the Hebrew word *keleb* could be used inclusively of all *canid* species including domestic dogs, jackals, and wolves. The English word *dog* can be used in this way.[79] The Hebrew Bible, however, often contrasts the *keleb*, "dog," with *wild* animals and birds. In 1 Kgs 14:11 and 16:4 the dogs are "in the city" and are contrasted with birds "in the country." Jer. 15:3 distinguishes dogs from birds of the field and wild animals. It seems likely, therefore, that the normal usage of *keleb* refers to dogs that are not wild.

Is there an historical dog behind these references? Commentators do not specify what they mean by "wild dogs," but the behaviors in Psalm 59 do not match the behaviors of wolves or jackals. Wolves do not normally scavenge around cities and the subspecies of wolf common to contemporary Israel–Palestine does not howl.[80] Wolves hunt in small family groups or alone and do not normally hunt humans.[81] In fact, wolves have high "flight distance." They run at the first scent or sound, while humans are still far away. Then they do not stop running until they are far away. And they wait a long time before they return. Wolves, therefore, do not usually approach cities and, if they did, would seldom be seen by humans.

---

78. Hyenas might be included under dogs in the ancient world, though we know from contemporary genetic analysis that the similarity of hyenas to dogs is an example of convergent adaptation. Genetically hyenas are closer to mongooses than dogs. And even without genetic analysis, some of their morphology and behaviors are closer to cats than dogs.

79. Wang and Tedford use this inclusive definition of *dog* in their book *Dogs: Their Fossil Relatives and Evolutionary History*.

80. Barry Holstun Lopez, *Of Wolves and Men* (New York: Scribner, 1978), 320.

81. Edward R. Hope, *All Creatures Great and Small: Living Things in the Bible* (Helps for Translators; New York: United Bible Societies, 2005), 106.

Jackals also have high flight distance and do not hunt humans. They may sneak into villages at night to scavenge, but they usually scavenge alone, not in packs, and look much like a fox, so are not much of a threat to humans.

Commentators might be thinking of domestic dogs that have "gone wild." People may have experience with domestic dogs in contemporary, urban contexts that have been abandoned, run away, or gotten lost. These dogs may congregate in groups and scavenge for food. If they are large dogs that have been kept as hunting or guard dogs and poorly socialized or ill-treated, then they may act aggressively toward humans.[82] While there is evidence of large mastiff-type dogs in ancient Mesopotamia,[83] it is unlikely that enough of these dogs would be abandoned or go missing to form packs, and, if they posed a threat to humans, they would probably be killed. When dogs are allowed to breed on their own, they cease to look like large breed dogs within a few generations but instead look and behave like the village dogs common throughout the world.

If the question is the historical and ecological reality behind Psalm 59, then it is more likely that the dogs referred to in Psalm 59 are the village or pariah dogs still in evidence in contemporary, rural villages in the Two-Thirds World. These dogs are not dogs that have been abandoned, as the previous paragraph suggested, or as the name pariah, "outcast," might imply. They exist in places where there are few if any domestic dogs, and recent research in evolutionary ecology and DNA studies suggest that they are the modern descendants of the wolves that began following humans and scavenging at their encampments in the Stone Age.[84] Natural selection favored medium-sized, non-aggressive wolves, because they required fewer calories, and aggressive dogs would have been killed or driven away. Villagers do not usually keep these dogs as pets, but people are accepting of their presence, even on their doorsteps, and may feed them scraps. They may value the dogs for alerting the village to the approach of intruders or large predators, especially in the night. The Coppingers report that when they tried to pat village dogs, they would move out of the way at the last moment, but not very far.[85] In biological terms village dogs have a very short flight distance. They scavenge for

---

82. Coppinger and Coppinger, *Dogs*, 322–3.

83. Juliet Clutton-Brock, *Domesticated Animals from Early Times* (Austin: University of Texas Press, 1981), 45, fig. 3.12. Mastiffs from the palace of Ashurbanipal, Nineveh (Iraq), now in the British Museum, ca. 645 BCE; Oded Borowski, *Every Living Thing: Daily Use of Animals in Ancient Israel* (Walnut Creek, CA: Altamira, 1998), 137–9, figs. 4.3–4.5.

84. Pat Shipman thinks that the Coppinger's theory that village dogs are the evolutionary step between wolves and domestic dogs is wrong because archaeological evidence now indicates dogs were domesticated while humans were still hunter-gatherers (Shipman, *The Invaders*, 172–80; *The Animal*, 209–20). I think that if Australian Aborigines in their sparse environment are able to share their food with dingoes and some ancient hunter-gatherers were proficient enough to kill large numbers of mammals as big as woolly mammoths, then wolves could have scavenged enough food to make following humans worthwhile.

85. Coppinger and Coppinger, *Dogs*, 83.

food from latrines and garbage dumps. They congregate to beg for food where people regularly clean fish, hunt and butcher animals, or prepare meals. Or they may wait to pick up scraps when the humans are not looking or have moved on. The dogs in Psalm 59 may be gathering at evening, because that is when the main meal of the day is eaten and leftovers thrown out. Recent studies have shown that dogs are very sophisticated at reading human eye movements and emotions and these intelligences probably developed over millennia as they scavenged and begged for food. The village dog of Israel–Palestine is called the Canaan dog in both Hebrew and Arabic. The existence of the name in two languages may be an indication of how common they once were. A few survived into modern times around Bedouin encampments and recently some were captured to form a "breed."[86] The behaviors described in the Psalm 59, therefore, most closely match the Canaan dog.

Of course, the biblical writers and commentators may be associating the behaviors of a few ill-tempered dogs with all dogs, or the behaviors of wolves with their domestic cousins. They may be attributing the behaviors of wolves to domestic dogs. This occurs in contemporary society when people are told that their dogs are "pack" animals and the owner needs to be dominant. The fear that dogs are like wolves hovers beneath this widespread advice, which is actually based on early, mistaken studies of wolves and failure to recognize significant behavioral differences between wolves and domestic dogs.[87] But the point is that people may fear dogs because they look like a wolf, which society has constructed as ferocious. Thus, dogs may variously be viewed as faithful and ferocious. This generalizing of the behaviors of a few individuals to a whole group is in my understanding at the root of sexism, racism, and speciesism. Negative behaviors are generalized and understood as part of the *nature* of the others, while the same behaviors may be viewed as *unnatural* exceptions in the dominant group, or reframed. If a white person is lazy, this is viewed as an exception, or reframed as efficiency, or a well-deserved rest, or the like. If one dog bites a human, then all dogs are dangerous. Or, if a wolf attacks a human, then wolves and all dogs are dangerous. If some human attacks another human, we do not conclude that all humans are dangerous to us (though if that human is from a visible minority, members of the dominant group may decide the minority is dangerous). It is actually humans that endanger the psalmist in Psalm 59, but these behaviors are assumed by the use of the metaphor to be part of the nature of dogs. The presence of these verses in the sacred Scriptures of Judaism and Christianity and their repetition in worship could perpetuate a negative stereotype.

But, if the historical dog in Psalm 59 is the Canaan dog, then why is a stereotypical, negative view of dogs widespread in the Hebrew Bible and other ancient Near East cultures? A number of reasons have been suggested or could be suggested.

---

86. Myrna Shiboleth, *The Israel Canaan Dog* (2nd ed.; Loveland, CO: Alpine, 1996).

87. John Bradshaw, *Dog Sense: How the New Science of Dog Behavior Can Make You a Better Friend to Your Pet* (New York: Basic, 2011), xi, xx–xxii, 1–94.

Scientific, Religious, and Economic Reasons

Some have suggested that dogs were disliked because they spread rabies. But the earliest evidence for knowledge of rabies comes from Muslim scholars in the Middle Ages. The cross-cultural evidence is ambiguous as dog bites are sometimes considered "poisonous," but dogs may also be considered to have magical or healing powers. Even if ancient Israelites had some understanding of rabies, this alone would not explain the portrayal of dogs as enemies, because other commensal and domestic species, like sheep and goats, can transfer diseases to humans.

Religious reasons may have contributed to the dislike of dogs. The Hebrew Bible's negative attitude toward dogs might be a reaction against the association of Egyptian gods with dogs. Anubis is often portrayed with a dog or jackal's head. But this could not be the only reason, because Egyptian gods are associated with a plethora of animals, including cows, hawks, crocodiles, lions, and hippopotami[88] that do not necessarily carry negative associations in Israelite religion. In a later period, the Genesis account of the creation of humans in the image of God to have dominion over other creatures contributed to an instrumental view of animals, which would contribute to a low view of dogs. But this does not explain why dogs were especially reviled, when Genesis provides a better textual basis for a dislike of snakes. In any case, Psalm 59 is probably earlier than Genesis 1. The opinion is often expressed that the negative perception in Judaism and Islam is because dogs were considered unclean or potentially unclean. Yet there is no clear textual basis for this. Leviticus does not list dogs or for that matter wolves or jackals among unclean animals. Cats are also not mentioned. So, the question remains why dogs in particular came to be considered unclean as well as having a number of other negative associations attached to them.

The relationship of dogs to polytheism might have intersected with issues of social justice and national identity. Wealthy Egyptians kept dogs as pets, and ancient Israelites may have associated dogs with Egypt and the wealthy elites who kept them as slaves. At a later time, several rabbinic authorities discouraged the keeping of dogs as "the abhorrent behavior of the uncircumcised."[89] Dogs might have symbolized wealth and bondage and been disparaged because of the self-understanding of Israel as a more egalitarian nation.

In this regard, one wonders if the general population might have resented dogs because they saw them as competing for food. This would fit with the statement in Psalm 59 that the dogs seek food (v. 15). Dogs might have been seen as competitors for food, especially if many of the population were barely eking out a living. Yet anthropologists report that Australian aborigines sometimes keep dingoes. If

---

88. Menache, "Dogs," 4.

89. Nahmanides in M. Slay, *Chayto Aretz: Animals of the Land* (in Hebrew) (Jerusalem: Sham, 1986); See also Rabbi Yaakov Emden, *Sheilot u-Teshuvot Yaavetz*, 17; both cited in Menache, "Dogs," 4.

Aborigines living in one of the scarcest environments on Earth have enough food to keep dingoes, then ancient Israelites would have had enough food to keep dogs.

While these medical, religious, and economic factors may have contributed to the negative view of dogs in the Hebrew Bible, Psalm 59 shows evidence of several other social-symbolic factors. These are primary factors in other cultures, so there is some reason to think they were primary factors in ancient Israel.

The Dog as Liminal Figure

Anthropologists identify the dog as a liminal figure in many cultures, including ancient Israel. Dogs inhabit and guard boundaries that construct human societies. *Liminal* is from the Latin for threshold, and this symbolic role of dogs is related to their literal use guarding the "threshold" of homes. The comparison of the psalmist's enemies to dogs appears to mark a number of boundaries in the Psalm 59.

First, the enemies seek to kill the psalmist, so comparing them to dogs may place them in the liminal space between life and death. Or, in other words, their link with dogs may evoke the role of dogs as gatekeepers on the road between life and death. Dogs guard the threshold between life and death in the myths and legends of a number of peoples. In ancient Egypt the Dog Star Sirius marked the flooding of the Nile, the beginning of a new planting season, and the transition between life and death. The dog- or jackal-headed god Anubis was the god of death and guide to the underworld.[90] The god Khenti-Amentiu was the ruler of the dead and depicted with a jackal or dog head. The god Wepwawet was depicted as a wolf or dog and associated with war and death.[91] In Ancient Ugarit a dog guarded the underworld.[92] In Hellenistic culture the three-headed dog Cerberus guarded the entrance to the underworld.[93] (A three-headed dog reappears in J. K. Rowling's *Harry Potter* series serving in a similar capacity.) These mythic and symbolic dogs are obviously interrelated with lived relationships with dogs guarding the thresholds of houses, their use in war, and the experience, referred to repeatedly in the Bible, of dogs eating the bodies of the dead that had not been buried. Whatever their social symbolic role in ancient Israel, many modern readers will tend to interpret them as liminal figures because of the use of dogs as liminal figures in contemporary cultures.

Significant for an ecological hermeneutic is that dogs serve as social symbolic markers of the boundary between nature and culture, civilization and wilderness, partly because of their kinship with wolves. Jack London's book *The Call of the Wild* (1903) is an example. The main character of the book is a mixed-breed dog

---

90. McHugh, *Dog*, 40.
91. Botterweck, "Keleb," 148.
92. B. Margalit, "Studia Ugaritica II: 'Studies in Krt and Aqht,'" *UF* 8 (1976): 169–70, cited in Botterweck, "Keleb," 151.
93. McHugh, *Dog*, 41.

named "Butch" who is stolen from a ranch in California and shipped to Canada's Yukon to serve as a sled dog during the time of the Gold Rush. Butch is abused by a series of owners until his exceptional character is recognized by a prospector who liberates him from his abusive and ignorant owners and nurtures him back to health. When the owner Butch has come to love is killed, he decides to follow a timber wolf he has befriended and "return to the wild." The brutality of Butch's owners exposes the thin veneer of human civilization. The story is usually interpreted as autobiographical and thus not really about a dog but about humans and the Victorian myth of regeneration by return to nature and wilderness. Thus, the story is colored by Victorian ideals but is an example of the use of dogs to meditate symbolically and literally on the relationship between humans and animals, nature and culture, civilization and wilderness.

Dogs mark two more boundaries in many cultures that are particularly important for ecojustice. First, dogs mark the boundary between human and animal. An example is the phenomenon of cynocephaly, reports of people with dog heads and human bodies that date back to antiquity. Dogs in contemporary society live a contested space on either side of the boundary, as the examples that have already been mentioned have begun to suggest. On the one hand, the advice commonly given to pet "owners" that a dog is a wolf and needs to be dominated or they will dominate the owner, and the use of dogs as research *animals* maintains dogs on the animal side of the human/animal binary. On the other hand, the practice of considering dogs as members of (human) families allows them to transgress that boundary.

Second, the existence of dogs in this liminal space between other animals and humans is interrelated, sometimes simultaneously, with their use constructing and maintaining boundaries between human communities. Dogs are frequently used in contemporary societies to maintain social constructs of gender, race, and ethnicity, both literally and symbolically. The media pictures of police officers with German shepherds confronting protesters both in the United States and South Africa have become almost iconic. Many Jewish people have memories of the use of German shepherds in concentration camps. Even for the broader public, the fact that they are *German* shepherds continues to have associations with Germany's role in the Second World War. Here the literal use begins to shade over into the more symbolic uses of dogs. Several cultures, like the Han Chinese, refer to other peoples as dogs, designating them as subhuman. In English, the words "dog" and "bitch" have derogatory connotations that are related to the human/animal distinction and are used in the construction of gender and race. As I was editing this book, the president of the United States provided an unfortunate example the use of "dog" to enforce boundaries of race and gender by referring to an African American woman critically as "that dog." These uses of dogs to legitimate social *and* ecological exploitation are interrelated.

Psalm 59's comparison of the enemies to dogs may have similar socioecological functions. The superscription may obscure these functions. The superscription places the psalm in the context of Saul having David's house watched in order to kill him. In this context, David is a victim or potential victim. The psalm, however, would have been used in ancient Israel, and many contexts since, when a king was in power and far from a victim. In these contexts, anyone opposing the king within the country or any external enemies could become the enemies of the psalm. In these contexts, the psalm would function to maintain the king's power. Those who were poor, seeking food like the dogs in the psalms, or foreigners, literally or metaphorically outside the walls of the city, like the dogs, would be labeled as enemies of the king. It seems plausible that in this psalm *dog* could have functioned to construct the marginalization of the poor, foreigners, and anyone else deemed a threat to the monarchy. And that *dog* could function that way in many other contexts the psalm has been used in since. This would be an early example of a dynamic that continues to this day—the use of *dog* to construct social inequality.

Summit Socioecology

Any number of the factors mentioned above might contribute to the negative attitude toward dogs in Psalm 59, but there is one other ecological factor that may have been decisive, and that ecological factor is evident in the rhetoric of the psalm. It has to do with the way the metaphors *dog* and *summit* interact in the psalm mentioned earlier. The metaphor of God as a *Summit* runs through the psalm. The opening cry for help asks God to be a *Summit* for the psalmist (v. 2[1]). Although "lift me up to a *summit*" may sound a little awkward in English, I have used the word "summit" to indicate that the word used here is a verb from a root that occurs three more times as a noun later in the psalm. At the heart of the psalm, the psalmist confesses trust in God "my *Summit*" (v. 10[9]). And two times at the end of the psalm, the poet praises God who is a "*Summit*" (vv. 17[16] and 18[17]). So, the psalm moves from prayer for God to raise the psalmist to a secure *summit* (v. 1), through expression of trust in God as a *Summit* (v. 10[9]), to praise of God who is a *Summit* (vv. 17[16] and 18[17]).

The organizing function of the metaphor, however, is more than a repeated word. A group of recurring words and images are related to *summit* and reinforce its organizing influence. Secure height is elaborated and reinforced by the words *my strength* (*'uzi*) and *my loyal* (*khasdiy*) God at the end of the first section, when the psalmist expresses trust in God:

> *My strength*, for you I will watch,
>   For God is *my Summit*.
> *My loyal* God will go before me. (vv. 9-10a)

The relationship between strength, loyalty, and summit is reinforced by parallelism and the repetition of *my*. The psalmist trusts in a personal relationship with the God of strength, loyalty, and security.

These same words are repeated twice in the concluding vow to praise God. The words are shown in bold, italics, and underlined in the following translation to show that the words that appeared once in the confession of trust are now repeated twice in the vow to praise.

> But as for me, I will sing of your **strength**,
>   And cry for joy in the morning at your <u>loyalty</u>.
> For you are a *summit* for me,
>   And a refuge when I am in trouble.
> **My strength**, for you I will make music,
>   For God is *my Summit*,
>   <u>My loyal</u> God. (vv. 17-18[16-17])

To these repeated words is added *refuge* (*manos*; v. 17[16]) in parallel with *summit*. Thus, repeated words in the final verses bring the psalm to a crescendo of trust and praise for God's loyalty and strength as refuge and *Summit*.

The organizing function of *Summit* is reinforced by other vertical imagery in the psalm. The enemies *rise up* against the psalmist (v. 2[1]), which is immediately followed by a prayer for God to be a *Summit* (v. 2[1]). Later, the psalmist prays that God will cause the enemies to totter and bring them *low* (v. 12[11]). *Summit*, therefore, is not just a recurring word but what cognitive linguists call a *domain*. These words and images expand and reinforce the meaning of *Summit*.

The enemies as dogs is the other major metaphor in Psalm 59, and Brian Doyle has provided good evidence for seeing *dogs* as an organizing metaphor. The dogs appear twice in a refrain:

> They return at evening.
>   They whine like dogs,
> And go around a city. (vv. 7[6], 15[14])

This refrain is followed by different descriptions of the dogs. The first is focused on what comes out of their mouths (v. 8[7]) and the second on what goes into their mouths (v. 16[15]).[94] If one considers the number of verses that are dedicated to describing the enemies (vv. 4-5[3-4], 13[12]) and dogs (vv. 7-8[6-7], 15-16[14-15]), then the importance of the metaphorical domain, enemies as dogs, begins to become evident.

In addition to repeated references, the structure of the psalm indicates the importance of the metaphors of God as summit and the enemies as dogs and their interaction. Recurring content, language, and grammar divides the psalm into two sections. After an introductory petition and address to God as "my Summit" (vv. 2-3[1-2]), the two sections (vv. 4-11[3-10], 12-18[11-17]) have a similar structure—enemies ... petitions ... selah ... dogs ... but ... my Summit. The psalm could, therefore, be outlined as follows:

A Introductory Petition & Address to "my **Summit**" (vv. 2-3[1-2])

---

94. Doyle, "Howling like Dogs," 68.

B Enemies (vv. 4-5a[3-4a])
C Petitions (vv. 5a-6[4a-5]) **Selah**
D Dogs (vv. 7-8[6-7])
E "**But** as for you" ... Trust in God as "my **Summit**" (vv. 9-11[8-10])
B' Enemies (v. 13[12])
C' Petitions (v. 14[13]) **Selah**
D' Dogs (vv. 15-16[14-15])
E' "**But** as for me" ... Praise of God as "my **Summit**". (vv. 17-18[16-17])

As McCann notes, "this repetitive structure, including the refrains, reinforces the content of the first refrain ... The structural elements of the psalms 'return' (vv. 7[6], 15[14]) just as the psalmist's enemies 'return' every evening." Content and structure emphasize the persistence of the threat.[95] At the same time, God as Summit is repeated and elaborated as the answer to the threat of the dog-like enemies.

Although Earth creatures, dogs, and a part of Earth, a summit, are important metaphors in the psalm, this does not make this a green text. The problem for a contemporary, ecological interpretation is that the world constructed by the vertical imagery and its relations to dogs/enemies could reinforce the idea that humans are above and separate from other species. The interaction of the metaphorical domains creates a world in which the psalmist wants to be on a summit, with God who is a Summit, away from the dogs/enemies who surround the city. Humans seek to be in a city on a hill separate from enemies conceived of as below and outside the city and the uncritical repetition of this metaphorical world in religious settings could provide ideological support for exploitation of Earth creatures. Given the cultural influence of the Bible, this psalm may be one of the sources of contemporary worldviews that see humans as above and separate from nature.

The metaphorical domains of the summit and dogs map the *natureculture* of the priests in Jerusalem. They live in Jerusalem on the Holy summit. They are part of Earth's early urban populations, still a rather small percentage of the total number of humans in the world at that time but, I would submit, beginning to show the alienation from Earth that may come from living in a city. They no longer live in rural areas or villages where they might appreciate the help of dogs herding, hunting, disposing of waste, and warning of intruders. I imagine the process of sacrificing animals in the temple may have made Canaan dogs begging for food or sneaking food a nuisance. It is in this socioecological context, perhaps combined with other cultural factors named above, that dogs could come to be viewed as enemies.

Although dogs can be used to maintain the boundaries that legitimate social and ecological exploitation, the fact that dogs are liminal figures creates possibilities for subversion of the boundary between humans and animals and, perhaps, construction of a more biocentric understanding of humanity. For

---

95. McCann, "The Book of Psalms," 912.

instance, the feminist historian of science, Donna Haraway, holds out hope that developing better relationships with dogs could help develop better material symbolic relationships with the many other companion species.[96]

Earth Creatures and Earth

The discussion thus far skipped over several Earth creatures mentioned in Psalm 58. The wicked are compared to venomous snakes:

> Their venom is like the venom of a snake,
>   Like a deaf cobra that stops its ears,
> That does not hear the voice of a whisperer
>   The spells of a wise person. (vv. 5-6[4-5])

After the already-mentioned prayer that God smash the teeth of young lions (v. 7[6]), the psalmist prays that God punishes them "as a melting snail moves along" (v. 9[8]). According to George Cansdale, "the predominantly limestone rocks of Palestine make it easy for snails to find the calcium for shell-building, with the result that many kinds live in most regions, even in the desert."[97] It is clear that in Psalm 58 this is considered negative and associated with death, because it is sandwiched between grass withering in the previous verse and a woman's miscarriage in same verse. The writer seems to relate the loss of bodily fluids with loss of life, but this is the snail's method of locomotion. The slimy secretion aids their movement.[98] They appear to misunderstand snails by projecting human concerns about the loss of bodily fluids on them.

The first example may also be based on a misunderstanding of snakes. It refers to a snake charmer. The snake is probably an Egyptian cobra, whose range extended into Israel and could grow up to 8 feet.[99] What the verse says about the cobra may be another human projection. George Cansdale says, "It is now agreed that all snakes are deaf, though they have some capacity to sense vibrations received through the ground, and the charmer holds their attention by the movement of his pipe, not its music."[100]

The snake and the snail join the lion and the dog as images of the enemy in this group of songs and implied representation of Earth and Earth community as enemies.

---

96. Donna Haraway, *The Companion Species Manifesto: Dogs, People, and Significant Otherness* (Chicago: Prickly Paradigm, 2003).

97. George Cansdale, *All the Animals of the Bible Lands* (Grand Rapids, MI: Zondervan, 1970), 231.

98. Ibid.

99. Ibid., 206.

100. Ibid.

This group of psalms culminates with God attacking Earth in Psalm 60. The psalmist says to God,

> You make Earth quake and break her open.
>   Heal her fracture for she staggers (v. 4[2])

The people here identify with Earth as a subject. In fact, the poetry places the staggering of Earth in the center of the people's troubles: In v. 3[1], the psalmist says God has rejected the people and broken their defenses. In v. 3[1], God has made the people "suffer hard things." In the center, in v. 4[2], Earth is quaking, broken open, and staggering. The destinies of people and Earth are interrelated and interdependent. God's rejection of the people causes Earth to shake and collapse. They pray for the healing of Earth, so that God will be present with them. Their rejection and healing are tied up with the healing and restoration of Earth.

Unfortunately, the imagery is of a God from the skies attacking Earth. An earthquake may lie behind the imagery, but it is also imagery commonly found with the myth of the divine warrior. That myth of a divine warrior approaching in a storm with earthquakes to do battle against enemies/chaos is found in the ancient Near East broadly and appears in the Hebrew Bible and the Psalms. As Hossfeld and Zenger observe, God strides "like a divine warrior over the land ... splitting it in two, like an earthquake would."[101] What is horrifying is that the divine warrior attacks a woman. Earth appears without an article as a subject. And the repeated personal pronouns emphasize that Earth is female: "*her* fracture ... break *her* ... *she* staggers." An ecological reading is deeply suspicious of a portrayal of God as a warrior abusing a woman. This makes it difficult to retrieve an ecological reading. Though Earth is a subject and the people identify with Earth as a subject recognizing their interrelationship and interdependence.

There is implied here a host of ethical issues around the fact that they are praying for success in war and all the violence that does to other humans, Earth, and Earth community. Contemporary warfare has huge ecological costs and does extensive damage, but, even in the ancient world, war might be accompanied by cutting down fruit trees and destroying crops.

This image of a warrior God violently attacking Earth is disturbing from an ecological perspective. Today, however, it is humans, not God, that are destroying Earth. As I write, the skies in Winnipeg are sepia brown from the many forest fires burning hundreds and thousands of kilometers away. The summer of 2018 has been a summer of catastrophic forest fires in Canada and the United States, record-breaking heat waves around the world, and devastating floods. Even if humans could reduce the emissions of greenhouse gases immediately, forest fires, heat waves, and flooding will grow worse over the next 150 years because of the greenhouse gases already in the atmosphere. We cannot blame this destruction of Earth on God or nature, and it is humans who will need to act rapidly to maintain a habitable biosphere.

---

101. Hossfeld and Zenger, *Psalms 2*, 99.

Chapter 7

GOD AS ROCK AND EARTH'S JOY
(Pss. 61-64 AND 65-68)

The next two groups of Davidic psalms are a tale of two different genres and two different ecologies. The first group of psalms (Pss. 61-64) are individual laments that use Earth metaphors for God but otherwise make little mention of nonhuman animals except for one mention of jackals. The next group of psalms (Pss. 65-68) are community laments with a pastoral socioecology and many references to nonhuman animals. The contrast between these two groups is like the difference between city and country. This difference will prove significant in the movement toward the final psalm of Book Two.

Psalms 61-64 are psalms "of David" like those around them, but they do not have the designation *miktam* like those that precede them and the designation *shir*, "a song," like those that follow them. For the ancient compilers of the Psalter who added the superscriptions, something different was going on in Psalms 61-64. Their modern genre designations also distinguish them from the psalms that follow. Psalms 61-64 are individual laments, though Psalm 63 is largely a prayer of trust, a subspecies of individual lament. Whereas the psalms that preceded them were individual or community laments, those that follow them are communal thanksgivings (Pss. 65-67) and a hymn or liturgy (Ps. 68). For modern-genre critics, Psalms 61-64 are different than those that follow them.

Rock

For the ecological reader, there are a couple of Earth metaphors for God that run through the first group of psalms—Rock and Wings. Psalm 61 combines both. *Rock* is an important part of Psalm 62 and *wing* an important part of Psalm 63. I will discuss each in turn beginning with *rock*.

The psalmist prays in Ps. 61:3[2] that God will "lead me to a rock that rises above me." The Hebrew has "a rock," but some English translations have "the rock." Hossfeldt and Zenger say this is "connected with the hypothesis that the psalm is here speaking of the 'rock' on which the Jerusalem Temple (really or mythically) stands."[1] Similarly, both Tate and LeMon see an allusion to the cosmic mountain in this reference.[2] The prototypical rock of protection and salvation in the context of the Psalter's geography is the temple mount. Psalm 61 is an individual lament, and, as mentioned in Chapter 2, a rock is a natural part of the typical narrative of an individual lament. In this narrative, the psalmist is sinking in mire, up to their neck in water, and the rock is a place God puts them on, or God as Rock is the place of salvation and security. Much of that plot and imagery is not present in this psalm but, because it is typical, might be heard behind the image of rock.

The addition of a definite article to "rock," however, obscures the fact that rock is the subject of an active verb, "rises up." The same verb and form of the verb appears with humans as the subject, and, depending on the context, English translators may choose English translations that are either passive, "is exalted," or active, "rise up." The lack of an article and the active verb could, therefore, be interpreted as a representation of rock as a subject. Rocks, of course, do not move, but the understanding of the rock as an active subject may not be so far-fetched when one considers that God is a Rock in the following psalm and that there is some overlap between the two metaphorical uses of rock.

The interrelationship between the rock on which God puts the psalmist and God as Rock is evident in the presence of language in this psalm that is part of the domain of God as Rock. Following the psalmist's prayer to "lead me to a rock that rises above me" (v. 3[2]), God is addressed as "my refuge" and "tower of strength" (v. 4[3]). Thus both the rock and God as Rock are part of the metaphorical domain of refuge, protection, and security in God.

> This imagery is grounded in the land of Israel. As Hossfeld and Zenger say,
>
> He prays that God will place him upon a high rock where he will be safe from chaos. That is a metaphor that, first of all, connects with experiences found in a number of biblical narratives, in which someone pursued by enemies flees to mountain regions and is able there to conceal himself in such a way that he cannot be found. It can also contain a hint of the experience of achieving the summit of a high cliff.[3]

I would add that it could also relate to the experience of the security and protection from enemies of a walled city like Jerusalem on a rocky hill. A high rock is, therefore, especially meaningful in the socioecology of ancient Israel.

---

1. Frank-Lothar Hossfeld and Erich Zenger, *Psalms 2: A Commentary on Psalms 51–100*, trans. Linda M. Maloney, in *Hermeneia: A Critical and Historical Commentary on the Bible*, ed. Klaus Baltzer (Minneapolis, MN: Fortress, 2005), 104.

2. Marvin Tate, *Psalms 51–100* (Word Biblical Commentary, vol. 20; Dallas, TX: Word, 1990), 114; Joel M. LeMon, *Yahweh's Winged Form in the Psalms: Exploring Congruent Iconography and Texts* (Orbis Biblicus et Orientalis, 242; Fribourg: Academic), 148.

3. Hossfeld and Zenger, *Psalms 2*, 107.

The prayer in Ps. 61:3[2] for God to "lead me to a rock that rises above me" is followed by multiple confessions of faith in God, My Rock, in Psalm 62.

Surely [God] is my Rock and my salvation,
> my refuge, I will not be shaken. (v. 3[2]).
. . .
Surely [God] is my Rock and my salvation,
> my refuge, I will not be shaken.

Upon God my salvation and glory [I rely],
> my Rock of strength, my refuge [is] in God. (vv. 7-8[6-7]).

The same Hebrew word for rock (*tsur*) occurs each time. God as Rock has here all the features mentioned in Chapter 2 where it appeared in the psalm that introduces Book Two of the Psalter (Ps. 42:10[9]). It is part of a metaphorical domain of salvation and security. The many parallel terms and multiple associations indicate that it is a living metaphor. Once again Rock is associated with "salvation" and "refuge." Once again the many personal pronouns on both Rock and accompanying words indicate the psalmist has an intensely personal relationship with "my Rock." This understanding of God arises out of a particular ecosystem and expresses the sacred, intrinsic value of that ecosystem.

This divine metaphor that connects the psalmist with Earth and a specific socioecology is an important one for Book Two of the Psalter. The image of Rock as a place of salvation and security and God as Rock runs through Book Two. Psalm 42 serves as an introduction to Book Two and introduces this metaphor for God (v. 10[9]). God as Rock is centered in Psalms 61 and 62 where it appears repeatedly. It is then repeated twice toward the end of Book Two in Ps. 71:3. Human metaphors for God tend to foster an anthropocentric theology and ethics that connects the righteous person only with God and other humans. This nonhuman metaphor for God also has the potential to connect the righteous person with all Creation.

Perhaps it is appropriate in the context of laments that this seems to be a barren rock. There is an allusion to birds in the reference to God's wings that will be discussed below but, otherwise, no plants or animals are mentioned in these psalms. The imagery of these psalms reflects the alienation of an anthropocentric, urban socioecology.

Wing

Psalm 61 combines the already mentioned prayer for "a rock that rises" (v. 3[2]) with a second Earth metaphor for God. The psalmist prays to "find refuge under cover on your wings" (v. 5[4]). The reference to God's wings is unusual. It speaks of the "cover" rather than the more common "shadow" of God's wings (Pss. 17:8; 36:8[7]; 57:2[1]; 63:8[7]).[4] The unique expression emphasizes that God's wings are protective (covering). LeMon emphasizes that the metaphor is defensive rather than aggressive and that, therefore, the types of ancient Near Eastern iconography

---

4. LeMon, *Yahweh's Winged Form in the Psalms*, 148.

Figure 1. Horus Falcon Protects Pharaoh Kehfren (2600–2480 BCE). Othmar Keel, *The Symbolism of the Biblical World: Ancient Near Eastern Iconography and the Book of Psalms* (Winona Lake, IN: Eisenbrauns, 1997), 190, fig. 260, 399.

of wings that this psalm most likely alludes to are either the falcon associated with the Sun god Re or the winged sun disk.[5]

Then in Psalm 63 the psalmist sings for joy "in the shadow of your wings." But before turning to a discussion of the wings in this psalm, it is important to note that the psalm begins with the psalmist identifying with Earth.

> God, My God, I search for you, my being thirsts for you,
>   my flesh faints for you, in a dry and weary Earth without water. (v. 2[1])

There is no definite article on Earth in Hebrew.[6] The Earth is treated as a subject who is "weary." The motif of thirsting for water was introduced at the beginning of Psalm 42, which introduced Book Two of the Psalter. There I noted that the frequent reference to water issues in the Hebrew Bible reflected the ecology of ancient Israel. In Psalm 63, the psalmist identifies with Earth as a subject. Humans and Earth are interdependent in their need for water.

Psalm 63 portrays a very intimate relationship between God and the psalmist. The pronouns in the above quote speak of desire and relationship. "*My* being thirsts for *you*, *my* body yearns for *you*." This use of pronouns extends through the psalm.

---

5. Ibid., 150.

6. There is a prefixed preposition on Earth so it is the Masoretes who have pointed it without a definite article.

In addition, the repeated mention of "my being" (vv. 2[1], 6[5], 9[8], and 10[9])[7] creates a sense of intimacy. The mention of thirst is followed by a reference to the psalmist's lips: "my lips will praise you" (v. 4[3]). Thirst changes to satisfaction in v. 6[5]: "As with rich cream, my being is satisfied, with joyful lips my mouth praises you." The psalmist calls from bed at night (v. 7[6]) and is protected by the wings of God (v. 8[7]). Strikingly, the psalmist's being "clings" to God whose right hand holds the psalmist up (v. 9[8]). This sounds like a child "clinging to a parent."[8]

LeMon suggests that taking all these intimate images together, the psalm may be alluding to a nursing goddess (*dea nutrix*). This image of a goddess nursing a worshipper is common across the ancient Near East. One wonders if the tendency of (male) scholars to refer to these figures by the Latin, *dea nutrix*, reflects a discomfort with the human body in general and female bodies in particular. In any case, the portrayal of the psalmist's relationship to God in Psalm 63 has striking similarities to the nursing goddess image.

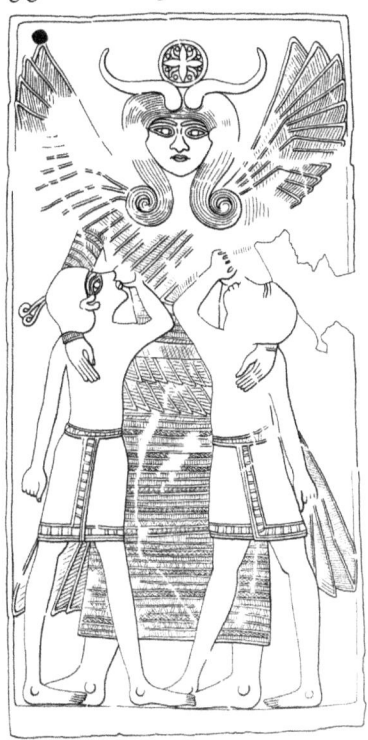

Figure 2. Late Bronze Age Ivory Relief from Ugarit. Urs Winter, *Frau und Göttin: Exegetishce und ikonographische Studien zum wieblichen Gottesbild im Alten Israel und in dessen Umwelt* (OBO 53; Fribourg: Universitätsverlag, 1983), Abb. 409.

---

7. Hossfeld and Zenger, *Psalms 2*, 123.
8. LeMon, *Yahweh's Winged Form in the Psalms*, 161.

The goddess has wings as does God in Psalm 63. The worshipper's hands are raised as are the psalmist's in Ps. 63:5[4]. The hand of the goddess holds the worshipper as in Psalm 63. The psalmist thirsts at the beginning of the psalm and is then satisfied by God in verse 6[5]:

As with rich cream, my being is satisfied,
   with joyful lips my mouth praises you.

LeMon argues that the peculiar Hebrew that I translated, "rich cream," above could refer to milk.[9] The Hebrew has two words for fat that Hossfeld and Zenger translate as "marrow and fatness."[10] Many take this as a reference to a cultic meal and translate it as "rich feast."[11] LeMon, however, notes that the verb translated as "satisfied" often refers to drinking one's fill of liquids (Isa. 66:11; Amos 4:8; Ps. 104:16) and that the first word has the same consonants as milk.[12] Thus, LeMon thinks the reference could be to milk. I have translated "rich cream" to attempt to capture the associations with both fat and milk. Psalm 63, therefore, has several features that could allude to a winged goddess and nursing mother.

The imagery of winged goddesses and gods is widespread and frequent in the ancient Near East, so that is probably the first association ancient readers would have with the reference to the wings of God. However, if an ancient reader were to associate this imagery with a bird, the pigeon/dove would be a good candidate, particularly in Israel. In the ancient Near East, the pigeon/dove is often associated with goddesses or represents goddesses, as Chapter 5 pointed out. Within the Israelite religion, the pigeon/dove was one of the common sacrificial animals in the temple. They were specified as an option for poor people and so may not have been considered as valuable as sheep, goats, or cattle. Nevertheless, people sacrifice what is valuable and meaningful to them. Although the pigeon/dove being sacrificed may not have appreciated this, their choice as a sacrificial animal indicates worshippers understood them as having intrinsic value and perhaps symbolic associations beyond that of many other birds. Pigeons/doves mate for life, take turns sitting on the nest until their young are almost fully grown, and frequently begin building a second nest while they are still raising the first brood. Pigeons/doves therefore have associations with love and parenting across cultures that are suitable to a psalm with the imagery of a nursing goddess. The pigeon/dove creates a natural connection between God as Rock and wings, because pigeons/doves nest on the rocky ledges of cliffs. Within the ancient Israelite context, therefore, the pigeon/dove might be the bird that one would associate with God's wings in Psalm 63.

9. LeMon, *Yahweh's Winged Form in the Psalms*, 160.
10. Hossfeld and Zenger, *Psalms 2*, 119.
11. Ibid., 124.
12. LeMon, *Yahweh's Winged Form in the Psalms*, 160.

Jackals

There are few references to nonhuman animals in this group of psalms, but Psalm 63 does mention one, along with a reference to Earth:

> May those who seek to ruin my life,
>   May they go into the depths of the earth
> May they be poured out by the power of the sword,
>   May they be food for jackals (Ps. 63:10-11[9-10])

For an Earth being, these lines are disturbing. Earth appears with a definite article. Earth is treated as an object and the place of judgment and death. This could too easily fit into modern, Christian ideas about heaven and hell, good and evil, spiritual and material. These ideas sometimes serve in contemporary contexts to legitimate exploitation of Earth understood as an evil object.

Second, an Earth creature is associated with death, wilderness, and God's judgment. The Hebrew word translated as "jackal" here, *shu'alim*, is a word that is used to designate any of the three species of fox in Israel and the jackal (*Canis aureus*). The jackal is genetically closer to a dog but looks like a large fox. The KJV had "foxes" here because there was no word for jackal in English at the time. The word jackal came into English later from Arabic *jakal*, which is from the same Semitic root as the Hebrew word used here.[13] Unlike foxes that tend to be solitary, jackals live in family groups and sometimes gather in larger groups "when many pairs are attracted to the same burrows, carrion, refuse dumps, or potential prey."[14] And unlike foxes, they are scavengers. Thus, the translation "jackal" suits this passage because the noun is plural, indicating a family or large group, and eating dead bodies fits jackal behavior.

Jackals live in burrows abandoned by other animals and sometimes abandoned and ruined human buildings. Thus, in the Hebrew Bible they are associated with ruins and desolation (Isa. 13:22; Jer. 49:33; 9:11). Psalm 63 has in view the other main association with jackals in the Hebrew Bible, their eating of human corpses. In this way their literal and symbolic roles on the boundary between life and death are similar to those of the dogs discussed in Chapter 6. The jackals are used in Psalm 63 to construct boundaries between life and death, civilization and wilderness, and place the enemies on the side of death and destruction.

In summary thus far, this group of psalms has a largely barren ecology. The psalmist appears to live in a socioecology that tends to objectify Earth and is largely devoid of nonhuman animals except one that represents death, wilderness, and desolation. The image of God as Rock, however, has potential to connect

---

13. George Cansdale, *All the Animals of the Bible Lands* (Grand Rapids, MI: Zondervan, 1970), 124.

14. Edward R. Hope, *All Creatures Great and Small: Living Things in the Bible* (Helps for Translators; New York: United Bible Societies, 2005), 66.

the reader with all creation. The image of the protective wings of God may be connected to an image of God as nursing mother and the pigeon/dove that nests on rocky cliffs and whose paternal care is well known. The landscape of these psalms are rather barren, but the Earth images for God have potential for human identification with Earth and Earth community.

Thanksgiving and Earth's Joy

The next group of Davidic psalms, however, are characterized by a different genre and different socioecology. The barren landscape of the laments in Psalms 61–64 shifts to a pastoral landscape, with many references to Earth's creatures, in the community thanksgivings in Psalms 65–68. The reader's transition from lament to thanksgiving is like walking out of a city and into the countryside. Psalms 61–64 were individual laments. Psalms 65–68 include three community thanksgiving psalms (Pss. 65–67) and a hymn or liturgy (Ps. 68). Psalms 65–68 are also distinguished from the psalms before and after them by being designated *shir*, "song" in their superscriptions.

Psalms 65–68 contain creation imagery that is common in the ancient Near East and in the Psalter. This is not imagery of the original creation of the world but the creation and maintenance of order. This creation imagery has a typical narrative pattern and imagery. Frank Moore Cross calls it the divine warrior pattern.[15] First, the divine warrior marches forth from the divine mountain to do battle. The approach of the divine warrior is accompanied by thunderstorms and earthquakes. Second, the divine warrior does battle with gods and nations that threaten the order of Creation. The enemies flee in fear at the rebuke of the divine warrior or are defeated. Third, the divine warrior returns in triumph, ascends the holy mountain and builds a temple. Fourth, the god's word goes forth from the temple and Earth responds with fertility and joy. For instance, in the Mesopotamian story of creation, the Enuma Elish, the god Marduk defeats Tiamat the Sea goddess and constructs the world from her body and is proclaimed king of the gods. In Canaan myth, the storm god Baal marches to battle with either Yamm (Sea) or Mot (Death) and returns triumphant to the divine mountain, and Earth responds with joy and fertility. This pattern and imagery are used repeatedly to describe Israel's God.[16]

The divine warrior pattern is clear in Psalms 65 and 68 and alluded to in Psalms 66 and 67. Psalm 65, thus, contains a type of creation imagery that is common in the ancient Near East:

---

15. Arthur Walker-Jones, *The Green Psalter: Resources for an Ecological Spirituality* (Minneapolis, MN: Fortress Press, 2009), 48; Frank Moore Cross, *Canaanite Myth and Hebrew Epic: Essays in the History of the Religion of Israel* (Cambridge, MA: Harvard University Press, 1973), 162–3.

16. Pss. 18:15-18[14-19]; 24; 46:3-7[2-6]; 65:7-14[6-13]; 68:8-19[7-18]; 74:12-17; 76; 77:16-21[15-20]; 89:6-15[5-14]; 104:2-9, 31-32; 114:3-7.

⁶Awesome in righteousness answer us, God of our salvation,
> The confidence of all extremities of Earth and far reaches of Sea,[17]

⁷who establishes Mountains by divine strength,
> who is girded with might.

⁸who stills the roar of Seas,
> the roar of the waves,
> and the murmur of peoples

⁹Those who inhabit the extremities are awed by your signs.
> You make the lands of morning and evening shout for joy.
> (vv. 6-9[5-8])

Several elements of the divine warrior myth are present in these lines. God appears as a warrior "girded with might" and "stills the roar of Seas." Seas represent chaos and instability, and the stilling of Seas creates stability and "establishes Mountains." Unfortunately, the parallel between roaring Seas and murmuring peoples in this passage is part of a typical pattern where enemy peoples are identified with chaos and have to be defeated to restore order. This myth justifies violence against foreigners. It may be significant, however, that God's stilling does not seem to involve violence or war in Psalm 65. Moreover, Earth, Sea, and Mountains appear without definite articles, and Sea even has a voice.

A definite article, however, appears on Earth in the following section where God stills Sea, stabilizes the world, and provides rain and fertility:

¹⁰You visit the Earth and water it, you greatly enrich it,
> with a divine canal full of water.
> You establish their grain[18] for so you have established it.

¹¹Watering its furrows, saturating its ridges,
> With abundant showers you soften it, you bless its sprouts.

¹²You crown the year with your good things,
> and your encampments overflow with rich food.

¹³The abodes of the wilderness overflow.
> Hills gird themselves with joy.

¹⁴Pastures clothe themselves with the flock,
> And Valleys robe themselves with grain,
> they shout for joy and sing.

The repetition of the same word in v. 10[9]—"establish ... established"—may seem to be poor English, but the Hebrew repeats the same verb. A participial form of the same Hebrew verb is used in v. 7[6] for God who "establishes" Mountains. I have

---

17. Some ancient versions have "peoples" or "coasts of sea," and BHS suggests reading "far coasts." The MT is to be preferred as more difficult. It is also retained as it may portray Sea as a subject.

18. Symmachus's translation has the Greek for "her grain."

translated using the same English word in all three places to show that the Hebrew Bible understands maintaining the stability of Earth and the provision of fertility as interrelated aspects of God's creative work.

Significant for an Earth being is that parts of Earth are treated as subjects that provide fertility and shout and sing for joy. Hills, Pastures, and Valleys, but no members of Earth community, are treated as subjects responding to God with fertility and joy. Earth's shouting and singing for joy ends Psalm 65 and a call for Earth to praise God begins the next psalm, Psalm 66:

> [1] Cheer for God all the Earth.
> [2] Make music to [God's] glorious name.
>> Make [God's] praise glorious.
> [3] Say to God, "How awesome are your deeds
>> Because of your great strength, your enemies cower before you.
> [4] All the Earth bows before you,
>> They make music for you,
>>> They make music for your name.
> [5] Come and see God's works,
>> Awesome deeds on behalf of children of humanity.
> [6] [God] turned Sea to dry land,
>> Through the river they passed on foot,
>> There they rejoiced in [God].

The last verse refers to the Exodus. Unfortunately the references to Earth in the previous verses have definite articles, so they come from a context in which Earth is viewed as an object. Sea, however, does not have an article and so is treated as a subject. This mention of Sea as a subject is one of the allusions to the defeat of Sea in the typical divine warrior pattern. Other allusions to the typical pattern are the mention of God's "strength," the cowering of God's enemies, and the call for Earth to cheer for God followed by all Earth bowing and making music to God. Thus, the divine warrior pattern frames the Exodus as an act of God. This portrayal of the Exodus in the divine warrior pattern is not limited to Psalm 65. It is found elsewhere in the Hebrew Bible, for instance, in the ancient poetry of Exodus 15. Since the divine warrior myth has to do with creation, the Exodus is understood as an ongoing act of creation by God.

Several Earth creatures are mentioned in Psalm 66, though unfortunately they are present as sacrifices. The psalm also provides a glimpse of temple rituals and their relation to lament, thanksgiving, and sacrifice:

> [13] I will enter your house with burnt offerings.
>> I will repay my vows
> [14] that my lips pronounced,
>> my mouth spoke when I was in distress.
> [15] Burnt offerings of fatlings I will offer up to you, with smoke of rams
>> I will make an offering of cattle and male goats.

Sacrifice is abhorrent to many modern readers, and for that reason it was discussed at length in Chapter 4. Briefly, the ritual is part of maintaining an ecological niche that would require the death of some animals to keep populations within the carrying capacity of the land. Kosher regulations may have been humane in their day, and ancient Israelites may have understood themselves not as killing the sacrificial animal but as transferring their life to God. The care taken with blood in sacrificial rituals and the statements that Israelites are not to eat the blood because "their blood is their life"[19] (Lev. 17:14) may indicate such an understanding. This may have functioned to assuage the guilt of the person who sacrifices but may also express a recognition of their dependence on cattle, sheep, and goats, and indebtedness for their sacrifice. In contrast to the two previous psalms that mention no animals except jackals, these at least indicate an awareness of humans as part of a niche constructed with nonhuman animals.

Psalm 67 does not have any elements of the divine warrior pattern except for two verses on Earth's fertility:

⁶Earth has given her produce,
    God, Our God, has blessed us.
⁷May God bless us, that all the ends of Earth may revere [God].

Earth is mentioned twice with a definite article earlier in Ps. 67:3[2], 5[4]. Earth as a subject is the source of produce, and the ends of Earth respond with reverence for God.

The following psalm makes extensive use of the divine warrior pattern. Psalm 68 is a hymn or liturgy widely recognized as one of the oldest pieces of poetry in the Hebrew Bible. Because it is ancient Hebrew poetry, the text is at times difficult, and others have extensively discussed the text. Those discussions need not be repeated here. For the present purposes it is enough to present selected verses that illustrate the narrative pattern and associated images. Psalm 68 contains all the elements of the divine warrior pattern outlined above. First, the divine warrior marches forth from the divine mountain accompanied by the phenomena of storms and earthquakes to battle enemies:

²May God arise, may God's enemies scatter,
    and those who hate him flee before him.
                    . . .
⁵Sing to God, make music to the divine name,
    Praise the one who rides on the clouds,
        for the LORD is the divine name, exult before God.

---

19. The Hebrew has the pronoun "his," but English translations treat the sacrificial animal as an object by translating the pronoun as "its." I have translated the pronoun as "their" to treat the sacrificial victim as a subject and adopted the growing trend of using "their" as a non-gendered singular pronoun.

> [6] Parent of orphans, and champion of widows
>> is God in God's holy habitation.
>
> . . .
>
> [8] God, when you went out before your people,
>> when you marched through the desert. Selah.
> [9] Earth quaked, even Skies showered before God, the one of Sinai,
>> Before God, the God of Israel.
> [10] Rain freely you cause to fall, God,
>> Your inheritance was weary,[20] you established it.

The narrative begins with a call for the divine warrior to arise and battle enemies (v. 2[3]). The phrase translated "one who rides on the clouds" (v. 5[4]) is a designation of the Canaanite storm god Baal here applied to Israel's God. God is portrayed according to the ideology of just kings in the ancient Near East as "parent of orphans, and champion of widows" (v. 6[5]). The mention of "God's holy habitation" makes clear that the narrative begins on the divine mountain. The march of the divine warrior is accompanied by rain and the quaking of Earth (vv. 8-10[7-9]). Earth and Skies have no definite articles and are subjects of active verbs. This commentary has been tracing where Earth and other parts of Earth community are addressed without a definite article as subjects. The absence of definite articles here in ancient Hebrew poetry may indicate that the divine warrior myth is one of the traditional locations of an understanding of Earth as subject.

The second part of the pattern is the battle, or rebuke and fleeing of the enemies:

> [13] Kings of armies flee, they flee,
>> And those at home divide spoil
>
> . . .
>
> [15] When Shaddai scattered kings there,
>> snow fell on Zalmon.

There may be retrospective references to the battle later in the psalm when God smashes the head of enemies (v. 22[21]) and Sea is mentioned (v. 23[22]), their feet splattering blood (v. 24[23]), and God rebuking the animals of the reeds (v. 31[30]).

Third, the divine warrior returns victorious to the holy mountain:

> [19] You went up to the heights, having taken captives.
>> You received tribute from humanity,
>> Even those who resist the dwelling there of the LORD God.
>
> . . .
>
> [22] Surely God shatters the head of [God's] enemies,
>> The hairy crown of those who walk in their guilt.
> [23] The Lord said, "From Bashan, I will bring back,

---

20. Reading a *yod* instead of a *vav*. The two letters are easily confused.

>   I will bring back from the depths of Sea.
> ²⁴So that your feet splash²¹ blood,
>   the tongue of your dogs have their portion from [your] enemies.
> ²⁵They see your processions, God,
>   the processions of my God, my King, into the holy place,
> ²⁶In front singers, afterward musicians,
>   amid young women playing tambourines
>
>   . . .
>
> ³⁰From your temple above Jerusalem,
>   to you kings bring tribute.
> ³¹Rebuke the animal of the reeds,
>   the assembly of bulls, with the calves of the people,
>   Scatter those who degrade themselves²² for pieces of silver,
>   who delight in war.

The literal and symbolic role the dogs are playing here seems to be similar to their eating corpses after battles mentioned elsewhere in the Hebrew Bible and discussed in Chapter 6. Given the generally negative attitude toward dogs in the Hebrew Bible discussed at length in Chapter 6, it is interesting that this passage indicates the Israelites have a relationship with these dogs. They are "your dogs."

The fourth and final part of the pattern is not well developed in Psalm 68, but God's voice does issue from the temple:

> ³³Kingdoms of the Earth sing to God.
>   Make music to my Lord. Selah.
> ³⁴To the rider of the skies, the ancient skies.
>   Listen, [God] issues the divine voice, [God's] mighty voice.

After the Second World War, biblical scholars in the United States who were part of the biblical theology movement argued that Israel's God acted in history. Israel's historical religion was contrasted with the nature religions of the Canaanites. Creation was treated as secondary to the religion of Israel. The Exodus was touted as the paradigmatic act of God in history. The presence in the Hebrew Bible of the imagery of Baal as a storm god defeating Sea and Death to establish fertility tended to be regarded either as outdated remnants or imagery transformed by Israel's historical religion. Yet Terence Fretheim argued that the

---

21. The Hebrew word here means "strike." Some emend the text to read "bathe," but I have chosen not to emend and, instead, understand "splatter" as what happens when one "strikes" liquid with one's foot.

22. The Hebrew participle here has the sense of "humble oneself" and I am interpreting that in a negative sense as "degrade oneself" by going to war for money. I have taken the verb "scatter" that appears in Hebrew at the beginning of the second clause as governing both clauses and, therefore placed the English translation at the beginning of the two clauses.

story of the plagues that lead up to the Exodus are examples of God acting, not in history but as Creator.[23] There is now a growing recognition among Hebrew Bible scholars of the importance of God acting as Creator in and through nature.[24] From an Earth being's perspective, it is not accidental that a biblical theology focused on human history separated from and antagonistic to nature arose in a rising imperial nation at the beginning of an exponential growth of the agro-industrial complex's exploitation of Earth. Exploring God as Creator in the Hebrew Bible may be significant for overcoming the history/nature binary and for ecotheology in an age of ecological collapse.

---

23. Terence Fretheim, "The Plagues as Ecological Signs of Historical Disaster" *JBL* 110 (1991): 385–96.

24. Terence Fretheim, *God and World in the Old Testament: A Relational Theology of Creation* (Nashville, TN: Abingdon, 2005; William P. Brown, *The Seven Pillars of Creation: The Bible, Science, and the Ecology of Wonder* (Oxford: Oxford University Press, 2010); William P. Brown, *The Ethos of the Cosmos: The Genesis of Moral Imagination in the Bible* (Grand Rapids, MI: Eerdmans, 1999); J. Richard Middleton, *The Liberating Image: The Imago Dei in Genesis 1* (Grand Rapids, MI: Brazos, 2005).

Chapter 8

EMPIRE'S GREENWASH (Pss. 69-72)

Psalms 69-72 form the conclusion to Book Two of the Psalter. They are set apart from the psalms that precede them by their genres and their superscriptions. Psalms 69-72 consist of three individual laments (Pss. 69-71) and a royal prayer or blessing (Ps. 72). This contrasts with the community thanksgivings of the previous groups and creates a conclusion to Book Two that returns to lament and recapitulates earlier themes and motifs. The psalms in this group do not have the designation *shir*, "a song," that the group of psalms preceding them did. Psalms 61 and 70 are "of David." Psalm 71 does not have a superscription. Gerald Wilson has shown that psalms without superscriptions tend to appear at seams between books in the Psalter, as is the case with Psalm 71.[1] The compilers of the book of Psalms have given Psalm 72 a special position and status. They have identified it as one of only two psalms "of Solomon," appended the note "The prayers of David, son of Jesse, are complete" (v. 20), and made it the final, concluding psalm of the second book of the Psalter. At one time, it was probably the conclusion of an earlier collection of psalms. This chapter notes the Earth themes that are recapitulated in the individual laments and then gives more sustained attention to Psalm 72 because of the importance the editors of the Psalter have given it. The discussion shows that Psalm 72 tries to co-opt Earth to support the monarchy in what nowadays we might call a greenwash of empire.

Psalm 69

Psalm 69 begins the conclusion to Book Two by reiterating several topics from earlier in the collection. The portrayal of God as a divine warrior battling the forces of chaos appeared several times in Book Two (Pss. 46; 48; 60:4[2]; 65:7-10[6-9]; 66:1-6; 68) and reappears in Psalm 69:

Save me, God,
    for Waters have come up to my neck.

---

1. Gerald Henry Wilson, *The Editing of the Hebrew Psalter* (SBL Dissertation Series; Chico, CA: Scholars Press, 1985), 131.

> I sink in the muddy depths
>> without any foothold
> I have come into deep Waters
>> and a river flows over me. (v. 2[1])

I have capitalized Waters in the translation to indicate that Waters is without a definite article and the subject of a verb so may be being understood as an active agent. Later in the psalm this imagery appears again, and the reference to the mouth of Pit seems to allude to a particular version of the divine warrior pattern, Baal's battle against Death (Mot) in Canaanite myth. Death's city is in a swamp, and, in the myth, Baal descends into Death's mouth.[2] Psalm 69 tells a similar story:

> Rescue me from mud, let me not sink,
>> Let me be rescued from those who hate me and from deep Waters.
> Do not let rivers of water flow over me, Depths swallow me.
>> Do not let Pit close its mouth over me. (vv. 15[14]-16[15])

Here again Pit and Depths do not have definite articles and seem to be active subjects attempting to swallow the psalmist. While this language is a metaphor for enemies attacking the psalmist, the problem that has been mentioned before is that metaphors are interactive so that parts of Earth come to be viewed as enemies. In other words, the metaphor assumes a world where parts of Earth can be enemies. This is dangerous in contemporary contexts where there is a common narrative pattern that speaks of humans at war with Earth and conquering Earth. The contemporary narrative pattern legitimates exploitation of Earth and Earth community.

Several psalms in Book Two express the perspective that thanksgiving is more important than sacrifice (Pss. 50:8-15; 51:18-19[16-17]; 66:13-15), and Psalm 69 reiterates it:

> I will praise the name of God with a song,
>> I will exalt [God] with thanksgiving.
> That will please [God] more than oxen,
>> than a young bull with horns and cloven hooves. (vv. 31-32[30-31])

In its ancient context, this probably was not a rejection of sacrifice. Rather it was an understanding that sacrifice should be done in the context of a relationship with God characterized by thanksgiving. While moderns tend to find animal sacrifice abhorrent, Chapter 4 argued that it is less exploitative than factory farming and modern slaughterhouses and may have been part of a relationship of trust with these animals and recognition of human dependence on them. At a minimum,

---

2. Michael D. Coogan, *Stories from Ancient Canaan* (Lousiville, KY: Westminster, 1978), 106–7.

these lines reflect the socioecology of ancient Israel. Oxen provided labor to plow and harvest more land, and sustain more humans in the land. Oxen and humans coevolved and constructed the ecological niche of ancient Israel.

Finally, Psalm 69 hits a note that sounded weakly earlier in Book Two (Pss. 65:14[13]; 66:1-4) but will expand and grow louder toward the end of the Psalter:

> Skies and Earth will praise [God],
>> Seas and all that moves in them. (v. 35[34])

Heaven, Earth, and Seas are all without definite articles, all subjects actively praising God. More voices will join this chorus as the reader moves through the Psalter, coming to a crescendo that takes up all of Psalm 148. I have suggested before that all Creation's praise of God could serve as a theological metaphor for overcoming alienation and integrating the righteous person into Earth community. Those who care for Creation maintain God's choir and learn to sing in unison with it.

Psalm 71

Several Hebrew manuscripts read Psalms 70 and 71 together, because Psalm 71 has no superscription.[3] Psalm 70 is a fairly brief and urgent call for help with no references to Earth or Earth community. Psalm 71 is a longer and less urgent plea for help. It includes the imagery of God as Rock:

> Be my Rock of dwelling[4] that I may always enter,[5]
>> Command my salvation, for you are my Cliff and my Stronghold. (v. 3)

Psalm 71 thus recapitulates the image of God as Rock found earlier in Book Two (Pss. 42:9[10]; 61:3[2]; 62:3[2]). As with other occurrences it appears with a cluster of words that reinforce the metaphorical domain—Cliff and Stronghold. The language of "dwelling that I may always enter" stands out as unique. It gives the sense of God as a home that is always there and may be particularly appropriate for a psalm that in the movement of the Psalter comes near the end of David's life. This is an image of God as a part of Earth and the psalmist dwelling in both. The psalmist dwells in the divine Rock that is in Earth.

At the same time, the psalm reflects alienation from Earth. The psalm has one reference to Earth as an object: "From the depths of the Earth raise me up"

---

3. Wilson, *The Editing of the Hebrew Psalter*, 131.

4. Many Hebrew manuscripts have *ma'oz*, "refuge" (cf. 31:3[2]), but *ma'on*, "dwelling," is slightly more difficult and, therefore, more likely original.

5. The Septuagint has "as a stronghold" with Ps. 31:3[2], but the Hebrew is more likely original on the principle that it is the more difficult reading and more reliable source.

(v. 20). This is an allusion to the divine warrior pattern, but Earth is not a subject. These psalms have no other explicit references to Earth or Earth community. As with earlier psalms in this collection, they construct a rather anthropocentric and barren, urban socioecology.

Psalm 72

In contrast to the barren, rocky landscape of Psalms 70 and 71, Psalm 72 has a pastoral landscape and treats Earth and parts of Earth as subjects. The editors of the Psalter, by placing Psalm 72 as the final psalm of David as king, indicate David has begun to understand Asaph's message in Psalm 50 about human relationship with Earth community.

Commentators have had difficulty discerning the structure of Psalm 72, but a complex and sophisticated structure is present. Commentators have pointed to the lack of repetitions and other typical indications of structure, and, indeed, there are no simple repetitions like refrains and inclusios, or other indicators like the word selah, or changes of voice, to indicate strophes. There are, however, more subtle repetitions and grammatical indicators of structure. James Kugel has characterized the idea of Hebrew poetic parallelism as two lines, where the second line typically repeats and advances the first line.[6] This same kind of parallelism exists not only between lines of the poetry in Psalm 72 but also defines larger sections.[7] As with the parallelism of lines, parallelism between verses and strophes both repeat and advance, often with new language. These repetitions both delineate and separate sections of Psalm 72.

The sections of Psalm 72 can be outlined as follows:

1) Ecojustice (vv. 1-7)
    a. Justice and righteousness (v. 1)
        b. Judge ... poor with justice (v. 2)
            c. Mountains bear peace (v. 3)
                d. Justice for the poor (v. 4)
            c'. Sun and Moon (v. 5)
        b'. Rain and Showers (v. 6)
    a'. Righteousness and Peace till Moon is no more (v. 7)

2) Empire (vv. 8-11)
    a) Rule (v. 8)
    b) Beasts and Enemies (v. 9)
    c) Tribute and service (vv. 10-11)

---

6. James L. Kugel, *The Idea of Biblical Poetry: Parallelism and Its History* (New Haven: Yale University Press, 1981), 1–58.

7. I am indebted for this concept to Brian Doyle who notices this parallelism between strophes in Psalm 59.

3) Empire's Justice (vv. 12-14)
    "For" ... Needy (3x)

4) Empire's Ecology (vv. 15-17)
    d) "Therefore" ... life, gold and prayers (v. 15)
    e) Plenty of grain and people (v. 16)
    f) Name endure, nations blessed (v. 17)

Some would divide the first section in two: vv. 1-4 and 5-7, and there is some advance in thought between the two sections, but there are no grammatical indicators or major shifts in content, and the entire section (vv. 1-7) is tied together by frequent references to justice. The connection between the ruler and justice is emphasized by repetitive, legal language in the first strophe. The above outline laid this section out in chiastic form to highlight the repetitions, and I will use a bold font for **justice** and underlining for <u>righteousness</u> to highlight their repetition in my translation.

> God, give your **justice** to a ruler,
>> And your <u>righteousness</u> to a ruler's heir.
> May they judge your people with <u>righteousness</u>,
>> And your poor with **justice**.
> May Mountains bear PEACE for the people,
>> And Hills <u>righteousness</u>.
> May the ruler[8] provide **justice** for poor people,[9]
>> Save needy children,
>> And crush one who does wrong.
> May they revere[10] you with Sun
>> And before Moon, many generations.
> May the ruler fall like rain on a mown field,
>> Like abundant showers drop[11] [to] Earth.
> May <u>righteousness</u> blossom in the ruler's days,
>> And abundant PEACE, till Moon is no more. (vv. 1-7)

Justice and <u>righteousness</u> appear in the first line and are repeated in the second line in reverse order. <u>Righteousness</u> appears again in v. 3 and **justice** in v. 4. I have

---

8. The Hebrew has the third masculine singular verb, "he," but I have translated here and elsewhere with "the ruler" or the "the monarch" to be more inclusive.

9. Hebrew "poor of people." While "poor people" may not exactly capture the Hebrew, I wanted to avoid adding definite articles here and in the next two lines of the translation, which are not in the Hebrew.

10. NRSV has "may he live," following the Septuagint rather than the MT.

11. The Hebrew is difficult with a plural noun, two singular nouns, and no verb. BHS suggests emending the first singular noun to a plural verb.

used capitals for PEACE to note that in the midst of the repetitions of justice and righteousness, the central location and solitary use of peace may highlight its centrality. It reappears in the concluding verse. Although the focus of these verses, and the psalm, is justice, the central and concluding appearances of the Hebrew *shalom*, "peace," indicate that is the overarching and central state of being that justice makes possible.

Justice reappears in v. 4 and the ruler's provision of justice for the poor introduced in v. 2 is elaborated. Verse 4 is central to the chiastic structure and its content; the ruler's provision of justice for the poor is central to the section. Verse 4 is surrounded by Mountains and Hills on one side (v. 3) and Sun and Moon on the other (v. 5). The provision of justice to the poor is central and extends to all creation. Verse 6 may be a metaphor for the ruler's justice, or the metaphor of ruler as rain showers may hint at the fertility that results from justice and righteousness and will be elaborated later in the psalm. Verse 7 forms a conclusion that includes words from each part of this section: righteousness from vv. 1, 2, and 3; peace from v. 3; and Moon from v. 5. Thus, repeated words tie the section together and highlight both the centrality of justice for the poor and the extension of justice, righteousness, and peace to all Creation.

Along with repetitions there are also advances in thought between the lines. The first time "righteousness" is used is as a masculine noun, the second time feminine. The first time "justice" is used it is as a singular, the second as a plural. These may come with new nuances of meaning. The first verse has to do with God's gift of justice and the second with the ruler's actions. The gift of God's justice (singular) thus becomes effective in the ruler's legal judgments (plural). Verse 4 continues the theme of justice, forming an inclusio with justice in the first verse, but the language becomes much more specific and graphic. The children of the poor people and the oppressor are introduced. The language moves from rather abstract legal language to the strong and graphic language of crushing the one who does wrong. The contrast between the poor and their children (plurals) and the one who does wrong (singular) may hint at the harm that can be done to many in a community by one person, or a small group of people, who do wrong. The language of this verse anticipates the similar, emotive language of vv. 12-14. The repetitions and their development, therefore, introduce the themes of governance and justice.

The *vav*, "and," at the beginning of v. 8 marks the beginning of a new section and the second section of the psalm.

> And may the sovereign rule[12] from sea to sea,
>   And from River to the ends of Earth.
> Before the ruler may desert animals[13] bow down,
>   And royal enemies lick dust.

12. Apocopated, jussive form.
13. Most translations assume the text *tsiyyim* could not be referring to wild animals and is therefore a corruption of *tsarim* "foes." Wild animals bowing down to kings is well attested in ANE iconography.

> Rulers of Tarshish and islands, tribute may they offer.
>> Rulers of Sheba and Seba, a gift may they bring.
> And may all monarchs worship the ruler,
>> all peoples serve the ruler. (vv. 8-11)

In addition to the "and," *vav*,[14] the beginning of a new section is indicated by language, content, and style. The language of justice that was so prevalent in vv. 1-7 disappears and the concern for justice does not reappear until the following section (vv. 12-14). This corresponds to a shift in content from just rule in vv. 1-7 to rule of an empire covering a large area (v. 8) with subject kings and their peoples paying tribute (v. 10) and worshipping and serving the ruler (v. 11). The style also becomes more expansive, with themes being elaborated at greater length.

The place names represent the margins of empire. "Tarshish is usually located in Spain."[15] Sheba is usually taken to be an area in the south of the Arabian peninsula known for its wealth (Isa. 60:6; Jer. 6:20; Ezek. 27:22-25), and Seba is probably either in southern Arabia or North Africa.[16] Tarshish, Sheba, and Seba all appear to represent remote lands and thus the "ends of Earth." Islands were evidently understood as on the margins of empire as they are in the contemporary world. The islands of Oceania where I taught for six years often appear on the margins of world maps created by France, Britain, and the United States.

"For," which translates Hebrew *ki* and begins v. 12, is a much stronger marker of a new section and the content returns to justice for the poor.

> [12]For the ruler delivers a needy person who cries for help,
>> And an oppressed person who has no helper.
> [13]The ruler has compassion on the weak and needy,
>> And saves the lives of needy people.
> [14]From violent oppression[17] the ruler redeems their life,
>> And their blood is precious in the ruler's eyes. (vv. 12-14)

---

14. "And," which translates a *vav*, may seem a rather subtle way to mark a major transition at v. 8, since *vav* at the beginning of verses is common in Hebrew. But a *vav* is unnecessary at the beginning of a verse in Hebrew poetry and rare in Psalm 72. Although there are a number in Psalm 72 joining the second or third poetical line to the first, this is one of only three in Psalm 72 that begin a verse (vv. 8, 11, and 15). The *vav* on the beginning of v. 15 also signals the beginning of a new section. The *vav* on v. 11 is an exception to this pattern because it is the final verse of a section, but the content of vv. 10 and 11 is closely related, so the *vav* may indicate that v. 11 is a continuation of v. 10. The *vav* on the beginning of v. 8, however, is just one indication of the beginning of a new section.

15. J. Clinton McCann, "The Book of Psalms: Introduction, Commentary, and Reflections," in *NIB*, vol. IV, ed. Leander E. Keck et al. (Nashville, TN: Abingdon, 1996), 964.

16. BDB, *HALOT*.

17. The Hebrew "oppression and violence" is probably hendiadys, thus the translation "violent oppression."

The use of "redeem" portrays the ruler as a family member rescuing another family member from slavery. The "needy" and "oppressed" were introduced in v. 4 and they reappear here in v. 12. Aristotle spoke of rhetoric in terms of logos, "reason," pathos, "emotion," and ethos, the "knowledge, authority, and ethical character" of the speaker. This section intensifies both the logic and the emotion of the discourse. The logic is signaled first by the word *ki*, "for." While the first section began to use strong, emotive language with "crushes those who do wrong," this section speaks of "one who cries for help," "one who has no helper," who suffers "violent oppression," and whose "blood is precious" (v. 14). This is vivid and emotional language. Although this section repeats language from vv. 1-4, it seems designed to make a stronger rhetorical appeal both to reason and emotion.

Another *vav*, "therefore," begins v. 15 and another section that returns to empire's wealth, fertility, and good reputation.

> Therefore, let the ruler live and receive gold of Sheba.
>> Let prayers be said continually on his behalf,
>> All day may blessing be invoked for the ruler.
> May there be plenty of grain on the Earth, to the top of hills may it wave,
>> may his produce be like the forests of Lebanon
>> And may they sprout from a city like green plants of the Earth.
> May the ruler's name endure and spread under the sun,
>> And may all nations bless themselves and be happy in the ruler.
> (vv. 15-17)

The language of justice disappears, and new language of blessing and happiness appears. Earth's produce is designated "his" produce. The disappearance of justice language might be merely the result of a change in topic, but the emphasis on gold and the ruler's ownership of Earth's bounty may unintentionally reveal the real concern of empire.

The following two sections are widely considered to have been added by the compilers of the Psalter and can be considered separately from the literary structure and rhetoric of vv. 1-17. They do, however, pick up language from the earlier part of the psalms and set it in a theological context. Empire becomes one of God's wonders and how God's name and glory "fill the whole Earth."

Empire

Traditional interpretations have long recognized the connection of Psalm 72 to kingship. As has already been mentioned, the psalm begins with the superscription "of Solomon" and ends with the note. "The prayers of David, son of Jesse, are completed." These are evidence of very early interpretation of the psalm, and interpreters through the centuries have followed this lead and interpreted the psalm as David's prayer for Solomon. Modern historical-critical scholarship showed that the superscription "of David" in most cases did not indicate the historical David had written them. Recently, canonical criticism has emphasized the importance of the superscriptions as clues to theological interpretation. They are evidence of what David came to mean to Judaism as a literary and theological figure. At the risk of stating the obvious, the monarchy is also a major concern of the psalm itself. The first verse, for instance, introduces the psalm as a prayer for the monarchy.

> God, give your justice to a ruler,
> And your righteousness to a ruler's heir.

Because of the royal content, form critical scholars generally designate this as a "royal psalm" and think the psalm shows indications of having been used in the installation ceremonies of kings in Jerusalem. Thus, traditional exegesis, form criticism, and canonical criticism all recognize the close connection of this psalm to the monarchy.

Only recently, however, have scholars begun to examine the ways in which Psalm 72 shows evidence of imperial ideology. David Jobling and Walter Houston examine the royal ideology of Psalm 72.[18] Both articles are helpful models of Marxist analysis of Psalm 72. Jobling's is a particularly detailed and sophisticated analysis using Jameson's method. Jobling looks at contradictions, or failures to close the semantic world, and make sense of the text, as reflections of contradictions in the modes of production that produced the text. His study is admirable for commenting on the importance of "natural wealth" in the psalm.[19] For Jobling the main contradiction in Psalm 72 is between the portrayal of the royal system in the first part of the psalm, vv. 1-7, and the remainder of the psalm. In the first seven verses the king's justice and rule are unconditional. God provides the king with justice, the king rules justly, while the people pray for God to give the king justice. It is in his words a "perpetual motion machine."[20] The second half of the psalm, however, prays that the king's rule will reach to the ends of Earth, "because he delivers the needy" (v. 12). The ruler's reign becomes conditional on caring for the poor and maintaining justice. If a ruler does not care for the poor, their rule and its divine sanction could be called into question. The ruler's justice "has been withdrawn from the perpetual motion machine, to become the machine's motor. From being part of a permanent, inevitable system, it has become a condition for the working of the rest of the system."[21] Jobling identifies this same contradiction

---

18. David Jobling, "Deconstruction and the Political Analysis of Biblical Texts: A Jamesonian Reading of Psalm 72," *Semeia* 59 (1992): 95–127; Walter Houston, "The King's Preferential Option for the Poor: Rhetoric, Ideology and Ethics in Psalm 72," *Biblical Interpretation* 7 (1999): 341–67.

19. Jobling, "Deconstruction and the Political Analysis of Biblical Texts," 100–15.

20. Ibid., 101–3.

21. Ibid., 103.

in the ideology of royal psalms and suggests it correlates to tensions between coexisting modes of production in Ancient Israel.

Houston identifies the main contradiction in Psalm 72 as the moral contradiction between the repeated prayers for the ruler to provide justice and righteousness for the poor and needy of God's people and the collection of tribute from faraway places, because tribute is by its nature oppressive.[22] The ruler's justice and care for the poor and needy is woven through the rhetoric of Psalm 72 with recurring vocabulary. Verse 1 begins as follows:

> God, give your justice to a ruler,
> And your righteousness to a ruler's heir.

Verses 2 and 4 then pray for the ruler to rule with justice and righteousness, and care for the poor and needy. Verse 7 prays righteousness and peace will flourish during their reign. The first half of v. 12, "for he delivers the needy," has already been mentioned. The second half of the verse continues with "the oppressed," and v. 13 mentions "the weak" once and "the needy" twice. Houston points out that, in addition to repetition, the logical and emotional rhetoric increases in vv. 12-14 with the use of *ki*, "because," and the emotional force with the mention of the poor and needy "who cries for help" and "has no helper" (v. 12). The ruler has "compassion" (v. 13) and the use of "redeems" has the ruler acting as a close family member (v. 14). The emotive language climaxes in v. 14 with the statement that "their blood is precious in his eyes." As a person who is constantly bombarded with advertising, even oil companies claiming to be green, all this repetition and appeals to reason and emotion makes me suspicious.

Houston notes that the section that comes between theses sections with their emphasis on the ruler's justice, creates a moral contradiction because it says:

> Rulers of Tarshish and islands, tribute may they offer.
> Rulers of Sheba and Seba, a gift may they bring. (v. 10)

Tribute can be collected from foreign rulers, but they tend to transfer the burden of taxation down the social hierarchy until it reaches those who cannot transfer it any further, the poor and needy at the bottom of the social system. Houston does not mention that in such a scenario the poor may feel forced to transfer the burden further by exploiting Earth and Earth's creatures. The "people" whom the king provides justice for do not include the people of foreign lands or Earth's creatures.

Beyond the contradictions Jobling and Houston identify, Psalm 72 contains a glaring, ecological contradiction. It can be characterized by the contrast between v. 3 and v. 16. Verse 3 says,

---

22. Houston, "The King's Preferential Option for the Poor," 350.

> May Mountains bear peace for the people,
>   And Hills righteousness.

Most English translations add definite articles to mountains and hills. They also add definite articles to the sun, the moon (vv. 5, 7), and the river (v. 8). There are no definite articles in Hebrew. Much has been made in biblical studies of Sun and Moon being called "the greater light" and "the lesser light," respectively, in Genesis. The fact that the priestly writer does not want to treat them as gods, however, does not mean the writer does not think they are alive. They are still agents in Genesis. God creates them to rule the day and to rule the night (Gen. 1:16). David Abram argues in *The Spell of the Sensuous* that many oral cultures perceive all parts of Earth, even so-called inanimate parts of the world, as alive and in dialogue with them. He points to the phenomenologist Merleau-Ponty who argued that even contemporary people continue to perceive the world as alive and in dialogue with them.[23] It seems possible to me, then, that in Genesis and Psalm 72 this type of worldview is retained, because names of parts of creation do not have definite articles and Mountains and Hills are clearly the subjects of an active verb. Mountains and Hills are treated as alive and supporting justice and shalom.

The ecology of v. 3 is contradicted by the ecology of v. 16 near the end of the Psalm:

> May there be plenty of grain on the Earth, to the top of hills may it wave,
>   and his produce be like the forests of Lebanon,
>   and may they sprout from a city like green plants of the Earth.[24]

The Hebrew of the verse is difficult to decipher, but commentators are clear that it is a prayer for fertility, and the words "his produce" are not in dispute. Hills are no longer the subject of a verb and the produce they support now belongs to the king. It is royal produce. The ruler, not Hills, is the source of fertility. Earth has definite articles. This translation usurps the role of Earth community, including small farmers and animals, in the flourishing of the land. The grain is produced by, and rightly belongs, to a flourishing Earth community, not to a human ruler. Empire attempts to control and take credit for Earth community's produce. The rhetoric of the psalm has been moving the reader towards this imperial view of the world in which the monarch takes credit for fertility and gains ownership of Earth's produce.

Another way the rhetoric does this is by likening the ruler to a god. Jobling notes that after the address to God in v. 1, "O God," God is largely absent. Houston

---

23. David Abram, *The Spell of the Sensuous: Perception and Language in More-Than-Human World* (New York: Random House, 1996).

24. André Caquot has a detailed discussion of the history of interpretation and interprets the king as the subject of the verbs ("Psaume LXXII 16," *Vetus Testamentum* 38 (1998): 214–20).

objects that God is still present because the psalm is a prayer to God.[25] But Jobling's observation still has some validity, because the focus of the prayer does shift away from God toward the monarch.

As the focus shifts away from God, the ruler takes on divine characteristics. Verse 5 says,

> May they revere you with Sun,
>   and before Moon, many generations.

My literal translation of v. 5 differs from many English translations. The "you" in the Hebrew is problematic, because there has been no second person, direct address to God since vv. 1-2 and the surrounding verses (4 and 6) refer to the works of the king in the third person. Most translators and commentators, therefore, assume that a metathesis of *'aleph* and *resh* has created the Hebrew (MT), and the Septuagint reflects an original with the verb *'rk*, "may he lengthen," rather than *yr'kh*, "may they revere you" (with the *kalph* being the suffix "you"). Sun is a symbol of longevity elsewhere and the moon symbolizes a long reign two verses later, so many translate "May the ruler live while the sun endures, and as long as the moon, throughout all generations" (NRSV). The grammar of the revised text is difficult. "With" becomes "as long as." But the Hebrew (MT) is *lectio difficilior* and it is possible that "you" refers either to God or, if the psalm was used in the court, addressed to the king. Either might cause theological problems for scribes. If "you" refers to God, it seems a diminution of God to be compared to Sun and Moon. If "you" refers to the ruler, then this attributes a semidivine status to the ruler. This might explain why the Septuagint chose differently or used a Hebrew text that had been changed. But the ruler is compared elsewhere to the sun (2 Sam. 23:3-4). I am suggesting, therefore, that copyists and translators may have consciously or unconsciously obscured a comparison of the ruler to Sun and Moon as cosmic rulers.

While it is difficult to be certain that v. 5 compares the ruler to Sun and Moon understood as cosmic agents because of the difficult text and grammar, there is no question that the next verse, v. 6, compares the ruler to showers on agricultural land:

> May he fall like rain on a mown field,
>   like abundant showers drop [to] Earth.

The ruler is likened to a storm god who provides rain and fertility. While the verse says "like" showers, the imagery has the rhetorical function of preparing the reader to accept the idea that the ruler is responsible for the fertility of the land and therefore can lay claim to its produce toward the end in v. 16.

Another place the psalm fails to close its semantic system is in the relationship between Earth and justice. Again, the first seven verses contrast with the rest of

---

25. Houston, "The King's Preferential Option for the Poor," 350.

the psalm, so the rhetoric can be seen as attempting to shift the reader's perception of reality. The first seven verses pray for God's justice to be given to the ruler. Words for righteousness and justice for the poor and needy appear over and over. In the center of these verses appears the already cited verse: "May mountains bear shalom for the people, and hills righteousness." Earth is integral to God's justice and righteousness. In the next section (vv. 8-11), which speaks of the extent of empire and alludes to the mechanisms of empire—conquest and tribute—justice, peace, and righteousness are not mentioned.

A concern for the poor and needy returns in the third section (vv. 12-14). Though, interestingly, the language of justice and righteousness does not reappear. The section begins with "Because," which attempts to tie the description of empire in the previous section to the ruler's care for the poor in this section but actually weakens the connection, as Jobling has pointed out as part of the contradiction he sees in the psalm. Ironically, "Because" opens the possibility that the king's reign depends, or is conditional, on the king's care for the poor.

The final section (vv. 15-17) brings together elements from throughout the psalm, but justice, righteousness, and care for the poor are absent. The poetry is not as tight as in earlier parts of the psalm and it is as if the lack of semantic closure is reflected in the inability to create the same quality of poetry as in earlier sections. Verse 15 returns to tribute from Sheba. Verse 16 returns to fertility, but Hills are now objects, not subjects, and the image in the MT, "they sprout from cities like green plants," is awkward and has puzzled interpreters. A new language of blessing and happiness has appeared—blessing for the ruler (v. 15) and blessing for the nations through the ruler (v. 17), but the poor and needy, justice and righteousness are not mentioned. There is an interesting slippage here. When the prayer is for the geographical extent and longevity of the empire, justice and peace are not mentioned. It is as if the two cannot be reconciled or integrated, even in prayer. The psalm is unable to fully integrate the poor and needy into its vision of empire and create semantic closure.

This inability to close the semantic system may relate to the almost complete absence of animals. The only mention of animals is in v. 9:

Before him may desert animals bow down
    And his enemies lick dust.

Most translators erase the nonhuman animals from this verse. They assume this could not refer to animals and emend the text to "foes." But we have already seen other cases in Book Two where enemies are identified with animals. The word, *tsiyyim*, is often used in parallel with animals representing wild and desolate places (Isa. 13:21) and seems to be etymologically related to the word for "dryness" and "drought," so I have translated desert animals. The desert animals in this translation are in parallel with the enemies that have been conquered to create an empire. Aside from this identification of desert animals with enemies, there is no mention of the sheep, goats, pigeons, and cattle that have appeared elsewhere, much less the dogs, lions, and jackals. Earth has fallen strangely passive and silent before empire.

I have been using the language of "closing the semantic world," and semantic worlds do construct reality, but not entirely. An ecological hermeneutic cannot limit reality to an anthropocentric world of language. In order to "make sense," Psalm 72 must enliven our senses to Earth. And Earth is often experienced by our senses as resisting worlds created by human language. Psalm 72 likens the ruler to rain, but rain can also be a destructive force. Psalm 72's portrayal of the ruler as gentle, fructifying rain, contrasts with other storm god passages in the Hebrew Bible that portray storms as awe inspiring and destructive. Sticking with other royal texts for fairly close parallels, Psalm 18 has a storm theophany that includes: "Earth reeled and rocked ... mountains trembled" (v. 8[7]). Psalm 144 also has a storm theophany that includes "touch the mountains so that they smoke ... Bow your heavens, O Lord, and come down; touch the mountains so that they smoke" (v. 5). A little further afield, texts like Psalms 42 and 104 integrate both the life-giving and life-destroying sides of water into one psalm. These correspond to our senses and, therefore, make sense. Empire attempts through the rhetoric of the psalm to domesticate Earth in service of the ruler, but the next big storm will deconstruct that semantic world. Earth can and will deconstruct the incomplete, contradictory, and distorted reality of Psalm 72.

One aspect of Jobling's work that I found particularly suggestive for an ecological hermeneutic was his discussion of Susan Newman's survey of preindustrial societies, because she correlates different types of agriculture with different types of human social structures.[26] Newman includes agriculture as a force within modes of production and distinguishes between wet intensive agriculture and dry intensive agriculture. Intensive agriculture is defined as the repeated use of limited land. Wet intensive agriculture depends on extensive irrigation. Newman notes that wet intensive agriculture has a higher correlation with social stratification and state formation. Dry intensive agriculture correlates with chieftainship or paramount chieftainship. Chieftainship is less centralized than a royal kingdom. Paramount chieftainship is midway between chieftainship and a royal kingdom. Jobling finds suggestive the note by Islamoğlu and Keyder that fiefdoms, which tend to form within the Asiatic Mode of Production (AMP), try to imitate the political structure and ideology of the central state.[27] Similarly, Newman says that paramount chieftainship "resembles the image of a royal kingdom, though in practice it is more decentralized than this vision suggests."[28] AMPs that have sufficient internal resources do not need to collect tribute, so the mention of tribute in Psalm 72 suggests a paramount chieftainship that needs tribute in

---

26. Katherine S. Newman, *Law and Economic Organization: A Comparative Study of Preindustrial Societies* (Cambridge: Cambridge University Press, 1983), 137–202.

27. Huri Islamoğlu and Cağlar Keyder, "The Ottoman Social Formation," pp. 301–24 in *The Asiatic Mode of Production: Science and Politics*, ed. Anne M. Bailey and Josep R. Llobera (London: Routledge & Kegan Paul, 1981), 308, cited in Jobling, "Deconstruction and the Political Analysis of Biblical Texts," 116.

28. Newman, *Law and Economic Organization*, 91.

order to imitate a royal kingdom. Solomon's kingdom seemed to rely on tariffs on international trade, tribute, and corvée labor and heavy taxation of its citizens, even to survive for a short period. Therefore, Israel along with other Canaanite city-states may have been "petty political units pretending to be Egypt."[29]

Jobling thinks the contradictions in Psalm 72 reflect a conflict between the monarchy and the local elders, who represented an older, tribal mode of production, and whose local accumulation of land and power could threaten the centralized monarchy. Psalm 72 prays for the ruler to "crush the oppressor." Jobling suggests that this may have referred to local elders, and the psalm attempts to subvert the elders and portray the ruler as the hope of the poor. Jameson says that, in order to be effective, the ideology of the dominant class needs to include the ideologies of the classes they are attempting to rule, but their inclusion can also be used against the dominant system.[30] I suspect that Psalm 72 attempts to include the world view of peasants, which included Mountains, Hills, Sun, Moon, and rivers that were alive and the source of well-being.

Psalm 72's attempt to greenwash the monarchy creates several contradictions that can be used to deconstruct imperial propaganda. I've suggested that in addition to the contradictions Jobling and Houston identified, there is a major ecological contradiction between the portrayal of the Hills and Mountains as agents supporting shalom and righteousness in the first part of the psalm, and the attempt of empire to remove the agency of Hills and Mountains, take credit for fertility, and claim to possess Earth's produce. This major contradiction is compounded by the absence of animals, except as enemies, and the domesticated picture of gentle rain fructifying Hills. But thinking the deconstruction of this propaganda relies on human ingenuity may be anthropocentric. The reader does not need to deconstruct empire's logic; Earth will deconstruct this Psalm with the next experience of wild animals or storms and the truth that will emerge from the rubble is, "Mountains bear shalom, hills righteousness."

Conclusion

This commentary can be summarized by retelling Book Two of the Psalter's story about ancient Israel, the Davidic monarchy, priests, and their ambiguous relationship to Creation. Current psalms scholarship understands the first three books of the Psalter as telling the story of failure of the covenant with the Davidic monarchy. This commentary shows that part of that failure is an ambiguous relationship with Earth and Earth community. Book Two of the Psalter begins with a collection of psalms with the superscription, "of the Korahites" and one psalm with the superscription "of Asaph." If one remembers that the Psalter was

---

29. Jobling, "Deconstruction and the Political Analysis of Biblical Texts," 117.
30. Fredric Jameson, "A Conversation with Fredric Jameson," *Semeia* 59 (1992): 228–9.

collected and used by priests in temple, then those psalms with superscriptions indicating they are psalms of the Korahites or Asaph are probably particularly close to a priestly self-understanding. While this commentary has not pointed to all the evidence of a priestly perspective, it has noted the references to sacrifices, thanksgiving, the temple, and closeness to God that reflect a priestly perspective. Furthermore, the psalms of the Korahites and Asaph reflect an understanding of priests as mediating not just between God and humans but between the Creator and all Creation. Thus, the psalms of Korah identify with deer as fellow creatures seeking God and water (Ps. 42:2[1]). They understand God as present in Creation as "My Rock" (Ps. 42:10[9]) and identify with sheep and goats with God as their shepherd (Ps. 44:12[11], 23[22]).

The ambiguity of the priest's position becomes evident when the psalms in the Korah collection shift to psalms whose genres and content focus on the monarchy and Zion (Pss. 45–49). The empire's exploitation of elephants and women is evident beneath the praise of Psalm 45, and Psalms 47–48 are set in the barren landscape of an urban, imperial ideology that objectifies Earth. Psalm 49's recognition that humans are embodied and die like all other species may, however, subvert this ideology and prepare for the judgment of Psalm 50.

Asaph is remembered in Chronicles as a chief priest appointed by David and a fellow composer of psalms. The superscription that connects Psalm 50 to Asaph gives it a particularly important place in the dialogue between priests and royalty and the prophetic genre makes it stand out from the collections of laments around it. Psalm 50 portrays Sun, Earth, and Skies, as subjects with agency and voices and God as in dialogue with them and in intimate relationship with even the smallest bugs. This portrayal of God suggests that priests and, by extension, all humans should be in right relationship with Earth and Earth community.

The priests carry out animal sacrifices, which are mentioned in these psalms, but these sacrifices are part of the socioecology and not as exploitative as contemporary factory farming. Humans, dogs, sheep, goats, and oxen coevolved and constructed an ecological niche in ancient Israel that supported larger numbers of both humans and domestic animals. They were not originally domesticated for meat but for dairy products and traction. The animals that were sacrificed were those that would need to be culled to maintain the carrying capacity of the land and prevent suffering in bad years. Among other things, the ritual care that was taken with their blood may indicate a culture of trust that recognized human dependence on domestic animals and expressed dependence, respect, and honor.

The superscription of Psalm 51 identifies it with David's response to the judgment of the prophet Nathan, and the content responds to Psalm 50. Psalm 51 is the first of the psalms "of David" that take up the rest of Book Two, apart from the last one, which is "of Solomon." Not just Psalm 51, but the rest of Book Two can be understood as David's response to the sons of Korah and especially Asaph and his attempt to integrate a priestly perspective on Creation.

The first group of Davidic laments (Pss. 51–55) makes steps in this direction as the psalmist identifies with a "green olive tree" (Ps. 52:10[8]) and wishes they had "wings like a dove" (Ps. 55:7[6]) to escape to the wilderness. The next group of Davidic petitions (Pss. 56–60), however, portrays enemies as lions (Pss. 57:5[4]; 58:7[6]) and dogs (Ps. 59:7[6], 15[14]). The problem with these metaphors is that they assume other Earth creatures are enemies and in contemporary contexts could legitimate their exploitation and killing. Many of the Davidic psalms are individual laments and the divine warrior narrative is typical of this genre. The use of it in these psalms shows its ambiguous relationship with Earth. While Earth and parts of Earth are sometimes portrayed as subjects, God is often portrayed as a storm god at war with them. At the same time, God as Rock has its home in this pattern and the metaphor identifies God with Earth. The divine warrior pattern is Creation imagery that includes the Creator providing water and fertility. These psalms also have imagery of God's wings that in Psalm 63 may allude to the ancient Near Eastern imagery of a nursing goddess and could give birds intrinsic value as images of God.

The commentary finished by arguing that the psalms that conclude Book Two, Psalms 69–72, and especially Psalm 72, show evidence of royal ideology taking credit for Earth's fertility. This coopting of Earth's bounty is framed in the Psalter as part of the failure of the Davidic monarchy and includes elements of a priestly understanding of right relationship with all Creation that could be recovered for an ecological reading. They acknowledge Mountain, Sun, and Moon as subjects and call Skies and Earth to praise God. In the following books of the Psalter, other voices will join all Creation's praise of God as David is transformed into a righteous person leading Israel's praise of the Creator.

BIBLIOGRAPHY

Abram, David. *The Spell of the Sensuous: Perception and Language in a More-Than-Human World.* New York: Random House, 1996.

Adams, Carol. *The Sexual Politics of Meat: A Feminist-Vegetarian Critical Theory.* 20th anniversary edition. New York: Continuum, 2010.

Agamben, Giorgio. *The Open: Man and Animal,* trans. Kevin Attell. Meridian, Crossing Aesthetics. Stanford, CA: Stanford University Press, 2003.

Allen, Barbara. *Pigeon.* Animal Series. London: Reaktion, 2009.

Armstrong, Philip. *Sheep.* Animal Series. London: Reaktion, 2016.

Ashkenazi, Eli. "Saving the Sturdy Little Cow that Fed Israel's Founders." *Haartez.com,* May 28, 2013 (https://www.haaretz.com/.premium-saving-the-sturdy-little-cow-that-fed-israel-s-founders-1.5270529, accessed December 29, 2014).

Bang, Ki-Min. "A Missing Key to Understanding Psalm 46: Revisiting the Chaoskampf." *Conversations with the Biblical World* 37 (2017): 68–89.

Baynes-Rock, Marcus. *Among the Bone Eaters: Encounters with Hyenas in Harar.* University Park: Pennsylvania State University Press, 2015.

Black, Max. *Models and Metaphors: Studies in Language and Philosophy.* Ithaca: Cornell University Press, 1962.

Bodenheimer, F. S. *Animal Life in Palestine: An Introduction to the Problems of Animal Ecology and Zoogeography.* Jerusalem: Mayer, 1935.

Bodenheimer, F. S. *Animals and Man in Bible Lands.* Leiden: Brill, 1960.

Borowski, Oded. *Every Living Thing: Daily Use of Animals in Ancient Israel.* Walnut Creek, CA: Altamira, 1998.

Bradshaw, John. *Dog Sense: How the New Science of Dog Behavior Can Make You a Better Friend to Your Pet.* New York: Basic, 2011.

Braude, William G. *The Midrash on Psalms.* Yale Judaica Series 13. New Haven, CT: Yale University Press, 1954.

Brown, William P. *The Ethos of the Cosmos: The Genesis of Moral Imagination in the Bible.* Grand Rapids, MI: Eerdmans, 1999.

Brown, William P. *Seeing the Psalms: A Theology of Metaphor.* Louisville: Westminster John Knox, 2002.

Brown, William P. *The Seven Pillars of Creation: The Bible, Science, and the Ecology of Wonder.* Oxford: Oxford University Press, 2010.

Brown, William P. "Thirsting for God in the Classroom: A Meditation on Psalm 42:1–8." *Teaching Theology and Religion* 6 (2003): 187–9.

Buss, Martin. "The Psalms of Asaph and Korah," *JBL* 82 (1963): 382–92.

Callender, Dexter E. Jr. *Adam in Myth and History: Ancient Israelite Perspectives on the Primal Human.* Harvard Semitic Studies, 48. Winona Lake, IN: Eisenbraous, 2000.

Cansdale, George. *All the Animals of the Bible Lands.* Grand Rapids, MI: Zondervan, 1970.

Caquot, André. "Psaume LXXII 16." *Vetus Testamentum* 38 (1998): 214–20.

Childs, Brevard. *Introduction to the Old Testament as Scripture.* Philadelphia: Fortress, 1979.

Clutton-Brock, Juliet. *Domesticated Animals from Early Times*. Austin: University of Texas Press, 1981.

Clutton-Brock, Juliet, and Caroline Grigson, eds. *Animals and Archaeology: 3. Early Herders and their Flocks*. BAR International Series 202. Oxford: B.A.R., 1984.

Coetzee, J. M. *The Lives of Animals*, ed. Amy Guzman. The University Centre for Human Values Series. Princeton, NJ: Princeton University, 1999.

Coogan, Michael D. *Stories from Ancient Canaan*. Louisville: Westminster, 1978.

Coppinger, Raymond, and Lorna Coppinger. *Dogs: A New Understanding of Canine Origin, Behavior, and Evolution*. Chicago: University of Chicago Press, 2002.

Coupe, Laurence. *Myth*, ed. John Drakakis. The New Critical Idiom. London: Routledge, 1997.

Creach, Jerome F. D. *The Destiny of the Righteous in the Psalms*. St. Louis, MO: Chalice, 2008.

Cross, Frank Moore. *Canaanite Myth and Hebrew Epic: Essays in the History of the Religion of Israel*. Cambridge, MA: Harvard University Press, 1973.

Dahood, Mitchell. "The Etymology of *Malta'ot* (Ps 58,7)." *CBQ* 17 (1955): 300–3.

Dahood, Mitchell. *Psalms 1–50; Introduction, Translation, and Notes*. Anchor Bible. Garden City, NY: Doubleday, 1966.

deClaissé-Walford, Nancy, Rolf A. Jacobsen, and Beth LaNeel Tanner. *The Book of Psalms*. The New International Commentary on the Old Testament. Grand Rapids, MI: Eerdmans, 2014.

Delitzsch, Franz. *Biblical Commentary on the Psalms*, trans. John Bolton. 3 vols. Edinburgh: T&T Clark, 1880.

Derr, Mark. *How the Dog Became the Dog: From Wolves to Our Best Friends*. New York: Overlook, 2011.

Derrida, Jacques. *The Animal That Therefore I Am*, ed. Marie-Louise Mallet. Perspectives in Continental Philosophy Series. New York: Fordham University Press, 2009.

Diez, Concepcion M., Isabel Trujillo, Nieves Martinez-Urdiroz, Diego Barranco, Luis Rallo, Pedro Marfil, and Brandon Grant. "Olive Domestication and Diversification in the Mediterranean Basin." *New Phytologist* 206 (2015): 436–47, doi: 10.1111/nph.13181.

Douglas, Mary. *Leviticus as Literature*. Oxford: Oxford University Press, 2001.

Doyle, B. "Howling like Dogs: Metaphorical Language in Psalm LIX." *Vetus Testamentum* 54 (2004): 61–82.

Feliks, Jehuda. "Dog," p. 733, in *Encyclopaedia Judaica*, ed. Michael Berenbaum and Fred Skolnik, vol. 5. 2nd ed. Detroit, MI: Macmillan Reference USA, 2007.

Fernandes, Salvador, OFM cap. *God as Rock in the Psalter*. European University Studies, Series XXIII Theology, vol. 934. Frankfurt am Main: Peter Lang, 2013.

Fletcher, John. *Deer*. London: Reaktion, 2013.

Frankfort, Henri. *The Art and Architecture of the Ancient Orient*. Pelican History of Art. Baltimore: Penguin, 1954.

Fretheim, Terence. *God and World in the Old Testament: A Relational Theology of Creation*. Nashville, TN: Abingdon, 2005.

Fretheim, Terence. "The Plagues as Ecological Signs of Historical Disaster." *JBL* 110 (1991): 385–96.

Frye, Northrop. *Anatomy of Criticism: Four Essays*. Princeton, NJ: Princeton University Press, 1957.

Fudge, Erica. *Animal*. Focus on Contemporary Issues. London: Reaktion, 2004.

Gadamer, Hans-Georg. *Truth and Method*. London: Continuum, 1975.

Gaiser, Frederick J. "The David of Psalm 51: Reading Psalm 51 in Light of Psalm 50." *Word & World* 23 (2003): 382–94.
Garrard, Greg. *Ecocriticism*. The New Critical Idiom Series, 2nd ed. London: Routledge, 2012.
Gilmour, Michael J. *Eden's Other Residents: The Bible and Animals*. Eugene, OR: Cascade, 2014.
Goddard, Burton L. *Animals and Birds of the Bible*. Mulberry, IN: Sovereign Grace, 2007.
Gottwald, Norman K. "Social Class as an Analytic and Hermeneutical Category in Biblical Studies." *Journal of Biblical Literature* 112 (1993): 3–22.
Gruenwald, Ithamar. "God the 'Stone/Rock': Myth, Idolatry, and Cultic Fetishism in Ancient Israel." *Journal of Religion* 76 (1996): 428–99.
Gunkel, Hermann, and Joachim Begrich. *An Introduction to the Psalms: The Genres of the Religious Lyric of Israel*, trans. James D. Nogalski. Macon, GA: Mercer University Press, 1998.
Habel, Norman C. *The Birth, the Curse and the Greening of Earth*. Earth Bible Commentary Series 1. Sheffield: Sheffield Phoenix Press, 2011.
Habel, Norman C., ed. *Readings from the Perspective of Earth*. Earth Bible series 1; Sheffield: Sheffield Academic Press, 2000.
Hackett, Jo Ann, and John Huehnergard. "On Breaking Teeth." *HTR* 77 (1984): 259–75.
Hansell, Peter and Jean Hansell. *Doves and Dovecotes*. Bath, UK: Millstream, 1988.
Harari, Yuval Noah. *Sapiens: A Brief History of Humankind*. Toronto: Signal, 2014.
Haraway, Donna. *The Companion Species Manifesto: Dogs, People, and Significant Otherness*. Chicago: Prickly Paradigm, 2003.
Haraway, Donna. "A Manifesto for Cyborgs: Science, Technology, and Socialist Feminism in the 1980s." *Socialist Review* 80 (1985): 65–107.
Haraway, Donna. *When Species Meet*. Posthumanities, 3. Minneapolis: University of Minnesota Press, 2008.
Hardwick, Paul. "The Monkey's Funeral in the Pilgrimage Window, York Minster." *Art History* 23 (2000): 290–9.
Hare, Brian, Michelle Brown, Christina Williamson, and Michael Tomasello. "The Domestication of Social Cognition in Dogs." *Science* 298 (2002): 1634–6.
Hart, George, ed. *The Routledge Dictionary of Egyptian Gods and Goddesses*. Routledge Dictionaries, 2nd ed. London: Routledge, 2005.
Hecke, Pierre van, and Antji Labahn, eds. *Metaphors in the Psalms*. Bibliotheca Ephemeridum Theologicarum Lovaniensium. Leuven: Peeters, 2010.
Hecke, P. van, ed. *Metaphor in the Hebrew Bible*. Bibliotheca Ephemeridum Theologicarum Lovaniensium, 187. Leuven: Peeters, 2005.
Henschel, P., H. Bauer, E. Sogbohoussou, and K. Nowell. "*Panthera leo* West Africa Subpopulation." The IUCN Red List of Threatened Species 2015 (https://www.iucnredlist.org/species/68933833/54067639, accessed August 15, 2018).
Hinson, Joy. *Goat*. Animal Series. London: Reaktion, 2015.
Hiebert, Theodore. "Air, The First Sacred Thing," p. 19, in *Exploring Ecological Hermeneutics*, ed. Norman C. Habel and Peter Trudinger. Atlanta: Society of Biblical Literature, 2008.
Hobgood-Oster, Laura. *The Friends We Keep: Unleashing Christianity's Compassion for Animals*. Waco, TX: Baylor University Press, 2010.
Hope, Edward R. *All Creatures Great and Small: Living Things in the Bible*. Helps for Translators. New York: United Bible Societies, 2005.

Hossfeld, Frank-Lothar, and Erich Zenger. *Psalms 2: A Commentary on Psalms 51–100*, ed. Klaus Baltzer, trans. Linda M. Maloney. In *Hermeneia: A Critical and Historical Commentary on the Bible*. Minneapolis: Fortress, 2005.

Houston, Walter. "The King's Preferential Option for the Poor: Rhetoric, Ideology and Ethics in Psalm 72." *Biblical Interpretation* 7 (1999): 341–67.

Ingold, Tim. "From the Master's Point of View: Hunting *is* Sacrifice." *Journal of the Royal Anthropological Institute* 21 (2015): 24–7.

Ingold, Tim. *The Perception of the Environment: Essays on Livelihood, Dwelling, and Skill.* London: Routledge, 2000.

Jackson, Deirdre. *Lion.* Animal Series; London: Reaktion, 2010.

Jameson, Fredric. "A Conversation with Fredric Jameson." *Semeia* 59 (1992): 227–37.

Jameson, Fredric. *The Political Unconscious: Narrative as a Socially Symbolic Act.* Ithaca, NY: Cornell University Press, 1981.

Jobling, David. "Deconstruction and the Political Analysis of Biblical Texts: A Jamesonian Reading of Psalm 72." *Semeia* 59 (1992): 95–127.

Johnston, Basil. *Ojibway Heritage.* Toronto: McClelland & Stewart, 1976.

Jones, Christine Danette Brown. "The Psalms of Asaph: A Study of the Function of a Psalm Collection." PhD dissertation, Baylor University, 2009.

Keel, Othmar. *The Symbolism of the Biblical World: Ancient Near Eastern Iconography and the Book of Psalms.* Winona Lake, IN: Eisenbrauns, 1997.

Keel, Othmar, and Christopher Uehlinger. *Gods, Goddesses and Images of God in Ancient Israel*, trans. Thomas H. Trapp. Minneapolis: Fortress, 1998.

Klawans, Jonathan. "Sacrifice in Ancient Israel: Pure Bodies, Domesticated Animals, and the Divine Shepherd." In *A Communion of Subjects: Animals in Religion, Science, and Ethics*, ed. Paul Waldau and Kimberley Patton. New York: Columbia University Press, 2006.

Knowles, Michael P. "'The Rock, His Work is Perfect': Unusual Imagery for God in Deuteronomy XXXII." *VT* 39 (1989): 307–22.

Koops, Robert. *Each According to Its Kind: Plants and Trees in the Bible.* UBS Technical Helps. Redding, UK: United Bible Societies, 2012.

Koosed, Jennifer L., ed. *The Bible and Posthumanism.* Atlanta: Society of Biblical Literature, 2014.

Kraus, Hans-Joachim. *Psalms 1-59: A Continental Commentary.* Minneapolis: Fortress, 1993.

Kugel, James L. *The Idea of Biblical Poetry: Parallelism and Its History.* New Haven: Yale University Press, 1981.

Laland, Kevin N., John Odling-Smee, and Marcus W. Feldman. "Causing a Commotion." *Nature* 429 (2004): 609, https://doi.org/10.1038/429609a.

Lambert, W. G. *Babylonian Wisdom Literature*, vol. 75. Oxford: Clarendon, 1967.

Leach, H. M. "Human Domestication Reconsidered." *Current Anthropology* 44 (2003): 349–68.

LeMon, Joel M. *Yahweh's Winged Form in the Psalms: Exploring Congruent Iconography and Texts.* Orbis Biblicus et Orientalis 242. Fribourg: Academic Press, 2010.

Levenson, Jon D. *Sinai & Zion: An Entry into the Jewish Bible.* San Francisco: HarperSanFrancisco, 1985.

Levenson, Jon D. "The Temple and the World." *The Journal of Religion* 64 (1984): 275–98.

Lopez, Barry Holstun. *Of Wolves and Men.* New York: Scribner, 1978.

Lovelock, James E. *Gaia: A New Look at Life on Earth.* New York: Oxford University Press, 1987.

Mason, I. L. *A World Dictionary of Livestock Breeds, Types and Varieties*. 4th ed. Wallingford: CABI Publishing, 1996.

Mays, James. *The Lord Reigns: A Theological Handbook to the Psalms*. Louisville: Westminster John Knox, 1994.

McCance, Erin C. "Understanding Urban White-Tailed Deer (*Odocoileus virginianus*) Movement and Related Social and Ecological Considerations for Management." Dissertation submitted to the University of Manitoba, 2014 (https://mspace.lib.umanitoba.ca/bitstream/handle/1993/23573/McCance_Erin.pdf?sequence=1, accessed January 11, 2018).

McCann, J. Clinton. "The Book of Psalms: Introduction, Commentary, and Reflections." Vol. IV in *The New Interpreter's Bible*, ed. Leander E. Keck et al. Nashville, TN: Abingdon, 1996.

McFague, Sallie. *Metaphorical Theology: Models of God in Religious Language*. Philadelphia: Fortress, 1982.

McHugh, Susan. *Dog*. London: Reaktion, 2004.

McHugh, Susan. *Animal Stories: Narrating Across Species Lines*. Minneapolis: University of Minnesota Press, 2011.

Menache, Sophia. "Dogs: God's Worst Enemies?" *Society and Animals: Journal of Human-Animal Studies* 5 (1997): 1–12.

Middleton, J. Richard. *The Liberating Image: The Imago Dei in Genesis 1*. Grand Rapids, MI: Brazos, 2005.

Miklósi, Ádám. *Dog Behaviour, Evolution, and Cognition*. Oxford Biology. London: Oxford University Press, 2007.

Miller, Patrick D., Jr. *The Divine Warrior in Early Israel*. HSM 5. Cambridge, MA: Harvard University Press, 1973.

Moore, Stephen D., ed. *Divinanimality: Animal Theory, Creaturely Theology*. Transdisciplinary Theological Colloquia. New York: Fordham University Press, 2014.

Moore, Stephen D. "Why There Are No Humans or Animals in the Gospel of Mark," pp. 71–93, in *Mark as Story: Retrospect and Prospect*, ed. Kelly R. Iverson and Christopher Skinner. Atlanta: Society of Biblical Literature, 2011.

Nasuti, Harry P. *Defining the Sacred Songs: Genre, Tradition and the Post-Critical Interpretation of the Psalms*. JSOTSup Series, 218. Sheffield: Sheffield Academic, 1999.

Nasuti, Harry P. *Tradition History and the Psalms of Asaph*. Atlanta: Scholars, 1988.

Newman, Katherine S. *Law and Economic Organization: A Comparative Study of Preindustrial Societies*. Cambridge: Cambridge University Press, 1983.

Odling-Smee, F. John, Kevin N. Laland, and Marcus W. Feldman. *Niche Construction: The Neglected Process in Evolution*, Monographs in Population Biology 37. Princeton, NJ: Princeton University Press, 2003.

Patte, Daniel. *Ethics of Biblical Interpretation: A Reevaluation*. Louisville: Westminster John Knox, 1995.

Peters, Joris, Angela von den Driesch, and Daniel Helmer. "The Upper Euphrates-Tigris Basin: Cradle of Agro-Pastoralism?" pp. 96–124, in *The First Steps of Animal Domestication*, ed. J.-D. Vigne, J. Peters, and D. Helmer. Oxford: Oxbow, 2005.

Pleins, J. David. "Death and Endurance: Reassessing the Literary Structure and Theology of Psalm 49." *Journal for the Study of the Old Testament* 69 (1996): 19–27.

Porter, Jody. "Ontario Announces $85M to Clean Up Mercury Near Grassy Narrows, Wabaseemoong First Nations." *CBC News/Thunder Bay* (http://www.cbc.ca/news/canada/thunder-bay/ontario-mercury-cleanup-1.4180631, accessed February 8, 2017).

Reitz, Elizabeth J. and Elizabeth S. Wing. *Zooarchaeology*. Cambridge Manuals in Archaeology. Cambridge: Cambridge University Press, 1999.

Ruse, Michael. *The Gaia Hypothesis: Science on a Pagan Planet*. Chicago: University of Chicago Press, 2013.

Ryder, Michael L. *Sheep and Man*. London: Duckworth, 1983.

Saint Augustine, Bishop of Hippo. *Expositions of the Psalms*, trans. Maria Boulding, OSB, ed. John E. Rotelle. 6 vols. Hyde Park, NY: New City Press, 2000–2004.

Sasson, Aharon. *Animal Husbandry in Ancient Israel: A Zooarchaeological Perspective on Livestock Exploitation, Herd Management and Economic Strategies*. Approaches to Anthropological Archaeology. London: Equinox, 2010.

Sheppard, Gerald. "Theology and the Book of Psalms." *Int* 46 (1992): 143–55.

Shipman, Pat. "The Animal Connection and Human Evolution." *Current Anthropology* 51 (2010): 519–38.

Shipman, Pat. *The Animal Connection: A New Perspective on What Makes Us Human*. New York: W. W. Norton, 2011.

Shipman, Pat. *The Invaders: How Humans and Their Dogs Drove Neanderthals to Extinction*. Cambridge, MA: Harvard University Press, 2015.

Singer, Peter. *Animal Liberation: The Definitive Classic of the Animal Movement*. Revised ed. New York: HarperCollins, 2009. Originally published 1975.

Snyder, Gary. *Turtle Island with "Four Changes."* New York: New Directions, 1974. Originally published in 1969.

Spiciarich, Abra, Yuval Gadot, and Lidar Sapir-Hen. "The Faunal Evidence from Early Roman Jerusalem: The People behind the Garbage." *Journal of the Institute of Archaeology of Tel Aviv University* 44 (2017): 98–117.

Stone, Ken. *Reading the Hebrew Bible with Animal Studies*. Stanford: Stanford University Press, 2018.

Strawn, Brent A. *What Is Stronger Than a Lion? Leonine Image and Metaphor in the Hebrew Bible and the Ancient Near East*. Orbis Biblicus et Orientalis 212. Fribourg: Academic Press, 2005.

Stutesman, Drake. *Snake*. London: Reaktion, 2005.

Tate, Marvin. *Psalms 51–100 in Word Biblical Commentary*, vol. 20. Dallas, TX: Word, 1990.

Twine, Richard T. "Ma(r)king Essence-Ecofeminism and Embodiment." *Ethics and the Environment* 6 (2001): 31–58.

Velten, Hannah. *Cow*. London: Reaktion, 2007.

Waal, Frans de. *Are We Smart Enough to Know How Smart Animals Are?* New York: W. W. Norton, 2016.

Waldau, Paul, and Kimberley Patton, eds. *A Communion of Subjects: Animals in Religion, Science, and Ethics*. New York: Columbia University Press, 2006.

Walker-Jones, Arthur. "Alternative Cosmogonies in the Psalms." PhD dissertation, Princeton Theological Seminary, 1991.

Walker-Jones, Arthur. "Ecological Biblical Criticism," in *Oxford Encyclopedia of Biblical Interpretation*, ed. Steven L. McKenzie. New York: Oxford University Press, 2013.

Walker-Jones, Arthur. *The Green Psalter: Resources for an Ecological Spirituality*. Minneapolis: Fortress, 2009.

Walker-Jones, Arthur. "Honey from the Rock: The Contribution of God as Rock to an Ecological Hermeneutic," pp. 91–102, in *Exploring Ecological Hermeneutics*, ed. Norman C. Habel and Peter Trudinger, Symposium Series, 46. Atlanta, GA: Society of Biblical Literature, 2008.

Walker-Jones, Arthur. "Naming the Human Animal: Genesis 1–3 and Other Animals in Human Becoming." *Zygon: Journal of Religion and Science* 52 (2017): 1005–28, doi: 10.1111/zoo.12375.
Walker-Jones, Arthur. "The So-Called Ostrich in the God Speeches of the Book of Job (Job 39, 13–18)." *Biblica* 86 (2005): 494–510.
Walker-Jones, Arthur. "'Words with Power' for Social Transformation: An Anatomy of Biblical Criticism for Theological Education." *Teaching Theology and Religion* 11 (2008): 75–81.
Wang, Xiaoming, and Richard H. Tedford. *Dogs: Their Fossil Relatives and Evolutionary History*. New York: Columbia University Press, 2008.
Wapnish, Paula. "Archaeozoology: The Integration of Faunal Data with Biblical Archaeology," pp. 426–42, in *Biblical Archaeology Today, 1990*, ed. A. Biran and J. Aviram. Jerusalem: Israel Exploration Society and Israel Academic of Sciences and Humanities, 1993.
Wapnish, Paula, and Brian Hesse. "Urbanization and the Organization of Animal Production at Tell Jemmeh in the Middle Bronze Age Levant." *Journal of Near Eastern Studies* 47 (1988): 81–94. http://www.jstor.org/stable/544380.
Weiss, Ehud, Wilma Wetterstrom, Dani Nadel, and Ofer Bar-Yosef. "The Broad Spectrum Revisited: Evidence from Plant Remains." *Proceedings of the National Academy of Sciences* 101 (2004): 9551–5, doi:10.1073/pnas.0402362101.
Westermann, Claus. *Genesis 37–50: A Commentary*. Minneapolis: Augsburg, 1986.
White, Lynn Jr. "The Historical Roots of Our Ecologic Crisis. *Science* 155, no. 3767 (1967): 1203–7.
Whitekettle, Richard. "A Communion of Subjects: Zoological Classification and Human/Animal Relations in Psalm 104." *BBR* 21, no. 2 (2011): 173–87.
Whitekettle, Richard. "All Creatures Great and Small: Intermediate Level Taxa in Israelite Zoological Thought." *SJOT* 16, no. 2 (2002): 163–83.
Whitekettle, Richard. "Bugs, Bunny, or Boar?: Identifying *Ziz* animals of Psalms 50 and 80." *CBQ* 67, no. 2 (April 2005): 250–64.
Whitekettle, Richard. "Forensic Zoology: Animal Taxonomy and Rhetorical Persuasion in Psalm 1." *VT* 58, no. 3 (2008): 404–19.
Whitekettle, Richard. "Like a Fish and Shrimp out of Water: Identifying the Dāg and Remeś Animals of Habakkuk 1:14." *BBR* 24, no. 4 (2014): 491–503.
Whitekettle, Richard. "Of Mice and Wren: Terminal Level Taxa in Israelite Zoological Thought." *SJOT* 17, no. 2 (2003): 163–82.
Whitekettle, Richard. "One If By And: Conjunctions, Taxonomic Development, and the Animals of Leviticus 11,26." *ZAW* 121, no. 4 (2009): 481–97.
Whitekettle, Richard. "Oxen Can Plow, but Women Can Ruminate: Animal Classification and the Helper in Genesis 2.18–24." *SJOT* 23, no. 2 (2009): 243–56.
Whitekettle, Richard. "Rats Are Like Snakes, and Hares Are Like Goats: A Study in Israelite Land Animal Taxonomy." *Biblica* 82, no. 3 (2001): 345–62.
Whitekettle, Richard. "The Raven as Kind and Kinds of Ravens: a Study in the Zoological Nomenclature of Leviticus 11,2–23." *ZAW* 117, no. 4 (2005): 509–28.
Whitekettle, Richard. "Taming the Shrew, Shrike, and Shrimp: The Form and Function of Zoological Classification in Psalm 8." *JBL* 125 (2006): 749–65.
Whitekettle, Richard. "Where the Wild Things Are: Primary Level Taxa in Israelite Zoological Thought." *JSOT* 25, no. 93 (2001): 17–37.

Willerslev, Rane, Piers Vitebsky, and Anatoly Alekseyev. "Sacrifice as the Ideal Hunt: A Cosmological Explanation of the Origin of the Reindeer." *Journal of the Royal Anthropological Institute* 21 (2014): 1–23.

Willerslev, Rane, Piers Vitebsky, and Anatoly Alekseyev. "Response: Defending the Thesis on the 'Hunter's Double Bind.'" *Journal of the Royal Anthropological Institute* 21 (2015): 28–31.

Williams, Peter. *Snail*. London: Reaktion, 2009.

Wilson, Gerald Henry. *The Editing of the Hebrew Psalter*. SBL Dissertation Series. Chico, CA: Scholars Press, 1985.

Wimsatt, William K., and Monroe Beardsley. "The Intentional Fallacy." *Sewanee Review* 54 (1946): 468–88. Revised and republished in Wimsatt, William K. *The Verbal Icon: Studies in the Meaning of Poetry*. Lexington: University of Kentucky Press, 1954, 3–18.

Winter, Urs. *Frau und Göttin: Exegetishce und ikonographische Studien zum wieblichen Gottesbild im Alten Israel und in dessen Umwelt*. OBO 53. Fribourg: Universitätsverlag, 1983.

Yee, Gale A. "The Author/Text/Reader and Power: Suggestions for a Critical Framework in Biblical Studies," pp. 114–15, in *Reading from This Place: Social Location and Biblical Interpretation*, ed. Fernando F. Segovia and Mary Ann Tolbert. Minneapolis: Fortress, 1995.

Zohary, Michael. *Plants of the Bible: A Complete Handbook to All the Plants with 200 Full-Color Plates Taken in the Natural Habitat*. Cambridge: Cambridge University Press, 1982.

AUTHOR INDEX

Note: Locators followed by n refer to notes.

Abram, David 13, 13 n.35, 143, 143 n.23
Ackroyd, Peter 22 n.69, 62 n.3
Adams, Carol 53, 53 n.9
Agamben, Giorgio 11, 11 n.23
Alekseyev, Anatoly 67 n.25, 67 n.26
Allen, Barbara 82, 82 n.20, 84 n.34, 84 n.35, 85 n.36, 85 n.39, 86 n.44
Anderson, James 106, 106 n.76
Armstrong, Philip 10 n.19, 44, 44 n.81, 44 n.83, 44 n.86, 50 n.103
Ashkenazi, Eli 71 n.49
Augustine of Hippo 27–8, 27 n.9, 28 n.14

Bang, Ki-Min 56 n.11
Baynes-Rock, Marcus 95, 95 n.35, 96 n.36
Beardsley, Monroe 17 n.48
Black, Max 94, 94 n.28
Bodenheimer, F. S. 9, 9 n.12, 71, 71 n.48
Bökönyi, S. 38 n.50
Borowski, Oded 9, 9 n.15, 30, 30 n.21, 39 n.51, 41, 41 n.60, 41 n.63, 42, 42 n.69, 43, 43 n.78, 46 n.94, 48 n.98, 48 n.101, 71 n.44, 71 n.47, 108 n.83
Botterweck, G. 102 n.60, 102 n.61, 102 n.62, 103, 103 n.66, 104 n.67, 111 n.91, 111 n.92
Bradshaw, John 109 n.87
Braude, William G. 22 n.67
Brown, William P. 27, 27 n.6, 34 n.32, 37 n.42, 37 n.45, 80 n.7, 132 n.26
Buss, Martin 63 n.5

Callaway, Ewan 19 n.60
Callender, Dexter E., Jr. 80 n.9
Calvin, John 106, 106 n.76
Cansdale, George 9, 9 n.13, 42, 42 n.68, 82 n.19, 83 n.27, 116, 116 n.97, 125 n.15
Caquot, André 143 n.24
Childs, Brevard 22 n.69, 62 n.3

Clutton-Brock, Juliet 38 n.49, 38 n.50, 71, 71 n.45, 108 n.83
Coetzee, J. M. 11, 11 n.23
Cokinos, Christopher 86 n.42
Conrad, Edgar 14, 14 n.38
Coogan, Michael D. 134 n.2
Coppinger, Lorna 19 n.58, 100 n.55, 101, 101 n.57, 108, 108 n.82, 108 n.85
Coppinger, Raymond 19 n.58, 100 n.55, 101, 101 n.57, 108, 108 n.82, 108 n.85
Coupe, Laurence 18 n.51
Creach, Jerome F. D. 62 n.2
Cross, Frank Moore 57 n.13, 126, 126 n.17

Dahl, Gudrun 39 n.55, 40 n.57, 41 n.63, 49 n.102
Dahood, Mitchell 28, 28 n.16, 29 n.17, 91, 91 n.12, 105 n.71
deClaissé-Walford, Nancy 25, 59 n.16
Derrida, Jacques 11, 11 n.23, 14, 14 n.40, 15
Diez, Concepcion M. 80 n.11
Driesch, Angela von den 39 n.53
Douglas, Mary 66, 66 n.17, 68, 68 n.28
Doyle, Brian 97, 97 n.40, 98 n.46, 98 n.48, 99 n.51, 114, 114 n.94, 136 n.7

Ellis, Richard 86 n.41, 86 n.43

Feldman, Marcus W. 39 n.52
Feliks, Jehuda 101, 101 n.58
Fernandes, Salvador 36, 36 n.38, 36 n.40
Fisk, Robert 103 n.64
Fletcher, John 11 n.25, 26 n.5, 27 n.7, 28 n.13, 29 n.18, 29 n.19, 30, 30 n.22, 30 n.23
Frankfort, Henri 48 n.100
Fretheim, Terence 131, 132 n.25, 132 n.26
Frye, Northrop 18

Gadamer, Hans-Georg 17, 17 n.47
Gadot, Yuval 84 n.32
Gaiser, Frederick 77, 77 n.2
Garrard, Greg 12 n.31, 16, 16 n.46
Gaulin, S. J. C. 47, 48 n.97
Gilmour, Michael J. 12, 12 n.29
Ginsberg, H. L. 29 n.17
Gruenwald, Ithamar 35, 35 n.37
Gunkel, Hermann 97 n.44

Habel, Norman C. 2, 2 n.1, 14 n.38, 14 n.39, 15, 15 n.42, 23, 24 n.70, 36 n.39
Hackett, Jo Ann 91 n.12
Hahn, Eduard 70, 70 n.42
Harari, Yuval Noah 20, 20 n.64
Haraway, Donna 11, 11 n.24, 13, 13 n.33, 13 n.34, 116, 116 n.96
Hardwick, Paul 16, 16 n.43
Hare, Brian 19 n.59
Hart, George 44 n.84
Hayes, William C. 93 n.24
Helmer, Daniel 39 n.53
Henschel, P. 94 n.29, 96 n.38
Hesse, Brian 46, 46 n.91
Hiebert, Theodore 14, 14 n.39
Hinson, Joy 44 n.82, 44 n.89
Hirsch, S. 41 n.63
Hjort, Anders 39 n.55, 40 n.57, 41 n.63
Hobgood-Oster, Laura 41 n.67, 66 n.20
Hope, Edward 9 n.14, 107 n.81, 125 n.16
Hossfeld, Franz-Lothar 77, 77 n.1, 105, 106 n.75, 117, 117 n.101, 119, 120, 120 n.1, 120 n.3, 123 n.8, 124, 124 n.12
Houston, Walter 141, 141 n.18, 142, 142 n.22, 143, 144, 147
Hrabel, Bohumil 85, 85 n.38
Huehnergard, John 91 n.12

Illman, Karl-Johan 63, 63 n.10
Ingold, Tim 66, 67, 67 n.22, 68, 68 n.27
Islamoğlu, Huri 146, 146 n.27

Jackson, Deirdre 94 n.30
Jacobsen, Rolf A. 25 n.2, 59 n.16
Jameson, Fredric 18, 18 n.50, 18 n.52, 147, 147 n.30

Jobling, David 14 n.18, 52 n.4, 141, 141 n.19, 142, 143, 144, 145, 146, 146 n.27, 147, 147 n.29
Johnston, Basil 7, 7 n.8

Keck, Leander E. 25 n.3, 52 n.3, 74 n.52, 106 n.73, 139 n.15
Keel, Othmar 27 n.43, 37, 38, 38 n.46, 80 n.8, 91, 91 n.10, 105, 106 n.72, 122 n.6
Keyder, Çağlar 146, 146 n.27
Kirkpatrick, A. F. 106, 106 n.74
Klawans, Jonathan 65, 65 n.15, 66, 68, 68 n.29
Knowles, Michael 35, 35 n.36
Koops, Robert 53, 53 n.6, 53 n.7, 78, 78 n.3, 78 n.6, 81 n.15, 81 n.16
Koosed, Jennifer L. 12, 12 n.28, 66 n.18
Kraus, Hans-Joachim 97 n.44, 105 n.70, 106, 106 n.73
Kugel, James 136, 136 n.6
Kwakkel, G. 90, 90 n.2, 90 n.3, 90 n.4

Laland, Kevin N. 39 n.52
Lazare, Bernard 84 n.33, 85
Leach, H. M. 40 n.58
LeMon, Joel M. 89, 89 n.1, 90 n.2, 90 n.6, 91, 91 n.7, 91 n.11, 120 n.2, 121 n.4, 123 n.9, 124 n.11, 124 n.14
Leopold, Aldo 2, 3, 3 n.3, 4, 4 n.4, 8, 17
Levenson, Jon D. 14 n.37, 32 n.26, 37 n.44
Lopez, Barry Holstun 107 n.80
Lovelock, James E. 64, 64 n.12

Maloney, Linda M. 77 n.1, 105 n.70, 120 n.1
Margalit, B. 111 n.92
Mays, James 22 n.69, 62 n.3, 105 n.70
McAdams, Sylvia 5
McCance, Erin C. 31, 31 n.25
McCann, J. Clinton 25 n.3, 52, 52 n.3, 57, 57 n.12, 57 n.14, 74 n.52, 105, 106 n.73, 115, 115 n.95, 139 n.15
McFague, Sallie 34 n.33
McHugh, Susan 96 n.39, 103 n.64, 105 n.69, 111 n.90, 111 n.93
Menache, Sophia 102 n.63, 110 n.88, 110 n.89

Middleton, J. Richard 132
Miklósi, Ádám 100 n.55
Milgrom, Jacob 68
Moore, Stephen 11, 11 n.26, 11 n.27, 57 n.13, 126, 126 n.17

Nasuti, Harry P. 22 n.46, 62 n.3, 63, 63 n.7–9
Newman, Katherine S. 52, 52 n.4, 146 n.26, 146 n.28

Odling-Smee, F. John 39 n.52
Ornan, Tallay 90 n.6

Pitts, Michael 29 n.18
Pleins, David J. 59, 59 n.15, 60 n.17
Porter, Jody 34 n.34

Rothschild, Miriam 84 n.33, 85 n.36
Ruse, Michael 64, 64 n.13
Ryder, Michael L. 38 n.48

Sapir-Hen, Lidar 84 n.32
Sasson, Aharon 9, 9 n.16, 20 n.63, 39 n.54, 39 n.55, 40 n.56, 40 n.57, 40 n.59, 41 n.63, 41 n.64, 43, 43 n.80, 47, 47 n.95, 48 n.97, 49 n.102, 66 n.19, 71 n.46, 71 n.47
Seesengood, Robert 66 n.18
Shell, Marc 101 n.56
Shiboleth, Myrna 109 n.86
Shipman, Pat 18 n.55, 19, 19 n.56, 19 n.57, 20 n.62, 21, 21 n.65, 21 n.66, 45 n.90, 93 n.26, 94, 94 n.27, 108 n.84
Singer, Isaac Bashevis 85
Singer, Peter 11, 11 n.23
Snyder, Gary 6, 6 n.6, 6 n.7
Spiciarich, Abra 84 n.32
Stone, Ken 11 n.22, 12 n.30
Strawn, Brent 9, 9 n.17, 10, 10 n.18, 91, 92, 92 n.13, 92 n.15, 92 n.18, 93 n.20, 93 n.23, 93 n.24, 93 n.25

Tanner, Beth LaNeel 25 n.2, 59 n.16

Tate, Marvin 97 n.44, 106, 106 n.74, 106 n.77, 120, 120 n.2
Tedford, Richard H. 19 n.61, 101 n.55, 107 n.79
Thomas, Elizabeth Marshall 95, 95 n.35
Tompkins, Jane 17, 17 n.49
Trapp, Thomas H. 91 n.10
Twine, Richard 60, 60 n.18

Uehlinger, Christopher 91 n.10

Velten, Hannah 69, 69 n.33, 69 n.37, 70 n.42, 70 n.43
Vitebsky, Piers 67 n.25, 67 n.26

Walker-Jones, Arthur 18 n.53, 24 n.71, 26 n.4, 34 n.31, 36 n.39, 36 n.41, 57 n.13, 62 n.4, 74 n.53, 126 n.17
Wang, Xiaoming 19 n.61, 101 n.55, 107 n.79
Wapnish, Paula 41 n.62, 46, 46 n.91, 46 n.92, 46 n.93, 47
Weiss, Ehud 80 n.10
Weissert, Elnathan 93 n.23
Welch, Patricia Bjaaland 44 n.83
Westermann, Claus 10, 10 n.18, 22 n.68
White, Lynn Jr. 12, 12 n.32
Whitekettle, Richard 61 n.1, 65 n.14, 73 n.51
Willerslev, Rane 67, 67 n.25, 67 n.26, 68
Wilson, Gerald Henry 133, 133 n.1, 135 n.3
Wilson, Paul 85 n.38
Wilson, Robert 63
Wimsatt, William K. 17 n.48

Yalçin, B. C. 43 n.77
Yee, Gale 17, 17 n.49

Zenger, Erich 77, 77 n.1, 105, 106, 106 n.75, 117, 117 n.101, 119, 120, 120 n.1, 120 n.3, 123 n.8, 124, 124 n.12
Zeuner, F. E. 70 n.43
Zohary, Michael 53, 53 n.5, 53 n.7, 53 n.8, 78, 78 n.5, 80 n.12, 81 n.17

BIBLICAL REFERENCES

Note: Locators followed by n refer to notes.

Genesis		*Numbers*	
1	35	19	79
1:16	143	19:2	71
1:26-28	68	23:22	69 n.36
4:4	50	24:8	69 n.36
5:24	59		
9:4	68	*Deuteronomy*	
12:16	70	32:11	89
13:2	70	33:17	69 n.36
13:5	70		
15:9	42, 83	*Joshua*	
20:14	70 n.41	6:21	43
22:13	50		
24:35	70 n.41	*Judges*	
26:14	70 n.41	6:19	43
30:36	43	7:5	102
31:10	42	9:9	81
31:19	43	13:15	43
31:22	43	13:19	42
49:24	70		
		1 Samuel	
Exodus		6:7	71
11:7	103	17:43	102, 102 n.59
12:1-32	50		
12:5	42	22:19	43
12:21-22	79	24:14	102 n.59
15:14	57		
15:15	57	*2 Samuel*	
22:31	103	3:8	102, 102 n.59
29:39	42		
30:23	53	9:8	101, 102 n.59
		16:9	102 n.59
Leviticus		22:4	27
4:28	42	23:3-4	144
5:11	83		
12:8	83	*1 Kings*	
14:2-53	79	1:41	99
16:20	42	5:13[4:33]	78
17:14	68, 129		

Biblical References

14:11	102, 107	31:3[2]	35
16:4	102, 107	32:4[3]	35
21:19	102	35:16	29
21:23-24	102	36:8[7]	121
22:38	102	40:3[2]	35, 37
		42	25, 26, 27, 28, 29, 31, 34, 42, 81, 122
2 Kings			
8:13	102, 102 n.59		
9:10	102	42–44	51
36	102	42–49	61
		42–72	22
1 Chronicles		42:2[1]	9, 28, 31, 32, 33, 35, 148
9:19	26		
16:5	61–2		
16:7	62	42:6[5]	25, 100
26:1	26	42:8-9[7-8]	33
26:19	26	42:8[7]	37
27:29	70	42:10[9]	35–8, 121, 135, 148
29:30	26, 62		
		42:11[10]	26
		42:12[11]	100
2 Chronicles		42:23[22]	148
20:19	43	43	25, 26, 31
31:6	43	43:1	31
		43:2	26
Esther		43:3	37
2:12	53	43:5	25, 100
		44:12	8
Job		44:12[11]	8, 49, 148
30:1	103	44:12-13[11-12]	38
39:1	27, 102 n.59	44:13[12]	50
39:9	69 n.36	44:20[19]	9
		44:23[22]	8, 38, 49
Psalms		45	51–4, 148
1–41	22	45–50	51
17:5	29	45–49	51, 148
17:8	121	45:1	51
18:8[7]	146	45:9[8]	9
18:3[2]	35	45:9-10a[8-9a]	52
18:8[7]	146	45:10a[9a]	54
18:15-18[14-19]	126 n.18	45:10-11[9-10]	54
18:34[33]	27	46	51, 56
18:47[46]	35	46–48	54
22:17[16]	106	46:1	51
23:1-2	68	46:3[2]	55, 58
24	126 n.18	46:3-4[2-3]	55
28:1	35	46:3-7[2-6]	126 n.18
29:6	69 n.36	46:4[3]	99
29:7	63		

46:5[4]	54	50:16-22	63
46:6[5]	54	51	62, 77, 77
46:7[6]	55, 99		n.2, 78
46:9[8]	55	51–55	77, 148
46:10[9]	55	51–65	61
46:11[10]	55, 58	51–70	25
47–48	148	51–72	77
47:1	51	51:9[7]	78
47:3[2]	56	51:12-14[10-12]	79
47:8a	56	51:18[16]	77
47:10[9]	56	51:19[17]	77
48	51, 57	51:18-19[16-17]	134
48:1	51	51:21[19]	8, 77
48:3[2]	56, 57	52	79, 80, 82
48:6[5]	57	52–55	77
48:7[6]	57	52:9[7]	79
48:8[7]	57	52:10[8]	79, 148
48:9[8]	57	55	85, 86, 90
48:10[9]	57	55:7[6]	9, 82, 148
48:11[10]	58	55:18[17]	100
49	58	56	90
49:1	51	56–60	77, 149
49:1-5[1-4]	58	57	89, 90,
49:6-9[5-8]	58		91, 92
49:11[10]	59	57:2[1]	9, 89, 121
49:13[12]	9, 59, 60	57:5[4]	9, 89,
49:15a[14a]	58		91, 149
49:15[14]	8	57:7[6]	92, 116
49:16[15]	59	58	93, 116
49:21[20]	9, 59, 60	58:5[4]	9
50	51, 61, 62,	58:5-6[4-5]	116
	63, 64, 69,	58:7[6]	9, 89, 91,
	72, 74, 75,		116, 149
	77, 148	58:9[8]	9, 116
50:1	61, 64	59	60, 96, 97,
50:1-6	63, 64		97 n.40, 99,
50:3	63		100, 101,
50:4	64		105, 106,
50:6	63, 64		107, 108,
50:8-9	73		109, 110,
50:8-15	65, 73, 134		111, 114
50:9	8, 61, 69, 77	59:2[1]	113, 114
50:10	9, 61	59:2-3[1-2]	114
50:10–13	61, 63, 73	59:4[3]	100
50:11	9, 61	59:4-5[3-4]	114, 115
50:13	8, 61	59:4-5a[3-4a]	115
50:14	74	59:4-11[3-10]	114, 115
50:14-15	73	59:5a-6[4a-5]	115

59:5-6[4-5]	116	63:10[9]	123
59:7[6]	9, 89, 99, 100, 107, 114, 115, 149	63:10-11[9-10]	125
		65	127
		65–67	119, 126
		65–68	77, 119, 126
59:7-8[6-7]	114, 115		
59:8[7]	9, 114	65:6-9[5-8]	127
59:9-11[8-10]	115	65:7-14[6-13]	126 n.18
59:10[9]	113, 121	65:7[6]	127
59:9[8]	100	65:10[9]	35, 127
59:10-11a[9-10a]	113	65:14[13]	8, 135
59:12[11]	114	66	128
59:12-18[11-17]	114, 115	66:1-4	135
59:13[12]	114, 115	66:13-15	134
59:14[13]	115	66:15	8, 9
59:15-16[14-15]	114, 115	67	129
59:14[13]	9	67:3[2]	129
59:15[14]	89, 99, 100, 114, 115, 149	68	119, 129, 131
			61
		68–70	129, 130
59:16[15]	98 n.49, 107, 110, 114, 115	68:2[1]	129, 130
		68:5[4]	130
		68:6[5]	130
59:17[16]	107, 113, 114	68:8-10[7-9]	126 n.18
		68:8-19[7-18]	130
59:17-18[16-17]	114, 115	68:13[12]	9
59:18[17]	113	68:14[13]	130
60	117, 114	68:15[14]	130
60:3[1]	117	68:19[18]	130
60:4[2]	89, 117	68:22-26[21-25]	130
61	119	68:23[22]	130
61–64	9, 77, 119, 126	68:24[23]	9, 102
		68:24-26[23-25]	131
61:3[2]	35, 119, 120, 121, 135	68:30-31[29-30]	131
		68:31[30]	9, 131
	120	69	133–5
61:4[3]	9, 121	69–71	77, 133
61:5[4]	35, 121, 135	69–72	133, 149
62:3[2]	121	69:2[1]	134
62:7-8[6-7]	122, 124, 125	69:2-3[1-2]	37
63		69:15[14]-16[15]	134
	122, 123	69:31-32[30-31]	134
63:2[1]	123	69:32[31]	8, 9
63:4[3]	124	69:35[34]	135
63:5[4]	123	70	135
63:6[5]	123	71	133, 135–6
63:7[6]	9, 121, 123	71:3	35, 121, 135
63:8[7]	123	71:20	135–6
63:9[8]			

72	25, 52, 77, 133, 136–40, 141, 141 n.18, 142, 143, 145, 146, 149	72:20	133
		73	63
		73–83	61
		73–89	22
		74:12-17	63, 126 n.18
		75	63
72:1	136, 138, 143	75:4[3]	63
		76	126 n.18
72:1-2	144	76:9[8]	63
72:1-4	137, 140	77:4[3]	100
72:1-7	136, 137, 139, 140, 141, 142, 143	77:16-21[15-20]	126 n.18
		77:17[16]	63
		81	63
		82	63
72:1-17	140	84–85	25
72:2	136, 138	84–88	61
72:3	136, 137, 138, 142–3	87–88	25
		89:6-15[5-14]	126 n.18
72:4	136, 137, 138, 140, 144	90–106	22
		92:11[10]	69 n.36
		92:13[12]	79
72:5	136, 138, 143, 144	94:22	35
		95:1	35
72:5-7	137	96:12	80
72:6	15 n.41, 136, 144	104:2-9	126 n.18
		104:4	63
72:7	136, 143	104:10-11	35
72:8	15 n.41, 136, 138, 139, 143	104:14	74
		104:16	124
		104:21	74
72:8-11	136, 139, 145	104:26	74
		104:27	74
72:9	136, 145	104:29-30	35
72:10	139, 142	104:30	35
72:10-11	136	104:31	74
72:11	139	104:31-32	126 n.18
72:12	139, 140, 141, 142	107–150	22
		114:3-7	126 n.18
72:12-14	137, 138, 139, 142, 145	144:1	35
		144:5	146
72:13	142	148	135
72:14	140, 142	148:9	80
72:15	137, 139, 140, 145	*Proverbs*	
72:15-17	137, 140, 145	5:19	27
72:16	137, 142, 143, 144	7:17	53
		26.11	102
72:17	137, 145	30:31	42

Biblical References

Song of Solomon
1:13   53
3:6   53
4:6   53
4:14   53
5:13   53

Isaiah
1:24   70
7:1-16   57
13:21   145
13:22   125
16:11   100
17:12   99
22:2   99
38:14   84
40:11   68
49:26   70
51:5   99
53:7   42, 50
56:10-11 103
59:11   84, 100
60:6   139
66:11   124

Jeremiah
4:19   100
6:20   139
7:1-15   57
9:11   125
15:3   102, 107
31:20   100
31:35   99
35:1-11 42
48:36   100
49:33   125
50:42   99
51:55   99

Ezekiel
6:13   80
7:16   84, 100
27:22-25 139
34:15-16 68
47   32

Daniel
8:21   42

Joel
1:19   28
1:20   28, 34

Amos
4:8   124

Nahum
2:8[7]   84

Habakkuk
3:19   27

Matthew
2:11   53
6:26   74
7:6   102
15:26-27 102
23:37   89

Mark
7:27-28 102

Luke
16:21   102

John
19:29   78

Galatians
6:2   28

Revelation
18:13   53
22   32
22:1   35

Sirach
13:18   103
24:15   53
26:25   102

SUBJECT INDEX

Note: Locators followed by n refer to notes.

Aboriginal Peoples Television Network 5–6
Abraham 34, 39, 42, 56, 70, 70 n.41, 83
Achaemenid Persian Empire 83
agallochon 53
agar 52, 53
Agarwood trees (*Aquillaria agallocha* Roxb.) 53
aghal 53
agrarian 21, 51, 72
ahaloth 53
'aleka yhvh 'ekra' 28
aloe 53
Aloe vera 53
Amenhotep II 48, 93
Amenhotep III 69–70
American Museum of Natural History 95
Among the Bone Eaters: Encounters with the Hyenas of Harar 95, 96 n.36
animal rights activists 65, 75
animal(s) 1, 2, 15, 34, 35, 119, 125, 129, 145
  objectification 16, 21
animals, particular
  Aurochs 69, 69 n.35, 70
  bulls 8, 61, 65, 69–74, 77, 13, 134
  Baladi cattle 71, 71 n.47
  cattle 3, 20, 21, 30, 39, 43, 44, 48, 61, 69, 70–73, 70 n.40–3, 92, 124, 129, 145
  cows 69–72, 110
  deer 2, 3, 7, 8, 9, 25 n.1, 26–31, 35, 51, 54, 148
  divine warrior 55, 117, 126–34, 136, 149
  doe 25–34
  dogs 1, 9, 10, 18–20, 44, 84, 89, 96-116, 129, 131, 145, 148, 149
  donkeys 43, 48
  doves 9, 81–8, 90, 91, 124, 126, 148
  earthquake(s) 117, 126, 129
  elephants 54, 69, 148
  fish 30, 34, 92 n.19, 109
  foxes 7, 9, 9 n.11, 16, 108, 125
  goats 8, 19, 20, 21, 27, 30, 38–50, 54, 58, 61, 65, 66, 69–74, 77, 110, 124, 128, 129, 145, 148
  hyenas 95–6, 103, 107 n.78
  jackals 9, 9 n.11, 105, 107, 108, 110, 111, 119, 125, 129, 145
  lions 9, 10, 44, 89, 91–6, 110, 116, 145, 149
  monkeys 16, 16 n.43
  mountain goats 27
  nonhuman animals 1, 2, 15, 34, 119, 125, 129, 145
  oxen 9, 43, 69, 71, 134, 135, 148
  pigeons 82–8, 90–1, 124, 126, 145
  references in Psalms 8–9, 10
  reindeer 26, 30, 31, 67, 67 n.25
  scapegoat 44
  sheep 8, 10, 19, 20 21, 30, 38–50, 51, 54, 58, 59, 66, 70, 71, 72 n.50, 74, 103, 110, 124, 129, 145, 148
  snails 9, 116
  snakes 9, 28, 110, 116
  wild dogs 105–7
  wild oxen *(Bos Primigenius) see* Aurochs
  wolves 2, 3, 6–8, 18, 18 n.54, 19, 19 n.60, 30, 104, 107, 107 n.80, 108–11
  young bulls 8, 69, 72, 77
animal studies 1–2, 7, 8–16, 21, 90
anthropocentrism 2, 4, 12, 28, 36
  and binaries 12–14
anthropomorphism 16
Asaph 23, 51, 61–3, 136, 147–8
  psalms of 61–3
Assiniboine River 4

Subject Index

Astarte 83
Astoreth 83
Aurochs 69, 69 n.35, 70

Baal 57, 126, 130, 131, 134
   battle against Death (Mot) 134
Babylonian Theodicy 92
Baladi cattle 71, 71 n.47
Bathsheba 45, 62
The Bible and Posthumanism 11–12, 12 n.28, 66 n.18
binary(ies) 2, 9, 12–15, 29, 31–2, 46, 81, 87, 90, 91, 112, 132
birds 9, 31, 61, 73, 82, 85, 86, 89, 90, 107, 121, 124, 149
   aquatic 4
   and bugs 73, 74
   and insects 73
   protecting their young 89
   sacrificial 83–4
bulls 8, 61, 65, 69–74, 77, 13, 134

Caesar, Julius 69
Call of the Wild, The (1903) 111–12
Canaan dog 109
Canaanites 43, 83, 130, 131
canon 21–4
canonical 22, 90
canonical criticism 22, 141
caper bush *(Capparis spinosa)* 78
capitale 70
caprine products 39–40
cassia 52, 53
cattle 3, 20, 21, 30, 39, 43, 44, 48, 61, 65, 69, 70–3, 70 n.40–3, 92, 124, 129, 145
Cher Ami 82–3
chicken bones 90
Christian animal ethics 12
Cinnamomum cassia 53
class-stratification 52
climate change 1, 3, 4, 17, 64
coevolution 18–21, 24, 39, 42, 45, 100
colonialism 5, 6, 8, 5, 86, 94
colonisation 5, 35
   and environmental issues 5
   racism and 5
Commiphora abyssinica 53
cosmic mountain 37, 56, 57, 120 *see also* Holy mountain; Holy summit

cow 69–72, 110
Cynegetica 28
cynocephaly 112

David 8 n.10, 22–23, 25, 26, 29, 45, 52, 61–3, 77–8, 87–88
Davidic monarchy 25, 52, 57, 147, 149
Davidic psalms 25–6, 89, 119, 126, 149
death, medical assistance in 1–2
deer 2, 3, 7, 8, 9, 25 n.1, 26–31, 35, 51, 54, 148
   symbolic associations in the Hebrew Bible 27
Deuteronomistic History 52, 52 n.2, 101, 102
divine warrior 55, 117, 126–34, 136, 149
Dodo bird 86
doe, 25, 34
dogs 1, 9, 10, 20, 44, 84, 89, 96–116, 129, 131, 145, 148, 149
   bites 110
   Canaan dog 109, 115
   domestication of 18–19
   expression of humility 102
   German shepherds 112
   as liminal figure 111–13
   low social status 102
   loyalty and servant 102
   polytheism 110
   pariah 108
   village 106, 108
   wild 105–11
Dog Star Sirius 111
domestication 18, 19–20, 45, 67, 83
   dogs 18, 19
   human 20
   pigeons 83, 84
   sheep and goats 21
domestic livestock 30
domestic pigeons 82
donkeys 43, 48
doves 9, 81–8, 90, 91, 124, 148
   wings of 9, 82, 84, 90–1, 98
dry intensive agriculture 52, 146
dryland farming 72

Earth 1, 2, 7, 14, 15, 16, 21, 27–9, 36, 37, 52, 54–8, 63–5, 72, 75, 119–32
   chaotic picture of 55

as enemy 89, 91–111
objectification of 58, 61
as a refuge 77–89
Earth Bible Commentary 1, 2, 2 n.1, 3, 7, 14, 15
Earth community 3, 7, 8, 13, 14, 15, 23, 24, 27, 51, 54, 56, 58, 61, 75, 76, 77, 81, 87, 88, 89, 94, 96, 116, 117, 126, 128, 134, 135, 136, 143, 147, 148
Earth metaphors for God 119
Ecocriticism 12, 14, 15, 16, 16 n.46
ecological hermeneutics 2, 3, 8, 17
Eden's Other Residents 12
'eleka, "to you" 28
elephants 54, 69, 148
ecology 1, 3, 4, 8, 13, 16, 21, 49 n.102, 52, 71, 108, 122, 125, 137, 143
embodiment 58–61
empire 8, 23, 24, 46, 47, 49, 51–60, 83, 133, 136–7, 133–45, 146, 147
Encyclopedia Judaica 101
English-Wabigoon river system 34
Enuma Elish 126
environment(s) 2, 5, 8, 20, 30, 40, 69, 87, 108
environmental crisis 3
environmental exploitation 94
environmentalism 86
"European hyssop" 78
Exploring Ecological Hermeneutics 14, 14 n.39, 36 n.39
'ezov 78

feminists 3, 94
fish 30, 34, 92 n.19, 109
forest fires 4
fortress 36, 96, 97, 99
The Four Stages of Cruelty 16
foxes 7, 9, 9 n.11, 16, 108, 125
fragrant anointing oil 53
fragrant resin 53

Gaia hypothesis 64, 64 n.13
Gallic Wars 69
garden hunting 31, 31 n.24
Garden of Eden 35, 80
genre 18, 21–4, 36, 51, 62, 77, 119, 126, 133, 148, 149
Gir National Forest in India 93

goatish 44
goats 8, 19, 20, 21, 27, 30, 38–50, 54, 58, 61, 65, 66, 69–74, 77, 110, 124, 128, 129, 145, 148
God as Rock 23, 35, 36, 36 n.39–40, 37, 38, 54, 85, 119–32, 135, 149
goddess nursing a worshipper 123
God's wings 89–91, 121–6, 149
Grassy Narrows community 34
green olive tree 79–81, 87, 148
greenwash 133–45, 147
guardians of Earth 56

Harry Potter series 111
Hebrew poetic parallelism 113, 136
Hercules 69
herders 46
  nomadic 42, 43, 49, 67
  sedentary 42, 43, 47
  transhumant 42–3, 47, 49
Hogarth, William 16
Holy mountain 37, 56, 57, 120 *see also* cosmic mountain
Holy summit 115
Homo sapiens 29
Horus falcon 91, 122
human/animal binary 2, 13, 14, 15, 32, 90, 96, 112
human-animal relations 10, 11
human civilization 19, 112
human-domestication hypothesis 40
Humane Society 1
humanities 11
human metaphors for God 121
humming 100
hunter-gathering 67–8
hunter-gatherers 19, 20, 66, 67, 108
hussopos 78 n.4
hyena 95–6, 103, 107n.78
hymn(s) 51, 54, 119, 126, 129
hymn to God as ruler (Psalm 47) 56
hyssop 78

identification 15–16, 28, 32, 38, 45, 49, 51, 53, 55, 79, 81, 90, 126, 145
identify 2, 3, 16, 44, 117
inanimate parts of the world 143
Indigenous culture 5

Indigenous Rights 35
  and environmental issues 5
Innana 83
interconnections of species 2–4
interhuman violence 66
internal emotions 100
I Served the King of England 85
Ishtar 83
ivory 9, 51–4, 123

jackals 9, 9 n.11, 105, 107, 108, 110, 111, 119, 125, 129, 145
Jerusalem 21, 48, 57, 61, 84 n.32, 115, 119, 120, 131, 141

kebeś 42
keleb 102 n.60–2, 104 n.64, 107, 111 n.91–2
Khenti-Amentiu 111
Khnum 44
Korah 51, 148
Korahite psalms 23, 25, 26, 62
Korahites 23, 25–6, 147, 148 *see also* sons of Korah
Kosher regulations 68, 129

Laban 43
Lake Winnipeg 4
Lamb of God 50
lament(s) 22–3, 22 n.68, 25, 26, 33, 36, 38, 51, 62, 74, 77, 79, 84, 87, 89, 119, 120, 121, 126, 128, 133, 148, 149
leprosy 79
lions 9, 10, 44, 89, 91–6, 110, 116, 145, 149
  as enemies 95
  as metaphors for God 92
  threat to 96
love *shīr* 51
liturgy(ies) 119, 126, 129

Majorana syriaca 78
Marduk 126
marjoram 78
market-age animals 46
Mary Poppins (1964) 85
maskils 23, 51, 77, 89
medically assisted death of nonhumans 1–2
messenger pigeons 83

Messiah 52
Midrash Tehillim 22
"A Mighty Fortress is Our God" 54
miktams 23, 77, 89, 97, 119
milk 20, 40, 41, 49, 70, 71, 72, 124
misgabbî 98–9
mizmor 51
mollusks 30
monkeys 16, 16 n.43
Moses 22, 39, 79
Mot 126, 134
mountain 3, 6, 8, 27, 37, 55–8, 73, 80, 85, 120, 126, 127, 138, 143, 145–7
mountain goats 27
Mount Hermon 33
Mount Zaphon 56–7
Mount Zion 56–8
myrrha 53

Nathan 45, 62, 148
natural sciences 11
naturecultures 13, 115
Netley Marsh 4
niche 8, 9, 10, 18–24, 39, 40, 72, 81, 84, 94, 129, 135, 148
niche construction, coevolution and 18–21, 24, 42, 45, 129, 135, 148
Ninurta 93
nomadic herding 42, 43, 47, 49
nonhuman animals 1, 2, 15, 34, 119, 125, 129, 145

objectification
  of animals 16, 21
  of Earth 58, 61
Odysseus 44
Ojibway *see* Saulteaux
Olea Europaea sativa 80
Olea Europaea sylvestris 80
olive tree 79–81, 87, 148
On the Waterfront 85
Origanum 78
Origanum syriacum 78
Origanum vulgare 78
Ostrich 2
oxen 9, 43, 69, 71, 134, 135, 148

pastoralism 68
pastoral socioecology 119

Paul J. Rainey's African Hunt (1912) 95
Pentateuch 63
perfume 51–4, 81
Pharaoh Kehfren 122
pigeons 82–8, 90–1, 124, 126, 145
   burnt or "holocaust" offerings 84
   in Hinduism 86
   messenger 83
   nest 85
   passenger 86
   racing 85
   for sacrifice 83
   of Trafalgar Square 87
   Winkie 83
Pilgrimage Window 16
Polyphemous 44, 45
Precambrian Shield 4, 6
preindustiral societies 52
principle of interconnectedness 7
principle of intrinsic worth 7
principle of mutual custodianship 7
principle of purpose 7
principle of voice 7
psalms of David 23, 26, 61, 62

Qetsiah 53

racism 35, 109
   and colonialism 5
Rameses III 69
Reading the Hebrew Bible with Animal Studies 11 n.22, 12
Red River 4
refuge 38, 54, 58, 121
reindeer 26, 30, 31, 67, 67 n.25
resh 29, 144
right relations 6, 13, 14, 61, 73–6
rock 6, 35–8, 51, 82, 85, 99, 116, 119–21, 126, 136
royal wedding hymn 51–2
ruakh 79

sacrifice 44, 50, 65–8, 74, 129
   of animals 65
   God rejects 77
   of human bodies 66
   pigeons/dove 83, 124
   reliance on sacrifice 73
   young bull 77

sacrificial animal 68, 76, 124, 129
salvation 36, 74, 85, 120, 121, 127, 135
Sand County Almanac, A 2, 3, 4 n.4
Saskatoon 5
Saul 26, 43, 97, 112
Saulteaux 5
scapegoat 44
schimperi 53
sedentary herding 42, 43, 47
Sennacherib 48
Sheba 139, 140
sheep 8, 10, 19, 20 21, 30, 38–50, 51, 54, 58, 59, 66, 70, 71, 72 n. 50, 74, 103, 110, 124, 129, 145, 148
   domestication 21
   Hebrew Bible, metaphorical uses 10
   perceived stupidity 10
shepherds 10, 39, 45, 46, 49, 58, 74
   God as 68, 72, 148
shir 51, 119, 126, 133
Shoal Lake 5, 35
Sierra Madre Mountains 4
Singh, Guru Govind 87
Sitz im Erde 34
slaughter houses 66, 76
small cattle 48, 71
snails 9, 116
snakes 9, 28, 110, 116
social sciences 11
socioecology 9, 10, 56, 58, 72, 113–16, 119, 120, 121, 125, 126, 135, 136, 148 135
Solomon 22, 23, 25–6, 47, 133, 140, 147, 148
sons of Korah 26, 51, 61, 148 *see also* Korahites
The Spell of the Sensuous 13, 13 n.35, 143, 143 n.23
spiritual/material binary 31–2, 79, 87
storm(s) 63, 117, 126, 129, 130, 131, 144, 146–7, 149
summit socioecology 113–16
superscription(s) 8, 8 n.10, 22–3, 25–6, 51, 61–2, 77, 89, 90, 112, 119, 126, 133, 135, 140–1, 147–8
sword(s) 43, 91, 98, 45, 125
"Syrian hyssop" 78

ta'arog 28, 29, 32, 34
teeth 54, 91, 92, 116

Tel Beer-Sheba 47
Tel-Dan 46
Tell Halif 39
thanksgiving(s) 23, 32, 74, 75, 119, 126, 128, 133, 134, 148
"think like a mountain" 2–4
Tiamat 126
Tiglath Pilesar I 69
Tiglath-Pileser 93
tooth 54, 93 *see also* teeth
traction 21, 70–2, 148
Trafalgar Square pigeons 82
transhumant herding 42, 43, 47, 49
Treaty One territory 5
trees 3, 6, 27, 53, 78 n.3, 79–81, 87, 105, 117, 148 *see also* olive tree
  socioecological importance 81
Turtle Island 5–6, 7, 24
Tutankhamun 93

urban socioecology 56, 58, 121, 136

Varro, Marcus Terentius 70
vav 138, 139

water 4, 5, 17, 20, 25, 27, 29, 30, 31, 32–37, 51, 54, 55, 63, 71, 72, 79, 81, 83, 87, 102, 120, 122, 127, 133, 134, 146, 148

Waters 134
wealthy elites 47, 110
wet intensive agriculture 52, 146
wilderness 26, 27, 35, 61, 85, 86, 88, 111, 112, 125, 148
wild ox *(Bos Primigenius) see* Aurochs
wild rock pigeon *(Columbia livia)* 82
wing(s) 9, 89, 119
  of the cherubim 90
  of a dove 82–4, 90–1, 148
  of God 89, 90, 121–6, 149
  of a pigeon 90–1
  winged female deities 91
  winged solar discs 89
Winnipeg 5, 31
wolves 2, 3, 6–8, 18, 18 n.54, 19, 19 n.60, 30, 104, 107, 107 n.80, 108–11

xylaloe 53

Yamm 126
young bulls 8, 61, 65, 69, 72, 77, 134

za'atar 78–9
  botanical identification 79
  use in purification 79
Zion 23, 37, 37 n.44, 51, 54–8, 148
zoomorphism 16

www.ingramcontent.com/pod-product-compliance
Lightning Source LLC
Chambersburg PA
CBHW052048300426
44117CB00012B/2022